Islamic Banking and Financial Crisis

Islamic Banking and Financial Crisis

REPUTATION, STABILITY AND RISKS

Edited by Habib Ahmed, Mehmet Asutay
and Rodney Wilson

EDINBURGH
University Press

© Islamic Research and Training Institute of The Islamic
Development Bank and The Durham Centre for Islamic
Economics and Finance, 2014

Edinburgh University Press Ltd
22 George Square, Edinburgh EH8 9LF
www.euppublishing.com

Typeset in Baskerville by
Servis Filmsetting Ltd, Stockport, Cheshire, and
printed and bound in Great Britain by
CPI Group (UK) Ltd, Croydon CR0 4YY

A CIP record for this book is available from the British
Library

ISBN 978 0 7486 4761 3 (hardback)
ISBN 978 0 7486 7237 0 (webready PDF)
ISBN 978 0 7486 7239 4 (epub)

The right of the contributors to be identified as authors
of this work has been asserted in accordance with the
Copyright, Designs and Patents Act 1988 and the Copyright
and Related Rights Regulations 2003 (SI No. 2498).

CONTENTS

FIGURES

TABLES

CONTRIBUTORS

Habib Ahmed holds the Sharjah Chair in Islamic Law and Finance at Durham University. He has authored/edited more than seventy publications, including articles in international refereed journals, books and other academic monographs/reports. His latest book is *Product Development in Islamic Banks*, published in 2011 by Edinburgh University Press.

Mehmet Asutay is a Reader in Middle Eastern and Islamic Political Economy and Finance at the School of Government and International Affairs, Durham University. He is also the Director of the Durham Doctoral Training Centre for Islamic Economics and Finance. His research interest is mainly on Islamic political economy, Islamic moral economy and empirical Islamic finance.

Rodney Wilson is Emeritus Professor in the International Centre for Education in Islamic Finance (INCEIF). Previously he was involved in research and teaching in Islamic economics and finance for over thirty years and he founded the Durham University Islamic Finance Programme. Before joining INCEIF he was a Visiting Professor at the Qatar Faculty of Islamic Studies.

Rafe Haneef is currently CEO of HSBC Amanah Malaysia. He has played a leadership role in developing Sukuk and Islamic structured and project finance since 1999 at HSBC, ABN AMRO and Citigroup. He is also a member of the Shariᶜah Advisory Council of Securities Commission Malaysia.

Edib Smolo is currently a PhD candidate at the International Centre for Education in Islamic Finance. He has worked as Shariᶜah Coordinator at the International Islamic Liquidity Management Corporation and prior to that as Researcher at International Shariᶜah Research Academy for Islamic Finance.

Rania Abdelfattah Salem is a Lecturer in Finance at the German University in Cairo. Prior to joining the academic field, she worked in the research area of financial firms. Her research in bank management and Islamic finance has resulted in a number of papers and participation in research projects. Her recent book *Risk Management for Islamic Banks* was published by Edinburgh University Press in 2013.

Ahmed Mohamed Badreldin is currently a PhD student at the Department of Finance and Banking, Philipps Universität Marburg. Prior to commencing his PhD, he completed his MSc from the German University in Cairo.

Matthias Verbeet studied History and Islamic Studies in Freiburg and Financial Management in Durham. Both of his studies focused on development of economic systems. He currently works in Oxfordshire in the automotive industry. Graduating during the peak time of the credit crisis resulted in an interest in researching alternative economic and financial models to a failing financial system.

Mohd Afandi Abu Bakar is a senior lecturer at the Faculty of Business Management, UiTM Perak, Malaysia. His research on empirical Islamic finance has been published in various outlets. He holds a Master Degree in Economics from the International Islamic University Malaysia.

Radiah Abdul Kader is an Associate Professor and Deputy Dean (undergraduate) at the Faculty of Economics and Administration, University of Malaya, Kuala Lumpur. She holds a PhD in Islamic Finance from Durham University.

Roza Hazli Zakaria is a senior lecturer at the Faculty of Economics and Administration, University of Malaya, Kuala Lumpur. She holds a PhD in Economics from Universiti Kebangsaan Malaysia.

Romzie Rosman currently works as researcher and consultant in 5R Strategic Consultancy, Malaysia. He also has presented papers at national and international conference, and published in international referred academic journals. He received his PhD (Islamic Banking and Finance) in 2012 from the International Islamic University Malaysia.

Abdul Rahim Abdul Rahman is currently a Professor of Accounting and Finance at the Kulliyyah of Economics and Management Sciences, International Islamic University Malaysia. He is also a member of the Shariᶜah Committee and a member of the Audit Committee of HSBC Amanah Malaysia. He has widely published papers in international refereed academic journals and has presented papers at national and international conferences.

Noraini Mohd Ariffin is an Assistant Professor in the Department of Accounting, International Islamic University Malaysia. Her research interest is in financial reporting of Islamic banks, mainly from the perspective of risk disclosure and risk management. She is currently teaching financial accounting and accounting for Islamic banks to undergraduate and postgraduate students and supervises Masters and PhD students in various areas relating to Islamic banking and *takāful*.

Salina Hj. Kassim is an Assistant Professor at the Kulliyyah (Faculty) of Economics and Management Sciences, International Islamic University Malaysia. Her research is mainly on the empirical aspects of Islamic banking and finance and her papers on these areas have been published in various international journals.

Sherin Binti Kunhibava is a Senior Lecturer in Faculty of the University of Malaya; previously she was a researcher at ISRA, Malaysia. Her research interests are on commercial law and legal aspects of Islamic banking and finance, and risk and risk management in Islamic banking and finance.

Zurina Shafii is the Director of Islamic Finance and Wealth Management Institute and an Associate Professor in the Faculty of Economics and Muamalat, Universiti Sains Islam, Malaysia. Her research interests are Shari\u02bfah audit, Halal traceability and compliance procedures, Islamic financial institutions' reporting and Islamic financial planning. She has co-authored the textbook *Governance and Shariah Audit in Islamic Financial Institutions* (2012).

Supiah Salleh is a lecturer at the Faculty of Economics and Muamalat, Universiti Sains Islam, Malaysia and currently pursuing her PhD in Economics and Muamalat (Accounting) there. She is co-author of *Governance and Shariah Audit in Islamic Financial Institutions* (2012).

Abdou Karim Diaw is currently a consultant and Lecturer in Islamic finance in Senegal, having completed his PhD in Islamic finance at the International Centre for Education in Islamic Finance. He has been published in refereed journals and has presented several papers at international conferences on Islamic finance.

Irawan Febianto is a lecturer and currently a deputy head of the Center for Islamic Economics and Business Studies, Padjadjaran University, Indonesia. He graduated from International Islamic University Malaysia and continues his studies under INCEIF, Malaysia. He has published several papers on Islamic management and finance in international journals.

Zulkifli Hasan is a Senior Lecturer at Shari\u02bfah and Law faculty of Islamic Science, University of Malaysia. He is a Shari\u02bfah committee member of Affin Islamic Bank Bhd and sits as a committee member for the Association of Shari\u02bfah Advisors. His research interest mainly lies in Shari\u02bfah and corporate governance and legal aspects of Islamic finance. His book, Shari\u02bfah *Governance in Islamic Banks*, was published by Edinburgh University Press in 2012.

Abdulazeem Abozaid holds a PhD, Masters, higher studies diploma and BA in Islamic financial law. He has both academic as well as practical experience in Islamic banking. Currently he is a faculty member of Damascus University and a Shari\u02bfah consultant to several Islamic financial institutions.

I

REFLECTING ON ISLAMIC BANKING AND FINANCIAL CRISIS: RISKS, REPUTATION AND STABILITY

Habib Ahmed, Mehmet Asutay and Rodney Wilson

1.1 Introduction

Do Islamic financial institutions perform better than their conventional counterparts during periods of financial stress? To what extent do systems for managing risk have to be adapted for Islamic financial institutions given the unique characteristics of their assets and liabilities and given the need for *Sharīʿah* compliance? The eleven contributors to this book address these issues, which have come to prominence since the global financial crisis of 2008 and the subsequent recession. The study explores the challenges for Islamic financial institutions in an international system where banks under Basel III are required to have more capital and liquidity to deal with future shocks. Governance issues are also examined, as these influence client and investor perceptions and ultimately have implications for institutional stability and sustainability.

The book is an outcome of a conference organised by the Islamic Research and Training Institute of the Islamic Development Bank Group and Durham University, both of which have been centres for research in Islamic finance for over three decades. As the Islamic finance industry has grown it has inevitably faced greater challenges, the most recent of which was the global financial crisis. Key features of the present study include:

(i) an in-depth assessment of how Islamic banks weathered the financial crisis and what lessons can be learned
(ii) an examination of whether Islamic banks are inherently more stable than conventional banks during periods of economic stress
(iii) an examination of how Islamic banks manage risk, with a particular focus on liquidity risk and the use of forward contracts to mitigate currency risk
(iv) an appraisal of the *Sharīʿah*-related issues in Islamic finance practice and an examination of the work of internal *Sharīʿah* audit units and the use of *Sharīʿah* reports to reduce non-compliance risks.

In other words, the major issues addressed include stability, financial sustainability, risk management, risk mitigation, *Sharīʿah* audit and governance – topics that have received increasing attention from both Islamic finance professionals and academics researching the subject.

1.2 Remit and Scope

The aim of the study is to provide an objective appraisal of how Islamic banks can cope during financial crises and to look at the extent to which the risks they and their clients face differ from those of conventional banks. Recent experience shows that Islamic banks and their regulators coped well during the 2008 financial crisis but they were not immune to the negative effects of the subsequent recession. The implications of business cycles for Islamic banks are explored, as is the issue of whether Islamic finance can act as a stabilising factor rather than being pro-cyclical. The strengths of the work include findings based on detailed empirical investigations of the behaviour and operations of particular Islamic banks. The methodology used should interest the reader and suggest how further follow-up studies can be conducted. The remit is international: Financial market issues and developments in many countries are discussed. The work makes a significant contribution to the empirical literature on Islamic finance by making data available that has not hitherto been analysed. At the same time the work should provide further knowledge of how financial risks can be managed and mitigated by Islamic banks and their regulators.

1.3 Financial Crisis – Causes and Evolution

While each financial crisis has its unique features, Reinhart and Rogoff (2008, 2009) and Reinhart (2008) conclude that many of these crises share some remarkable similarities. Observations demonstrate that crises start with innovation in some sector that creates potential for high returns and the financial institutions are attracted to these innovative schemes to reap a share of profits. Financial liberalisation and deregulation, on the other hand, provides incentives and facilitates the financial sector to increase exposure to these new profitable sectors. The increase in demand, as a result, is fuelled by increasing debt provided by the financial sector, causing an asset-price boom. Eventually, the price-bubble bursts due to some negative shock, creating a crisis in over-leveraged banks and causing economic downturn. The response to crisis in the banking sector by the government eventually leads to sovereign debt crisis.

The global financial crisis of 2008 originated in the United States as a result of the failure of risk assessment and management at the institutional (legal and regulatory), organisational and product levels. The regulatory and legal regimes under which the financial sector was operating underwent a shift towards deregulation and dependence on the market economy. In 1999 the Gramm–Leach–Bailey Act was passed, repealing portions of the Glass–Steagall Act that had prevented banks from intermingling. The Federal Reserve System endorsed the view that the financial institutions were capable of self-regulation (Fukuyama, 2008).[1] Similarly, the Securities and Exchange Commission (SEC) in the United States loosened capital requirements for large investment banks in 2004. Furthermore, there was resistance to control the fast-growing over-the-counter (OTC) derivatives market (Faiola et al., 2008), which further increased the vulnerability of the financial markets.

An urge to reap excessive profits by financial institutions in an unregulated environment led to innovations and the introduction of new products that changed the financial structure. The traditional financial intermediation model, in which depositors provided funds to the banks for investment, was replaced by raising funds from the market through securitisation. Loans were pooled and sold to investors as Mortgage Backed Securities (MBSs)/Collateralised Debt Obligations (CDOs). By the end of 2006 about 55 per cent of the estimated total of $10.2 trillion value of mortgage loans in the United States was packaged and sold to local and global investors (Norges Bank, 2007).

Another segment that expanded rapidly during the period preceding the crisis was the unregulated OTC derivatives market. The value of the overall notional amounts of OTC contracts reached $596 trillion by the end of 2007, with credit default swaps increasing by 36 per cent during the second half of the year to reach $58 trillion (BIS, 2008). While some of these products were used for hedging purposes, most of them were used for speculation. The lax regulatory environment allowed banks to hold many of these risky instruments off-balance sheet (OBS) with little capital to support them (Crotty, 2009).

The financial crisis of 2008 was triggered by the collapse of an investment bank, Lehman Brothers Holdings Inc., which blew the already bubbling financial markets. The key problem was the derivatives it issued and traded, in particular securitised packages of mortgages, many of which contained a significant sub-prime element, but yet were favourably rated, as they were collateralised by real estate assets that had enjoyed a substantial increase in value. The downturn in the real estate market in the United States caused many to question the value of this collateral, which became more apparent when sub-prime borrowers started to default on their payments and their property was re-possessed. These defaults were not because of fecklessness on the part of the borrowers, but rather because many had taken out interest-only mortgages on a floating basis, so that when rates rose, they could no longer afford the payments. Furthermore, as the economy started to slow down and contract, many lost their jobs or could only work for fewer hours at reduced pay. As a consequence their finances were squeezed and the mortgage charges became unbearable.

The idea of home ownership for the majority of Americans was a commendable goal for the United States, socially, politically and economically. Home ownership makes people feel that they have a greater stake in their societies; it can result in more responsible citizenship. It was evident with hindsight, however, that the means of achieving mass ownership were flawed and that many were encouraged to have unrealistic expectations and aspirations given their personal financial circumstances. What happened was not accidental, and it is evident that the banks that sold the mortgages had some responsibility for the financial difficulties their clients ultimately faced. In particular there was an incentive structure of salary bonuses, which encouraged bank employees to sign up as many mortgage clients as possible. As the banks subsequently sold on the mortgages to investment banks such as Lehman, they were unconcerned about whether their clients could meet their long-term commitments (Crotty, 2009).

1.3.1 An Islamic Perspective on the Causes and Consequences of the Financial Crisis

From both an Islamic and broader moral perspective there was much to criticise in the system that contributed to the 2008 financial crisis and the resultant misery for those whose properties were re-possessed. There was widespread criticism of the injustices that resulted in the poorer classes in society suffering the most while many of the senior bankers kept their substantial bonuses. Islamic finance, in an aspiration sense, involves profit and loss sharing (PLS), whereas the banking practices that contributed to the crisis involved the concentration of profit in the hands of a few rather than any wider social sharing. Losses in the conventional system were also not shared, as although admittedly the shareholders suffered substantial declines in the value of their holdings, and there were some redundancies among junior bank staff, many of the leading investment bankers kept their jobs or soon found others as equally well paid as business as usual was resumed once the crisis passed. The main losers were bank clients who got into difficulties and taxpayers, including those of modest means but above tax thresholds (Dowd, 2009).

In Islamic finance interest is equated with *ribā*, which is explicitly forbidden. In contrast, the banking relations before the crisis and subsequent to it were based on a lender and borrower relationship with interest at its core. However, the relationship was asymmetric and exploitative, with the interest charge for the borrowing quoted on a take-it-or-leave-it basis rather than the rate being agreed through a process of negotiation. Of course it could be argued that the borrower had choices and could shop around for different quotes. All too often the terms of the borrowing were deliberately complicated to prevent clients comparing like with like, with trade-offs between the interest charged and the level of arrangement fees and in addition exit or termination fees frequently levied. Front discounting and back loading were also used, so that the borrower may believe they had a cheap deal, whereas in reality the long-term charges were great. In short, the ignorance of borrowers was being exploited, which in Islam is referred to as *jahalah*, something discouraged in economic transactions.

1.4 Islamic Banking Factors Mitigating Financial Crises

The relationship between lenders and borrowers in conventional banking is based on risk transfer from the latter to the former rather than risk sharing. Risk transfers are, however, seen as unjust and exploitative in Islamic finance. The borrower who has signed a variable rate contract is vulnerable to rises in interest rates that result from monetary policy tightening that is totally exogenous from the lender–borrower contract. Of course borrowers can opt for fixed interest contracts, but these are usually more expensive and not necessarily advantageous, as borrowers can end up paying well over the market price should interest rates fall. In other words, with both variable and fixed interest contracts clients face pricing risk, but this is mitigated for the bank given its power to set interest rates unilaterally.

With Islamic personal and corporate finance, risks are shared between the bank and the client; indeed it is this sharing that justifies the bank's return (Iqbal and Llewellyn, 2002). In contrast with conventional corporate finance, risks are not shared; rather, business risks are entirely borne by the client. Of course there is the possibility of client default, which is admittedly a risk for the bank, although usually the consequences for the business client are much worse, as it is the client who becomes bankrupt, not usually the bank. In fact the injustices with defaults can also be regarded as perverse. Although large corporate borrowers are in a much stronger position to re-negotiate than medium- and small-sized businesses, their potential default could easily threaten the credit rating of the bank. The 'too big to fail' argument not only applies to banks but to their customers.

In contrast with Islamic corporate finance, through *mushārakah* and *muḍārabah* contracts business risks are shared, with the bank getting a lower return, or indeed no return at all if the business is performing badly. With these contracts the banks also share in losses; in fact under a *muḍārabah* contract the bank, as financier or *rab al maal*, has to cover the entire loss. This burden-sharing is of course welcomed by corporate clients, but from the bank's perspective these types of contracts also have advantages. The sharing in business risks, including losses, makes defaults much less likely. It means that the bank has a long-term relationship with the corporate client. With conventional banking the lenders rarely look beyond the next repayment that is due, whereas with *mushārakah* and *muḍārabah* contracts that can have a maturity of five years or more, Islamic banks can take a much longer-term perspective (Çizakça, 1996).

If all banks were Islamic, financial crises would be less likely. Islamic banks not only take a longer-term perspective beyond the relatively short five-year periods of most business cycles, but they have built-in stabilisers that lower the probability of crises. In particular, having investment depositors whose accounts are governed by *muḍārabah* contracts provides a safety net. If an Islamic bank finds its profits diminishing because of a worsening financial environment, not only will dividends to shareholders be reduced, but less will be paid out in profit shares to investment account holders. If losses occur, none of the bank's current revenue can be paid to these depositors; rather, any payouts can be financed from the profit equalisation reserve that most Islamic banks maintain (El Tiby, 2011: 124). If these reserves are insufficient the investment depositors will not receive a return, or in an extreme case could suffer losses through the bank writing down the value of their deposits, although this has never happened in practice.

1.5 Lessons for Islamic Banks in Retrospect

Islamic banks are in principle less vulnerable during financial crises and in practice no Islamic bank failed during the period of the 2008 crisis and its aftermath. Nevertheless, the boards of Islamic banks and their executives should not be complacent, and there are important lessons from the crisis for their future operations. First and foremost the case for close adherence to Islamic financial principles has been strengthened by the crisis, in particular those principles of profit and loss and risk sharing. Second, stressing that Islamic finance is about long-term relationship building, not simply short-term profits (Brown *et al.*, 2007: 97). If mortgages are sold to third parties, this breaks the relationship between banks and those they are financing. Securitising mortgages may be undesirable for Islamic banks, even though some had been adopting such practices prior to the financial crisis.

Although it is simplistic to blame the growth of derivatives for the crisis, the complex collateralised debt instruments and credit default swaps that won financial engineers many accolades turned out to be of doubtful merit. The behaviour of those involved in trading these instruments came very close to gambling, as the derivatives markets resembled a zero-sum game with gains for the winners being at the expense of the losers. Gambling or *maysir* is forbidden in Islamic teaching because of the inevitable injustices and the harm it can inflict on others (Rosenthal, 1975: 77). Clearly much pain was inflicted on the wider community because of the actions of a relatively small number of derivatives traders over the 2007–8 period, even though the traders' behaviour was within national laws.

Product pricing policies that simply mimic those for interest-based transactions are also undesirable and unjust. Of course it can be argued that in so far as Islamic banks are competing with conventional institutions, with the latter dominating the market, Islamic banks are price-takers rather than price-makers. However, Islamic banks are offering differentiated products, the competition being about quality rather than mere pricing. What matters is that the client should be able to negotiate prices, and that both parties believe they have reached a just outcome. To be able to negotiate effectively clients need full and timely information and the ability to understand its significance. The former depends on transparency and the prohibition of any attempt to conceal information from a client while respecting the confidentiality of both parties. The latter, being able to interpret the information provided, implies a degree of client education, for which the Islamic bank should have some responsibility. Clearly there should not be mis-selling with the bank receiving unjustifiable fees for inappropriate or irrelevant services. Such activity by the bank could be equated with *jahiliyah*, the exploitation of the ignorant.

One lesson from the financial crisis is that uncertainty feeds on itself and causes a massive loss of confidence in the financial system. Contractual ambiguity was a key contributor to the uncertainty, and if Islamic bankers are not to repeat the mistakes made they should be mindful of the prohibition of *gharar* when drafting contracts (Vogel and Hayes, 1998: 68–9). Indeed what happened during the crisis, when many contracts became valueless, vindicates the prohibition of *gharar*. It is morally objectionable if ambiguous contracts are deliberately offered so that the financier can avoid their contractual undertakings. Even if it is unintentional, but arises through careless legal drafting, this cannot be accepted as an excuse, especially if one of the parties to the contract ends up being worse off through no fault of their own. Banks either use law firms to draft their contracts or undertake the work in-house by their own legal departments. Most clients, however, take the contracts they are offered on trust, as they cannot afford to take legal advice on every contract they sign.

The effects of the global financial crisis should not be viewed as entirely negative, as the questioning of the weaknesses in the financial system that caused the failure has focused on the immorality of many of the systems used and the inappropriate reward structures, especially those determining bankers' bonuses. Islamic bankers can stress their moral and ethical credentials as employees of faith-based organisations. It is, however, important that Islamic banks live up to these values by demonstrating that there is a real alternative to the conventional financial system. The way of ensuring this is to stress the value of having a *Sharīʿah* board to provide moral oversight as well as systems of corporate governance that ensure that there are appropriate checks and balances, as may be expected by institutions guided by religious principles that stress the importance of following a straight and righteous path (Esposito, 1998). One consequence is to have executive pay based on fair and just remuneration rather than on greed, which was all too apparent during the financial crisis and in its aftermath.

1.6 Implications for Islamic Banks of Post-crisis Regulatory Developments under Basel III

Recapitalising banks that got into difficulties as a result of the 2008 financial crisis has imposed an enormous financial burden on governments and hence taxpayers. It is not only banks in debt-ridden countries such as Greece, Iceland and Ireland that became almost insolvent but also two of the UK's four largest banks – Royal Bank of Scotland and Lloyds TSB, while in the United States the Treasury had to buy Citibank Shares at a cost of $45 billion. No Islamic bank had to be bailed out in this way, although the specialist real estate financier Amlak had to be recapitalised by the government of Dubai where it is based.

In order to strengthen banks worldwide the capital adequacy requirements have been increased significantly by the Basel Committee on Banking Supervision (BCBS). National regulators, including central banks throughout the Muslim world, require all banks to adhere to the Basel II standards, and the new, tougher Basel III standards will have to be fully implemented by 31 December 2019. The G-20 countries representing the world's largest economies agreed to adopt Basel III in 2011, including Indonesia, Turkey and Saudi Arabia, the three most important economies in the Muslim world. Islamic banks already adhere to Basel II, but the implementation of Basel III will still be a major challenge, not least as the standards are designed for conventional banks, yet Islamic banks must also comply.

Under Basel III capital adequacy is set at 4.5 per cent of common equity in relation to risk-weighted assets compared to 2.0 per cent under Basel II (Basel Committee on Banking Supervision, 2011: 2). Islamic banks are generally well capitalised, but it is worth stressing that the investment *muḍārabah* accounts do not count as common equity, even though some in the Islamic finance industry argue that they should. Regulators treat these accounts as bank liabilities, not assets, even though in principle they have some ability to absorb losses, although this has never happened in practice. Banks are required to have a minimum of 6 per cent of risk-weighted assets accounted for by Tier 1 capital, which includes the 4.5 per cent common equity plus an additional 1.5 per cent as retained earnings. As already indicated Islamic banks maintain profit equalisation reserves in order to smooth out payments to investment *muḍārabah* depositors so that they can receive a profit share even when the bank is unprofitable or is suffering losses. One issue yet to be resolved is whether these reserves can count as retained earnings. Regulators may argue that because the profit equalisation reserves are earmarked for the benefit of investment depositors only, they cannot be counted as retained earnings. Islamic bankers may well disagree.

Additional buffers are also required under Basel III, the first being the mandatory capital conservation buffer of 2.5 per cent. Islamic bankers could argue that, if profit equalisation reserves are not allowed to count as retained earnings, then a fall-back position is that they could count for capital conservation purposes. Again regulators may assert that the capital conservation buffers are designed to reduce the need to call on equity investors for additional capital in the case of a crisis, and that reserves designed to protect depositors cannot fulfil that function. The second buffer, referred to as the discretionary counter-cyclical buffer, is also likely to be an issue for Islamic banks. This applies to banks with high credit growth, the concern being that this may make the banks more vulnerable to a cyclical downturn, especially if they are financing many new customers, some of whom may not be able to meet their repayments obligations. As many Islamic banks are expanding rapidly, regulators may insist that they set an additional 2.5 per cent of their capital aside for the counter-cyclical buffer. If the two buffers, plus the capital adequacy requirements under Basel III are applied, the capital ratio rises to 9.5 per cent of risk-weighted assets, plus the 1.5 per cent retained earnings requirement for Tier 1 capital.

Liquidity requirements have also been increased under Basel III with the introduction of a net funding ratio of thirty days' coverage, meaning that Islamic banks will have to calculate their net funding outflows and ensure they have sufficient liquidity to meet all depositor demands (Basel Committee on Banking Supervision, 2010: 3). This accentuates the difficulty that Islamic banks already have over liquidity, as the major qualifying assets include treasury bills on which interest is payable. At present Islamic banks manage their liquidity through deposits with the central bank that earn no return and by holding inter-bank deposits that are subject to *murābaḥah* contracts usually involving commodity trades on the London Metal Exchange (Ainley *et al.*, 2007: 6).

The Islamic banks earn a minimal return on these deposits, but the transaction costs are high. There is therefore dissatisfaction with this method of liquidity management, which will not be acceptable under Basel III rules in any case. Assets issued by banks are likely to be at risk in times of financial stress and there are concerns that in such circumstances the contractual obligations of the *murābaḥah* deposits could be breached.

Under Basel III banks are also obliged to maintain a Net Stable Funding Ratio (NSFR) for long-term assets and liabilities (Basel Committee on Banking Supervision, 2010: 25–6). The metric stipulates that the sum of stable funding divided by the sum of long-term assets should exceed 100 per cent. Stable funding is defined as customer deposits, long-term wholesale funding, usually through time deposits from other banks and equity. Short-term wholesale funding of the sort that dried up during the financial crisis is excluded. Such funding included the overnight and short-term *murābaḥah* deposits of Islamic banks. In the case of Islamic banks, most stable funding is from investment *muḍārabah* deposits, usually subject to periods of notice for withdrawals from thirty to 180 days. Islamic banks did not seek funding through the wholesale market as this would have involved interest transactions, although there were some fund placements on a long-term basis by other Islamic banks, including by parent banks in their subsidiaries, which will continue to comply with NSFR requirements under Basel III.

The denominator of the metric, long-term assets or 'Structural Term Assets' is defined as:

(i) 100 per cent of loans longer than one year
(ii) 85 per cent of loans to retail clients with a remaining life shorter than one year
(iii) 50 per cent of loans to corporate clients with a remaining life shorter than one year
(iv) 20 per cent of government and corporate bonds.

In the definition of 'Structural Term Assets', weighted off-balance sheet assets should also be included.

Islamic banks do not provide loans but their financing through *murābaḥah*, *ijārah*, *istisnā*, *salam*, *muḍārabah* and *mushārakah* is counted as equivalent to loans under Basel III in the same way as it had been under previous Basel standards. The fourth measured component, corporate bonds, cannot be held by Islamic banks as they pay interest. *Sukuk* are the recognised alternative, and with an active market in Malaysia such assets can be regarded as liquid, but this is not the case in the Gulf Cooperation Council (GCC), which raises questions about whether they can count as structured term assets for liquidity purposes (Ahmad and Mat Radzi, 2011: 1–14).

Islamic banks have few off-balance sheet items, the financing through the restricted *muḍārabah* deposits being the major item. The banks earn a fee for

administrating the deposits that fund the assets, but in the event of default it
is unclear whether it is the bank or the restricted *muḍārabah* depositors that
have a legal claim over the assets. For Basel III purposes such assets are best
excluded, not least as they are largely illiquid. What are included are revocable
and irrevocable lines of credit and liquidity facilities to clients. However, since
such credit types incur interest charges, they are not provided by Islamic banks,
while fee-based guarantees can be the *Sharīʿah*-compliant alternative.

A leveraging ratio of a minimum of 3 per cent has also been proposed under
the Basel III framework. This measures risk exposure in relation to total assets,
and is in addition to the capital adequacy ratios already discussed that measure
Tier 1 capital in relation to risk-weighted total assets. The aim of the leverage
ratio is to limit positions in financial derivatives and off-balance sheet exposure.
As neither of these applies to Islamic banks there is little need for a leverage
ratio to be imposed from their perspective. Setting the amount at 3 per cent
seems a modest goal, as with Islamic funds a leverage ratio of one-third is
applied as a screening criterion (Derigs and Marzban, 2007). In this case companies are ineligible for *Sharīʿah*-compliant investment if their debt to equity ratio
exceeds one-third, the aim being to encourage companies to raise funds through
risk-sharing equity rather than debt involving risk transfer, which increases cyclical vulnerability.

1.7 The Implications of Business Cycles for Islamic Bank Risk

The financial crisis highlighted the differences in risks in Islamic finance compared to conventional banking. Although – as the Islamic Financial Services
Board recognises – Islamic banks face similar categories of risk as conventional
banks, namely credit, liquidity, operational and market risk, the nature of the
risks differs within each category (Islamic Financial Services Board, 2005). The
credit risk on conventional interest-based loans differs from that on *murābaḥah*
and *ijārah* transactions, which involves the Islamic bank owning the asset being
financed. Of course the creditworthiness of the client has to be assessed in the
normal manner, but the legal position in the event of a default is completely different. With an unsecured interest-based loan there is no collateral, which can be
sold to realise some of the debt. Where a loan is secured the bank will have a legal
charge over the asset offered, which is not necessarily the same as what is being
financed. The conventional bank has no ownership rights.

The financial crisis was in part driven by credit risk, especially in the home
loan market where arguably the sub-prime lending should never have been
made. This, however, was a long-term issue. The immediate cause was liquidity
risk rising dramatically as market confidence evaporated and banks were unwill-
ing to transact with one another in wholesale markets. As Islamic banks were not,
as already indicated, involved in these markets, this was not really an issue as far
as they were concerned.

Most Islamic banks are retail institutions; hence the major liquidity risk is that they will not be able to meet their obligations to depositors seeking to withdraw their funds. In this context the Basel III thirty-day coverage of net withdrawals seems appropriate. In practice Islamic banks should not have much difficulty meeting this criterion as the velocity of circulation of their deposits is generally lower than for conventional banks, and hence net outflows are less (Wilson and Yusoff, 2005). Retail current account deposits with both Islamic and conventional banks tend to follow a monthly cycle with salary payments being credited each month followed by monthly housing and utility payments and cash withdrawals to cover everyday purchases. As Islamic current accounts do not offer overdraft facilities, the average monthly credit balance tends to be higher, and the accounts are managed more conservatively. The demand for liquidity is therefore lower relative to deposits and the calls on liquidity more predictable.

For many Islamic banks the amount of funds in *muḍārabah* deposits greatly exceeds that in current accounts. These accounts tend to be viewed by depositors as long-term savings accounts, a frequent motive for opening such accounts being the desire to save for the deposit on a house or a vehicle, which the Islamic bank may be asked to finance. The savings period may take years, during which there will be few or even no withdrawals from the accounts. This considerably reduces the need for Islamic banks to maintain liquidity buffers to cover withdrawals. Furthermore, as with most *muḍārabah* accounts, notice must be given for withdrawals with the periods usually ranging from thirty to 180 days as already indicated; this reduces the likelihood of unpredictable withdrawals. As a consequence Islamic banks are generally regarded as being subject to lower liquidity risks than their conventional counterparts.

The risks that Islamic banks have significant exposure to include ownership risk associated with *murābaḥah* and *ijārah*, market risk associated with *salam* and *istisnā* and venture capital risks, especially those associated with exit, in respect to *mushārakah* and *muḍārabah* financing. The latter can be regarded as similar to counter-party credit risk, although these are partnership and not purely financing contracts. Banking regulators are often uncertain of how to deal with such risks, which lie outside their normal areas of competency. Some informally argue that such risks can be more easily borne by ordinary companies that are only accountable to their owners, not banks with depositors who expect a higher degree of protection, including *muḍārabah* depositors. Fortunately, ownership risks are not primarily cyclical and nor are the commodity market risks from *murābaḥah*, which in so far as they involve commodities trading, may even be anti-cyclical. The risks of defaults on rental payments with *ijārah* are to some extent pro-cyclical, although during recessions more discounts may be offered on equipment and accommodation, which can result in *ijārah* risks being anti-cyclical. The venture capital exit risks from *muḍārabah* and *mushārakah* contracts are perhaps the most pro-cyclical.

It is important, however, to note that the change in the business cycles of a country does have implications for the operations of Islamic banks and financial institutions. Considering that the share of Islamic banking and finance is still lesser than its conventional counterpart, the causal relationship runs from the business cycle to Islamic banking and finance, implying that the effects of Islamic banking and finance on macro-economic variables are rather limited. The resilience of Islamic banking, hence, is very much related to its own internal dynamics, which should be strong enough, as explained, to respond to the external shocks created by the business cycles.

1.8 *Sharī͑ah* Governance Systems and Risk Mitigation

The role of *Sharī͑ah* supervisory boards is to ensure that the legal contracts offered by Islamic financial institutions are compliant with *fiqh* jurisprudence (Grais and Pellegrini, 2006). The board has no executive function, which is a matter for the management of the bank, or strategic role, which is the responsibility of the board of directors. The *Sharī͑ah* board has no responsibility for risk management, apart from those arising from their own rulings or *fatwā*. This exposure is referred to as *Sharī͑ah* risk, which arises when the boards issue *fatwā* that change or even contradict previous *fatwā*. This could be because of a lack of due diligence at the time of the first ruling, or simply because the *Sharī͑ah* board changed their mind when the consequences of what they approved was brought to their attention, usually by the internal *Sharī͑ah* audit team. In either case the outcome may render a previously approved contract *Sharī͑ah* non-compliant, a serious matter for an Islamic bank that could damage customer confidence and introduce reputational risk.

Fortunately, *Sharī͑ah* risk does not arise too often, recent examples being the condemnation of *mushārakah*- and *muḍārabah*-based *sukuk* because of the guarantees relating to the repurchase undertaking by the issuer. Sheikh Taqi Usmani, chairman of the *Sharī͑ah* board of the Accounting and Auditing Organisation for Islamic Financial Institutions (AAOIFI), criticised the *sukuk* contracts. These were subsequently modified, although not for existing *sukuk*. Although *Sharī͑ah* risk is not related to business cycles the timing of Sheikh Taqi Usmani's pronouncements was unfortunate, as it was in 2007, the year before the global crisis. New *sukuk* issuance in the GCC almost stopped in 2008, although this was more a result of knock-on effects from the global financial crisis rather than as a result of Sheikh Taqi Usmani's remarks and the subsequent clarification by AAOIFI.[2]

The other recent example of *Sharī͑ah* risk came in 2009 when the International Islamic *Fiqh* Academy issued a *fatwā* prohibiting *tawarruq*, a method of providing cash advances widely used by Islamic banks. As the International Islamic *Fiqh* Academy is the institution that provides rulings on Islamic finance on behalf of the Organisation of the Islamic Conference, a body representing fifty-six Muslim majority states, its *fatwā* carry significant weight. While *tawarruq* is not yet universally prohibited, its days as a financing method are certainly numbered (Bouheraoua, 2011).

While many banking laws pertaining to Islamic finance stipulate that Islamic banks should have a *Sharīʿah* board, most regulators are reluctant to get involved in matters of *Sharīʿah*, not least as with five major schools of Islamic thought worldwide there is a desire not to take sides in matters of dispute between *Sharīʿah* scholars. Malaysia is the exception, as its Central Bank has its own *Sharīʿah* board whose *fatwā* can overrule those of the Islamic bank *Sharīʿah* boards. This ensures consistency and arguably some risk mitigation, but it could potentially stifle future debate by centralising *Sharīʿah* decision making.

Sharīʿah governance, as part of the corporate governance system, is essential for ensuring *Sharīʿah* compliancy but also for helping to mitigate the effects of potential risks through due diligence by abiding the ethical foundations of Islamic moral economy. However, recent empirical evidences, such as by Hasan (2011), suggest that 'best practice' in *Sharīʿah* governance has not reached the level of sophistication and efficiency expected from Islamic banks. Islamic banks, thus, should aspire to reach to the *Sharīʿah* governance level as identified by Islamic moral economy to make sure that financial crises similar to the one that has engulfed the entire world should not emerge from the Islamic banking sector.

1.9 The Operations of Islamic Banks in Distressed Markets

In their last four decades of existence, the Islamic banks have experience in operating in distressed markets before the 2008 financial crisis. Kuwait Finance House was founded in 1977, four years before the *Souk al-Manakh* crisis that resulted in a catastrophic fall in stock market prices. This in turn caused a collapse of the real estate market and the bankruptcy of many Kuwaitis, including clients of the Kuwait Finance House (Wilson, 1983: 172–6). Nevertheless the bank survived, even though it was heavily exposed to the real estate market. No profit shares were paid to *mudॖ.ārabah* depositors for a two-year period, yet they stayed loyal while the bank rebalanced its books to emerge as a stronger institution.

In the case of Malaysia the Asia Crisis of 1997 drastically affected the economy and the banking sector, including Bank Islam Malaysia the country's first Islamic bank, which was established in 1983. Nevertheless the crisis brought opportunities for Islamic finance. Following a merger of two conventional poorly performing banks, Bank Muamalat was established, Malaysia's second largest exclusively Islamic bank. This increased client interest in Islamic finance, as most of the clients of the previous two conventional banks remained with Bank Muamalat (Kryst and Moore, 2001).

The global crisis of 2008 had only a limited effect on Islamic banks. This was partly because the effects were greatest in the developed markets of North America and Europe rather than in the emerging markets where most Islamic financial institutions are located. Malaysia's economy and financial system was buoyed up by the continuing growth in the East and Southeast Asian region and the country was less affected by the financial crisis than its more globalised neighbour Singapore. *Sukuk* issuance continued and the Islamic banking sector was more prepared for international setbacks, partly because of its restructuring in the aftermath of the earlier Asian crisis.

In the GCC the effect of the crisis was limited, not least because oil prices stayed firm because of sustained demand from China and India. Consequently trade continued and the *murābaḥah* contracts offered by Islamic banks to finance imports, including consumer durables, remained popular. Leasing activity was also buoyant and it was only in the construction sector that the global crisis had an effect; even in Dubai it was a correction in prices in the aftermath of the local real estate bubble rather than global factors that caused the problems. In Saudi Arabia, where oil prices and production levels drive government and consumer spending, which in turn determines activity in the financial sector, the global crisis had only a limited effect. Of greater recent concern has been the Arab Uprising as, although it is unlikely that there will be civil strife in Saudi Arabia, the government raised salaries for public sector workers in 2011 and increased welfare spending on its citizens to prevent discontent. The resultant fiscal stimulus has undoubtedly been helpful for the Islamic banking sector.

As has been pointed out, while no two crises are the same, it is possible to identify a number of common features in many crises (Reinhart and Rogoff, 2009). It is apparent that Islamic banks and Islamic finance more generally survive and cope with many different types of crisis (Chapra, 2008). The global financial crisis of 2008 was the most severe for almost eighty years; hence it was a challenging test. Future crises are inevitable, but Islamic finance is well established and Islamic banking strong enough to cope with future crises. Debt crises in the Eurozone periphery and the United States should not have an effect on the Islamic banking industry to a large degree, as its presence is marginal in these markets. Future possible conflicts and even wars within and between states in the Middle East are a concern, but they are unlikely to engulf the entire region and Islamic banking has a strong presence in other more stable regions in any case, notably Southeast Asia, which has a much larger Muslim population. There is good reason therefore to be cautiously optimistic about the future for Islamic finance given its resilience during past crises (Wilson, 2011).

1.10 The Book Contents

This work contains a selection of the papers presented at a conference hosted by Durham University in July 2010 and jointly sponsored with the Islamic Research and Training Institute of the Islamic Development Bank Group as already indicated. The table of contents demonstrates the scope of the discussions; this introduction and the remarks above, written one year after the conference, are an attempt to put the papers in context and to discuss the significance of the issues for the Islamic finance industry. The question of the stability of Islamic banks was first raised by Dr Mabid Al-Jarhi, president of the International Association of Islamic Economics, but not taken up by researchers until recently (Al-Jarhi, 2004). Apart from this book the other major studies on the stability of Islamic finance are by Askari *et al.* (2010), and a volume edited by Venardos (2010). This study seeks to complement these studies as an examination of the contents of all three volumes will show.

The contribution to this book by Rafe Haneef and Edib Smolo applies the lessons learned from the global financial crisis. The authors consider some of the major failings in the existing global financial system, notably how risk transfers result in imprudent economic growth. The inadequate standards of care of many of those selling conventional financial products is highlighted, a symptom of regulatory failure. Transparency and disclosure issues are also discussed, which will become even more important if the shift to equity-based finance, which the authors favour, occurs, given its greater compatibility with Islamic financial principles.

1.11 The Empirical Contributions on Stability

Three chapters are directly concerned with the resilience and stability of Islamic banks. Rania Abdelfattah and Ahmed Badreldin examine the performance of leading Islamic banks before and during the financial crisis using standard measures such as return on equity, cost–income ratios and risk provision margins. The empirical data show that Islamic banks have performed well during the financial crisis but reveals significant differences between the banks. Whether these differences reflect the environments in which the banks operate or their own management could be an interesting topic for further research with the evidence presented as its starting point.

Matthias Verbeet compares the stability of Islamic banks with that of their conventional counterparts using data from five Malaysian and two UK banks. Five of the banks are conventional, although they have some Islamic banking business, but this is not separately reported. The two Islamic banks are Bank Islam Malaysia and Bank Muamalat. As with the study by Rania Abdelfattah and Ahmed Badreldin, the data used to measure performance includes returns on equity but changes in capital structure are also analysed, including core capital ratios, the equity capital to total capital ratio, and the risk-weighted capital ratio – important variables from the perspective of Basel II and Basel III.

The third contribution on stability focuses on the cyclical behaviour of Islamic bank financing. Mohd. Afandi Abu Bakar, Radiah Abdul Kader and Roza Hazli and Hairunnizam Wahid use standard cyclical indicators distinguishing leading indicators such as money supply and the interest rate from lagging indicators such as commercial loans, the consumer price index (CPI) and unemployment. The bank indicators include reserve growth as a proportion of earnings, the ratio of bank capital growth to earnings asset growth and loan loss provisions to earnings asset growth, which would be expected to rise in a recession. The testing involved the use of panel data for the period from 1998 to 2008 for twenty-four Islamic banks. The findings show that financing growth accelerates as economic growth strengthens, which is similar to what occurs with conventional banks. The authors suggest that if Islamic banks relied more on profit and risk sharing their financing may be less pro-cyclical.

1.12 The Contributions on Risk Management

Effective risk management can mitigate the negative effects of cycles on banks, and perhaps even reduce the magnitude of an economic downturn. This study contains three contributions on risk management in Islamic banking, which involved detailed empirical research. The first by Romzie Rosman and Abdul Rahim Abdul Rahman involved an examination of the risk management practices of twenty-eight Islamic banks in sixteen countries using a questionnaire survey. The researchers sought information on the risk management practices used, how risks were measured and what techniques were used for risk mitigation. The findings revealed that overall risk management was treated seriously but managing liquidity risk was a challenge and the provision for rate of return risk was inadequate, indeed in some cases non-existent. The guidelines on displaced commercial risk provided by the Islamic Financial Services Board were not usually followed, leaving the banks vulnerable. Risk measurement was also revealed to be inadequate, and many Islamic banks were complacent about risk mitigation.

The contribution by Noraini Mohd. Ariffin and Salina Hj Kassim focuses on liquidity issues. The researchers analyse the implications of the maturity mismatches that inevitably arise in Islamic as well as conventional banks and how these are handled. In addition, the relationship is investigated between liquidity risk management and financial performance as measured by return on assets and return on equity. The period covered is from 2006 to 2008, with data and information collected from the leading six Malaysian Islamic banks. Although there was no clear increase in liquidity risk over the period, the return on equity of the banks declined as a result of the global crisis. As with conventional banks, it was apparent that investors in the banks with the highest liquidity risk expected and obtained the highest return on their equity. This was particularly apparent with Bank Islam Malaysia, the most exposed Islamic bank. However, as liquidity reporting appears to be far from adequate, the findings should be interpreted with caution.

Sherin Kunhibava's contribution concerns risk management and Islamic forward contracts, a topic not hitherto dealt with in the Islamic finance literature. *Fiqh* scholars have objected to forward contracts because of the implied uncertainty when the goods do not exist at the time the contract is agreed and the possibility of non-payment and non-delivery. *Salam* contracts eliminate the payments uncertainty and attempt to minimise the delivery uncertainty, although most Islamic banks do not use these contracts. Kunhibava examines the contracts that Islamic banks at present use including *bai muajjal* and *wa'd* as well as *bai al-sarf* for currency exchange. The author argues that there is a real need for hedging but further research is needed on suitable instruments. Bilateral promises would seem to be a way forward, although AAOIFI allows unilateral promises for currency exchange, which amount to guarantees with the guarantor charging a fee.

1.13 *Sharīᶜah* Governance of Islamic Financial Institutions

There are four contributions that are concerned with how Islamic financial institutions are governed. These only marginally touch on the corporate governance issues that arise with all financial institutions, but they need to be reconsidered for institutions such as Islamic banks because of their more complex stakeholder relations that involve a greater sharing of obligations and responsibilities. The four contributions focus on different aspects of *Sharīᶜah* governance, the *Sharīᶜah* board being the stakeholders with overall responsibility for *Sharīᶜah* compliance.

Zurina Shafii and Supiah Salleh examine the processes involved in internal *sharīᶜah* audit, a hitherto under-researched topic. *Sharīᶜah* audit practice is examined from the perspective of operational risk, which at present is seen as being rather restricted. In Malaysia, for example, it focuses on product design, structuring and legal procedures. The AAOIFI guidelines and those of Bank Negara Malaysia on the establishment of *Sharīᶜah* committees are much more comprehensive and are seen as the starting point for *Sharīᶜah* audit. Standard methods of internal control as applied by KPMG are used as a benchmark against which *Sharīᶜah* audit can be appraised. The authors devise a *Sharīᶜah* internal control checklist (ICC) comprising of forty-two items and take two case studies, Bank Islam Malaysia and Bahrain Islamic bank, to examine how they score. Bank Islam Malaysia scores significantly higher across most categories.

Irawan Febianto and Abdou Diaw examine how far *Sharīᶜah* reports can be used as an effective tool for managing non-compliance risks. Unfortunately the reporting is often too brief with the issues that are examined not reported in any detail. In short, the reports frequently lack depth and do not reflect adequately the discussions at the *Sharīᶜah* board meetings and the points raised by the members. AAOIFI provides some guidance on *Sharīᶜah* reporting and the authors examine how far this has been adopted by ten leading Islamic banks. The level of conformity varies considerably with the Al Baraka Group based in Bahrain scoring 100 per cent and Bank Islam Malaysia, Kuwait Finance House Malaysia and Bahrain Islamic bank scoring more than 90 per cent. At the bottom are the Kuwait Finance House parent company, scoring a mere 18.2 per cent and Bank Muamalat Malaysia and Al Rajhi Malaysia, both scoring 27.3 per cent. Clearly there is much need for improvement. The relevant reports are reproduced as an appendix so that the readers can judge for themselves.

Another worthwhile empirical investigation of *Sharīᶜah* governance was undertaken by Zulkifli Hasan who is writing a book on the subject for the Edinburgh Guides to Islamic Finance Series. His survey brought responses from thirty-five Islamic financial institutions in the United Kingdom, Malaysia and the GCC. The survey sought information on the internal arrangements for *Sharīᶜah* governance, disputes procedures and the legal authority of *Sharīʿah* boards, the work and operational procedures of the boards and their attributes in terms of competence, independence and confidentiality. There were the attributes identified by the Islamic Financial Services Board as being critical for effective *Sharīʿah* governance, so there is awareness in the Islamic finance industry of these issues. The survey showed that there were significant deficiencies in *Sharīʿah* governance, but that these were worse in the United Kingdom and the GCC than in Malaysia where the issues had received more attention.

The final contribution by Abdulazeem Abozaid is more concerned with the outcomes of *Sharīʿah* governance rather than the governance itself. He examines financial products that have raised objections from *Sharīʿah* board members, notably *eina*, or back-to-back sales that are widely used for housing finance, and *tawarruq*, which was discussed earlier. The author argues that the financial crisis has demonstrated the folly of such financing methods that closely resemble some of the conventional financing products that proved defective. Abozaid displays a good knowledge of *fiqh* as well as modern finance, which makes his arguments convincing that *eina* and *tawarruq* contribute nothing to *maslahah*, the goals of the *Sharīʿah*.

1.14 Reputational Perspectives

These eleven contributions to this book represent the results of painstaking research conducted by young academic scholars in the field of Islamic finance. There are clearly a large number of empirical and theoretical studies taking place that should contribute to the development of the discipline. The readers can judge the merits of the papers for themselves, but suffice it to say that there have been some benefits from the 2008 crisis, resulting not least in a rethinking of what financing methods can ensure a greater degree of justice. The Islamic banking industry continues to have many shortcomings as the contributors to this book point out, but academic research can help to steer it in a better direction and enhance its reputation, not only in Islamic finance circles, but in the wider world beyond.

Notes

1. One finds a similar viewpoint in the new regulatory standards issued by the Basel Committee on Bank Supervision (Basel II), which proposes market-based risk assessment and capital requirements for financial institutions.
2. www.aaoifi.com/aaoifi_sb_sukuk_Feb2008_English.pdfi

References

Ahmad, Wahida and Mat Radzi, Rafisah (2011). *Sustainability of Sukuk and Conventional Bonds during Financial Crisis: Malaysian Capital Market*, La Trobe University Faculty of Law and Management Working Paper, Victoria, Australia.

Ainley, Michael, Mashayekhi, Ali, Hicks, Robert, Rahman, Arshadur and Ravalia, Ali (2007). *Islamic Banking in the UK: Regulation and Challenges*. London: Financial Services Authority.

Al-Jarhi, Mabid Ali (2004). 'Remedy for banking crises: What Chicago and Islam have in common', *Islamic Economic Studies* 11(2): 23–442.

Askari, Hossein, Iqbal, Zamir, Krichene, Noureddine and Mirakhor, Abbas (2010). *The Stability of Islamic Finance: Creating a Resilient Financial Environment for a Secure Future*. Singapore: Wiley Finance.

Bank for International Settlements (2008). *OTC Derivatives Market Activity in the Second Half of 2007*, Press Release. Available at: www.bis.org/press/p080522.htm, last accessed 2 May 2008.Basel Committee on Banking Supervision (2010). *International Framework for Liquidity Risk Measurement, Standards and Monitoring*. Basel: Bank for International Settlements, December.

Basel Committee on Banking Supervision (2011). *Basel III: A Global Regulatory Framework for More Resilient Banks and Banking Systems*. Basel: Bank for International Settlements, June.

Bouheraoua, Said (2001). *Tawarruq in the Banking System: A Critical Analytic Study of the Juristic Views on the Topic*. Kuala Lumpur: International Shariah Research Academy.

Brown, Kym, Hassan, M. Kabir and Skully, Michael (2007). 'Operational efficiency and performance of Islamic banks', in Kabir Hassan and Mervyn Lewis (eds), *Handbook of Islamic Banking*. Cheltenham: Edward Elgar, pp. 96–115.

Chapra, M. Umer (2008). *The Global Financial Crisis: Can Islamic Finance Help Minimise the Severity and Frequency of Such a Crisis in the Future?* Paper prepared for the Islamic Development Bank Forum on the Global Financial Crisis, Jeddah, 25 October.

Çizakça, M. (1996). *A Comparative Evolution of Business Partnerships: Islamic World and the West, with Specific Reference to the Ottoman Archives*. Leiden: E. J. Brill.

Crotty, James (2009). 'Structural causes of the global financial crisis: A critical assessment of the new financial architecture', *Cambridge Journal of Economics* 33(3): 563–80.

Derigs, Ulrich and Marzban, Shehab (2007). 'Review and analysis of current Islamic equity screening practices', *International Journal of Islamic and Middle Eastern Finance and Management* 1(4): 285–303.

Dowd, Kevin (2009). 'Moral hazard and the financial crisis', *Cato Journal* 29(1): 141–66.

El Tiby, Amr Mohamed (2011). *Islamic Banking: How to Manage Risk and Improve Profitability*. New Jersey: Wiley Finance.

Esposito, John L. (1998). *Islam: The Straight Path*. 3rd edn. New York: Oxford University Press.

Faiola, Anthony, Nakashima, Ellen and Drew, Jill (2008). 'What went wrong?', *The Washington Post*, 15 October. Available at: www.washingtonpost.com/wp-dyn/content/article/2008/10/14/ AR2008101403343.html, last accessed 14 February 2010.

Fukuyama, Francis (2008). 'The fall of America, Inc.', *Newsweek*, 13 October.

Grais, Wafik and Pellegrini, Matteo (2006). *Corporate Governance and Shariah Compliance in Institutions Offering Islamic Financial Services*. World Bank Policy Research Working Paper No. 4054, November.

Hasan, Zulkifli (2011). 'A survey on Shari'ah governance practices in Malaysia, GCC countries and the UK critical appraisal', *International Journal of Islamic and Middle Eastern Finance and Management* 4(1): 30–51.

Iqbal, M. and Llewellyn, D. T. (2002). 'Introduction', in M. Iqbal and D. T. Llewellyn (eds), *Islamic Banking and Finance: New Perspectives on Profit Sharing and Risk*, Cheltenham: Edward Elgar, pp. 1–14.

Islamic Financial Services Board (2005). *Guiding Principles of Risk Management for Institutions Offering Only Islamic Financial Services*. Kuala Lumpur, Malaysia.

Kryst, Mark H. and Moore, Michael (2001). 'Financial Sector Issues', in Kanitta Meesook,

Il Houng Lee, Olin Liu, Yougesh Khatri, Natalia Tamirisa, Michael Moore and Mark H. Kryst (eds), *Malaysia: From Crisis to Recovery*. Washington, DC: International Monetary Fund, Washington, pp. 71–82.

Norges Bank (2007). *Financial Stability 2/2007*. Report from the Central Bank of Norway, No. 5/2007.

Reinhart, Carmen M. (2008). *Reflections on the International Dimensions and Policy Lessons of the US Subprime Crisis*, 15 March 2008. Available at: www.voxeu.org/index.php?q=node/988, last accessed 13 October 2011.

Reinhart, Carmen M. and Rogoff, Kenneth S. (2008). 'Is the 2007 US sub-prime financial crisis so different? An international historical comparison', *American Economic Review: Paper & Proceedings* 98(2): 339–44.

Reinhart, Carmen M. and Rogoff, Kenneth S. (2009). *This Time is Different: Eight Centuries of Financial Folly*. Princeton: Princeton University Press.

Rosenthal, Franz (1975). *Gambling in Islam*. Leiden: E. J. Brill.

Venardos, Angelo M. (2010). *Current Issues in Islamic Banking and Finance: Resilience and Stability in the Present System*. Singapore: World Scientific Publishing.

Vogel, Frank E. and Hayes, Samuel L. (1998). *Islamic Law and Finance: Religion, Risk and Return*. The Hague: Kluwer Law International.

Wilson, Rodney (1983). *Banking and Finance in the Arab Middle East*. London: Macmillan.

Wilson, Rodney (2011). *The Determinants of Islamic Financial Development and the Constraints on its Growth*, Islamic Financial Services Board 4th Public Lecture on Financial Policy and Stability, Amman, Jordan.

Wilson, Rodney and Yusoff, Remali (2005). 'An econometric analysis of conventional and Islamic bank deposits in Malaysia', *Review of Islamic Economics* 9(1): 31–49.

2

RESHAPING THE ISLAMIC FINANCE INDUSTRY: APPLYING THE LESSONS LEARNED FROM THE GLOBAL FINANCIAL CRISIS

Rafe Haneef and Edib Smolo

2.1 Introduction

In the last twenty-seven years, the world has witnessed more than 124 distinct financial crises. The financial meltdown caused by the current global financial crisis brought the financial world to its knees. Due to its severity, it has been labelled the worst crisis since the Great Depression (for example, see Jones, 2009; Nonomiya and Lanman, 2008; *The New York Times*, 2010; Volcker, 2010). It is now, more than ever before, clear that the current financial system is not flawless. The severity of the recent asset bubble burst has raised questions about the merits of *laissez-faire* capitalism and the theory of a rational market as highlighted in the Efficient Market Hypothesis (EMH). There has been growing interest in the work of Hyman Minsky and his financial instability hypothesis (Minsky, 2008) following the American sub-prime mortgage crisis. According to this hypothesis, the accumulation of debt is the initial trigger for financial crisis. Economic stability in the short run breeds instability in the long run as debt accumulates to unsustainable levels.

Notably, the prolonged period of 'moderation' following previous crises, such as the 2001 dot-com bubble, together with what is termed as 'the global saving glut', paved the way for the current crisis. In addition, easy money, uncontrolled growth of credit and debts, lax regulation and supervision, innovation of complex financial structures that far exceeded the real potential and needs of the economy, mismanagement of risks involved, lack of disclosure and transparency, predatory lending and high leveraging – among other factors – can be traced as the main culprits of the crisis. The distinguishing feature of the current financial crisis is that it originated in a developed economy, that of the United States of America, as compared to the other crises of the last half-century (Truman, 2009a, 2009b).

The global financial crisis also brought the Islamic financial industry (IFI) into the limelight as a possible and viable alternative. Its underlying principles, deeply rooted in the teachings of the *Sharīʿah* (Islamic law), proved to be a blessing for the IFI. The crisis had a limited effect on Islamic finance, although the sector did not emerge completely unscathed. At the same time the crisis provided a necessary shock for the Islamic finance industry to evaluate its own practices and position within the global financial architecture. Such an evaluation of current practices has to be performed from an ethico-legal perspective to ensure that the industry is not replicating the conventional path but adhering to the spirit of what the *Sharīʿah* intended in financial contracts.

In short, the global financial crisis offers both a challenge and opportunity for Islamic finance. How Muslim scholars will respond to these challenges will clearly define the future of Islamic finance. As Karuvelil stated (2000: 155): 'The [Islamic finance] industry faces considerable challenges; its response to them will determine whether it becomes a significant alternative to the conventional system in global financial markets.'

This chapter consists of five sections, including the introduction. Section Two highlights the main lessons from the financial crisis. As identifying the lessons from the crisis is only one part of the story, the redressing of issues and flaws in the current financial architecture is the focus of Section Three. Section Four focuses on reshaping the behaviours of the economic agents. Special focus is given to Islamic finance and the importance of ethico-legal principles necessary for building a healthier and more stable financial system.

2.2 Lessons Learned from the Current Global Crisis

The inherent features of the recent crisis, which commentators consider unique among other international financial crises of recent decades, provide a backdrop for framing an evaluation of the current financial architecture. First, the recent financial crisis originated in the United States – a seemingly highly developed financial and legal system – as compared to other past crises, which began in emerging markets. Second, the fact that a US sub-prime mortgage crisis evolved into a global financial crisis should not surprise us since the currency and the institutions of the United States are at the core of the global financial system. And, third, this recent crisis began in the financial sector and then moved to the real economy, creating a feedback cycle that further weakened the financial sector and real economy (Truman, 2009a).

Upon a review of the available literature on the current global financial crisis, it appears that there is no consensus on the causes of the current financial crisis. Some argue that the complexity and intensive use of structured financial products, derivatives and other assets with uncertain fundamentals played a key role in triggering the crisis (Aziz, 2008; FSF, 2008; Jordan and Jain, 2009; Mersch, 2009: 14; Mirakhor and Krichene, 2009; Mizen, 2008; *The New York Times*, 2010; Sarkar, 2009; Truman, 2009a, 2009b; Yellen, 2009). Other commentators note a combination of loose monetary policy, lax financial supervision and a trend towards deregulation (Aziz, 2008; Cooper, 2008: 171; Kashyap et al., 2008; Taylor, 2008; Truman, 2009a, 2009b), together with low interest rates, excessive leveraging and credit growth as the fundamental factors that ignited the crisis (Aziz, 2008; Bordo, 2008; Mirakhor and Krichene, 2009; OECD, 2009a, 2009b; Roubini, 2008; Truman, 2009a). This view has been endorsed in the World Economic Forum's *Financial Development Report 2008* as follows:

These crises [currency crises, sovereign debt crises, systemic banking or financial crises, systemic corporate crises, systemic household debt crises] are often preceded by asset bubbles and the credit bubbles that feed them . . . However, many asset bubbles have been associated with episodes of easy monetary policy and excessive credit growth.

The perverse interaction between easy money, asset bubbles, credit growth, and leveraging that feed asset bubbles has been observed in many episodes. The initial trigger for a bubble may (but not necessarily) be a period of easy money with relatively low real interest rates. Such a low cost of capital and easy liquidity may lead to an initial increase in the asset price above its fundamental value. Since asset purchases are often financed by credit, the initial increase in the asset prices allows borrowers to borrow more as the asset price rise increases the value of collateral that can be used to increase leverage. With higher asset prices, the collateral value of borrowing to finance further asset purchases is higher, with increased leverage allowing additional asset purchases that further increases the collateral that then allows further borrowing and leveraging, entering into a vicious circle . . . Thus, easy money and easy credit may be an initial trigger of a process of asset bubbles and excessive leveraging of the financial system and of the private non-financial sector.

(Roubini, 2008: 34–5)

The events of the last couple of years have revealed failures on two fronts: one of them is the failure of the risk management practices used by the private sector, and the other is the failure of the public sector's oversight of the financial system (Aziz, 2008; Bernanke, 2009). Among other things, the chairman of the Federal Reserve Ben S. Bernanke concludes that 'capital adequacy, effective liquidity planning, and strong risk management are essential for safe and sound banking; the crisis revealed serious deficiencies on the part of some financial institutions in one or more of the areas' (Bernanke, 2009). In other words, failure of one or more of these core elements of safe and sound banking would lead to a crisis. This is exactly what happened prior to the recent financial crisis.

One of the important lessons that emerged in the wake of the current financial crisis is the effect of globalisation. The globalisation of trade, finance, capital and labour has tied together countries all over the world. Countries are now more interlinked and interdependent than ever before. Modern technology has expedited the transfer of information instantaneously, for better or for worse. Consequently, any panic or any crisis that affects a major interlinked economy or a group of countries has the ability to spread to other countries in a so-called contagion effect (Aziz, 2008; Jones, 2009; Jordan and Jain, 2009; Kashyap et al., 2008; Truman, 2009a; Yellen, 2009).

Aside from the above-mentioned lessons, we would like to summarise here the major lessons that are common to all the cited authors.

2.2.1 *Risk Transfers and Imprudent Credit Growth*

The current financial turmoil is a direct result of an exceptional boom in credit growth and leverage within the financial system (Aziz, 2008; Financial Stability Forum, 2008: 1, 5). A low-interest-rate regime that lasted for too long and lax lending standards contributed to the current crisis (Bordo, 2008; Jones, 2009; Mizen, 2008; Nonomiya and Lanman, 2008; *The New York Times*, 2010). The low interest rate lured both borrowers to borrow more than they could handle and financial institutions to devise new products and grant excessively risky loans in search of high profits in a low interest-rate environment (Mizen, 2008).

This is not surprising, as conventional banking in particular and the financial industry in general is based on interest-based debt intermediation supported by deposit insurance schemes under the canopy of a lender of last resort. One of the main sources of income for conventional financial institutions is the interest charged on loans granted by banks to customers. More precisely, banks make their profit from the spread between the interest paid on deposits and the interest earned on loans. Given that banks will face losses if they are unable to recover their loans with interest, they are expected to carefully analyse each and every loan application so as to minimise the risk of loss.

However, banks, driven by shareholder interest and the desire for profit-maximisation, started to indulge in excessive and imprudent lending. Over the long period of a low-interest-rate regime, lenders were extending loans to borrowers who borrowed more than they could afford (Jordan and Jain, 2009). According to the Bank for International Settlements (BIS), the fundamental cause for the current global financial crisis lies in 'excessive and imprudent credit growth over a long period' (BIS, 2008: 143). Lionel Robbins remarked that 'the pursuit of self-interest, unrestrained by suitable institutions, carries no guarantee of anything but chaos' (Robbins, 1952 cited in Mirakhor and Krichene, 2009: 71). Furthermore, depositors were oblivious to the excessive risk-taking appetite of the banks, given that their deposits are either expressly guaranteed by deposit insurance schemes or implicitly by the lender of last resort, the central banks.

Nevertheless, banks alone should not be blamed for the current global crisis, as they were merely playing by the 'rules of the game' that governments had established in financial markets. If deposits were not guaranteed expressly or implicitly by the government, and if bank managers were to be made person-ally liable for their irrational and irresponsible decisions, they would obviously be more cautious in their lending decisions. There are, therefore, three factors that influence and explain the banks' imprudent lending practices: the first is the banks' ability to freely transfer their risk to third parties by selling their loan portfolios. In the past, when risk transfers were not prevalent, banks used to be more prudent in their lending practices, given that they would have to 'hold-to-maturity' their loan portfolios. When banks know that they can transfer their risks by way of securitisation, collateralised debt obligations and other risk-transfer mechanisms, they are incentivised to assume excessive risks in pursuit of greater profits.

The second factor is the sense of security that both banks and depositors acquire from the 'too big to fail' syndrome, whereby in the case of a crisis the central bank would assume the responsibility to bail the bank out in order to contain a systemic risk to the economy. Many commentators firmly believe that it is for this reason that banks ended up taking greater risks than they would have otherwise sustained independently (Chapra, 2008; Mishkin, 1997: 61–2).

The third factor is again related to the guarantee mechanism in the current financial framework: the deposit insurance companies that guarantee citizens' deposits. In the absence of such deposit insurance, banks would need to be more careful when investing depositor money, and, at the same time, depositors would be more cautious when choosing their banks (see Roubini, 2008: 41).

This leads us to the next lesson, which is the failure of risk management procedures by the major financial institutions.

2.2.2 Failure of Risk Management

As mentioned above by Bernanke (2009), risk management is paramount for safe and sound banking. Rapid financial innovation and product development, which seemed to have reached their pinnacle in the last decade, made risk management extremely challenging. While financial innovation brings improvements and benefits to market participants, problems arise if new products bring with them unnecessary complications resulting in new risks that are less understood, assessed and controlled. As a result, the inadequacy of risk management practices of many financial institutions was exposed (Ahmed, 2009; Aziz, 2008; Bernanke, 2009; FSF, 2008: 7; Mirakhor and Krichene, 2009; Trichet, 2009). The Financial Stability Forum concluded that '[t]he market turmoil has revealed weaknesses in risk management at the banks and securities firms at the core of the global financial system, and in the system of incentives that regulators and supervisors provide through capital and liquidity requirements and oversight' (FSF, 2008: 12).

The increased complexity of financial products and markets deteriorated the ability of market participants, regulators and supervisors to evaluate the risks. In other words, the risks inherent in these new products were mispriced (see Mizen, 2008: 554; Taylor, 2008). Consequently, risk management practices have to be regularly updated to reflect the changes in instruments, markets and business models. Regulators and supervisors should also make sure that financial institutions do not engage in activities without having adequate skills and controls (FSF, 2008).

This crisis revealed the importance of maintaining effective risk management practices. As Bernanke (2009) noted, 'It is precisely during those good times, when risks appear low and the financial horizon seems clear, that financial market participants can become overly optimistic and make costly mistakes' (Bernanke, 2009).

2.2.3 Liquidity and Leveraging

Risk-taking, from an Islamic finance point of view, is considered not only good but also necessary, based on the well-known legal maxim *al-kharāj bil-ḍamān*; that is, entitlement to profit or gain depends on the corresponding liability for loss. However, exposing oneself or one's wealth to unnecessary or excessive risk is seen as gambling (*maysir*), and such risk-taking is prohibited.

The European Central Bank (ECB) defines liquidity as 'the ease and speed with which a financial asset can be converted into cash or used to settle a liability. Cash is thus a highly liquid asset. The term "liquidity" is also often used as a synonym for money' (ECB, 2010). The current crisis revealed the importance of liquidity and liquidity risk management for efficient functioning of financial markets (Allen and Carletti, 2008; Aziz, 2008; Bernanke, 2009; Bordo, 2008; Mersch, 2009: 10; OECD, 2009a). It is believed that one of the triggers of the crisis was the excessive liquidity of financial institutions, a result of their search for high yield and extra profits (Mirakhor and Krichene, 2009). Liquidity risk management is important due to its role in maintaining institutional and systemic resilience in the face of shocks. Liquidity shortfall of even one institution can cause system-wide repercussions (Basel Committee on Banking Supervision, 2008: 1; FSF, 2008: 16).

Since the crisis, the Basel Committee on Banking Supervision has published a number of papers and principles on the issue, including: *Principles for Sound Liquidity Risk Management and Supervision, Sound Practices for Managing Liquidity in Banking Organisations* and *Liquidity Risk Management and Supervisory Challenges*. The studies showed the failure of many banks to take into account very basic principles of liquidity risk management when liquidity was plentiful (for details see Basel Committee on Banking Supervision, 2008: 3–5).

2.2.4 Lax Regulation and Supervision

According to Warren and Tyagi (2009), although many economists and financial experts have given different reasons for the current financial meltdown, they all failed to identify the major culprit: the weak 'legal structure governing the sale of mortgages, credit cards, and other consumer financial products' (Warren and Tyagi, 2009: 22).

Many experts, time and again, have highlighted the importance of the regulatory and supervisory framework for the smooth functioning of a stable system. Supervision and regulation of the financial sector, or rather the lack of both, played a role in the crisis (Bordo, 2008; Truman, 2009b). The limited scope of the regulatory framework allowed the growth of unregulated exposures, which led to excessive risk-taking and weak liquidity risk management (Aziz, 2008; FSF, 2008: 9).

It is now clear that the regulatory and supervisory frameworks of many countries in general, and of the United States in particular, were incomplete and inefficient (Jordan and Jain, 2009). Over the years, the so-called 'shadow financial system' – consisting of money market mutual funds, special purpose investment vehicles, hedge funds, private equity firms, among other vehicles and players – developed. As these institutions were less regulated, the traditional banks were motivated to shift to their use in pursuit of profit maximisation. In order to compete with these less-regulated institutions, traditional banks developed new models that led to the overleveraging of the global financial system, especially in the United States. Once the good days waned, the artificial financial system collapsed (Truman, 2009a).

Lax regulation and supervision led to extensive innovation, which far exceeded the real potential and needs of the economy. As a result, the financial crisis became an inevitable reality. It is true that lax regulations leave more space for the development of the financial system and that over-regulation may harm it, but it is also true that if proper regulatory framework had been in place the effects of the financial crisis could have been less devastating. In other words, as Mirakhor and Krichene (2009) stated, we need '"efficient", rather than "more", regulations and supervision that avoids excesses in risk-taking'[1] (Mirakhor and Krichene, 2009: 33). Therefore, what we need is a prudent and up-to-date regulatory and supervisory framework that will be able to cope with the ever-increasing needs of the financial market (Nier, 2009). We need to find a golden mean that will be equally applicable in good and bad times.

2.2.5 Transparency and Disclosure

Another lesson that can be drawn from the current turmoil is the issue of transparency and disclosure. It is inextricably related to all the previously highlighted lessons. The innovation that brought about new products with new, less understandable risks and exposures, combined with opaque disclosure of information by the financial system, led market players astray and played a decisive role in underestimation of the risks involved. The low level of transparency and disclosure that accompanied all the other factors damaged market confidence and contributed to panic in the market (see Aziz, 2008; OECD, 2009a: 36).

All of the above points to one conclusion: that reliable valuation, together with effective and usable disclosure of the risks associated with new products (especially structured credit products), is very important for a sound financial system. The Financial Stability Forum (FSF) concludes that 'sound disclosure, accounting and valuation practices are essential to achieve transparency, to maintain market confidence and to promote effective market discipline' (FSF, 2008: 22).

2.2.6 Debt- and Interest-based Financing

Muslim scholars and economists, as well as many Western economists and financial think-tanks, argue that the prevailing debt-based financial system and its financial instruments are among the causes (if not the main cause) of the current global financial crisis.

The interest-based financial system inevitably helps the rich to get richer while keeping the poor mired in poverty or driving them deeper into it. As Dusuki (2009) pointed out, over-emphasis on debt-based instruments in the economy would not help to remove the injustices, harm, inequity and inefficiency that are inimical to the objectives of the *Sharīʿah*. It is due to the interest-based system that we have the unjust and uneven distribution of wealth that damages the interests of common people. This has been criticised even by Western economists such as Robertson:

> The pervasive role of interest in the economic system results in the systematic transfer of money from those who have less to those who have more. Again, this transfer of resources from poor to rich has been made shockingly clear by the Third World debt crisis. But it applies universally. It is partly because those who have more money to lend, get more in interest than those who have less; it is partly because those who have less, often have to borrow more; and it is partly because the cost of interest repayments now forms a substantial element in the cost of all goods and services, and the necessary goods and services loom much larger in the finances of the rich. When we look at the money system that way and when we begin to think about how it should be redesigned to carry out its functions fairly and efficiently as part of an enabling and conserving economy, the arguments for an interest-free, inflation-free money system for the twenty-first century seem to be very strong.
>
> Robertson (1990: 130–1 cited in Usmani, 2010a)

The literature on the financial crisis has suggested a number of factors contributing to the emergence of the crisis. As stated by Mirakhor and Krichene, these include:

> extraordinarily high liquidity; rapid pace of financial engineering which innovated complex, opaque and difficult-to-understand financial instruments way ahead of the market; informational problems caused by lack of transparency in asset market prices, particularly in the market for structured credit instruments; outdated, lax or absent regulatory-supervisory oversight, which encouraged excessive risk-taking; faulty risk management and accounting models; and the emergence of an incentive structure that created a complicit coalition composed of financial institutions, real estate developers and appraisers, insurance companies and credit-rating agencies whose actions led to a deliberate underestimation and underpricing of risk.
>
> Mirakhor and Krichene (2009: 33)

2.3 Redressing the Current Financial Architecture

Identifying the lessons from the current global financial crisis is one side of the coin while the other side is implementing practicable measures to avoid the past mistakes. As Bernanke repeatedly asked (2008a, 2008b, 2009): 'What have we learned from this extraordinary episode? And how can we apply those lessons to strengthen our banking system and avoid or mitigate future crises?'

From an Islamic finance perspective, Mirakhor and Krichene (2009: 71) concluded that 'the most important lesson of the recent crisis for Islamic finance is an urgent need for the design, development and implementation of a comprehensive, unified, uniform, global and dynamic regulatory-prudential-supervisory framework'. This 'properly designed regulatory-prudential-supervisory framework,' the authors further argued, is 'essential to the orderly development and evolution of Islamic finance' (Mirakhor and Krichene, 2009: 68–9).

2.3.1 Shift towards Equity-based Financing

Shaykh Muhammad Taqi Usmani, in his address to the recent World Economic Forum in Davos, called for restructuring the international financial system in general and Islamic finance in particular. He proposed that the current debt-based system be replaced with an equity-based system that is more linked to the real economy. As mentioned earlier, there is a role for debt in every financial system (be it Islamic or otherwise), but it should not be predominant. In other words, the use of debt should be a last-resort approach, once all other options are exhausted (Usmani, 2010a, 2010b). Shaykh Taqi Usmani's recommendation has been supported by many Muslim scholars and economists.

However, debt-oriented financing has to be viewed in the context of a financial system based on a fractional reserve banking model. Debt financing has been accorded significant pricing advantages in the current financial system. Islamic finance cannot refrain from debt-based financing unless the government is prepared to replace the existing fractional reserve banking model with an entirely *Sharīᶜah*-based model. Until such time when a *Sharīᶜah*-based financial system is implemented, Islamic financiers must ensure that the scope of Islamic debt financing is limited for constructive and essential purposes only. Debt financing should not be extended for irrational and wasteful consumption or speculation. Islam has clearly laid down certain conditions to help prevent excessive expansion of debt. Some of these conditions are mentioned by Chapra as follows:

(i) The asset which is being sold or leased must be *real*, and not imaginary or notional.
(ii) The seller must own and possess the goods being sold or leased.
(iii) The transaction must be a genuine trade transaction with full intention of giving and taking delivery.
(iv) The debt cannot be sold, and thus, the risk associated with it cannot be transferred to someone else. It must be borne by the creditor himself.

Chapra (2008: 15–16; emphasis in original)

In order to prevent the recurrence of crises in the future, according to Chapra, we need the combination of three forces, namely:

(i) Establishing moral constraints on greed for maximum profits, wealth, and consumption.

(ii) The need for market discipline that will exercise a restraint on leverage, excessive lending and derivatives.

(iii) Reform of the system's structure, combined with prudential regulation and supervision, to prevent crises, achieve sustainable development and protect social interests.

Chapra (2008: 2)

2.4 Reshaping the Behaviour and Responsibilities of Economic Agents

As already mentioned, debt-based financing has a limited role in Islam. To understand the scope of debt in Islam, and its subsequent affect on the behaviour and responsibilities of economic agents in an Islamic financial system, we need to look into the primary sources of the *Sharīʿah*: the *Qur'ān* and *ḥadīth*.

The longest verse in the Holy *Qur'ān* is *Ayat al-Dayn* or the Verse on Debt (verse 282, *shūrā al-Baqarah*). From the layman's perspective, the length of this *ayat* is in itself an indication of its importance. *Allah (swt)* says in this verse: 'O you who believe! When you contract a debt for a fixed period, write it down . . .'

Abu Jaʿfar said that whenever there is a transaction involving debt for a specified period (whether it is created through sale or loan), it should be written down (Al-Tabari, 2000: 43). In short, this *āyah* lays down the foundation and fundamental principles when drafting the debt contract. Some of these principles are briefly mentioned here: first, it is obvious that the debt contract should be written down; second, the time period should be known and specified; third, the person writing down the contract (*kātib*) should be just and trustworthy; fourth, the *kātib* has to treat both seller (creditor) and buyer (debtor) fairly and not be biased towards either one of them. (For a full list of principles see Al-Sa'adi, 2000: 118.)

Aishah (may *Allah* be pleased with her) reported that the Prophet (*pbuh*) would frequently say in his prayers: 'O Allah, I seek refuge with You from the trial of the grave and from the trial of *Masīḥ al-Dajjāl* and from the afflictions of life and death. O Allah, I seek refuge with you from sins (*ma'tham*) and from being in debt (*maghram*).' When asked, 'Why do you so frequently seek refuge with Allah from being in debt?' the Prophet (*pbuh*) replied, 'A person in debt tells lies whenever he speaks and breaks promises whenever he makes (them)' (Al-Bayhaqi, 1994c:. 453; Al-Bukhari, 1987a: 286; *ḥadīth* no. 798).

In another *ḥadīth* narrated by Abu Saʿīd, the Prophet (*pbuh*) was once seeking protection from *kufr* (disbelief) and *dayn* (debt); a man asked him, 'Is *dayn* on a par with *kufr*?' The Prophet (*pbuh*) replied, 'Yes' (see Al-Nasa'i, 1420: 658). The Prophet (*pbuh*) also declined to perform funeral prayers for a companion who died with an outstanding debt.[2]

There appears to be only one instance in which the Prophet (*pbuh*) borrowed for his personal interest, and that was to buy food, which is an essential need. *Aishah* (may *Allah* be pleased with her) reported that the Holy Prophet (*pbuh*) bought food on credit from a Jew, for which he pledged his new armour (Al-Bukhari, 1987b: 887). The other instances in which the Prophet (*pbuh*) borrowed, he did so to help the poor and needy. In all these reports it is evidently clear that the Prophet (*pbuh*) only took debt for essential requirements and that he constantly sought *Allah*'s protection from debt.

Given the limited scope of credit (debt) in the *Sharīᶜah*, the bank (as seller) should be transparent, responsible and accountable for the credit facilities offered to the market. Similarly, the customers who seek credit must also be responsible and ensure that they do not resort to debt impulsively or capriciously. In addition, regulators have a responsibility to ensure that both sellers (banks) and buyers (customers) conform to these standards. The questions, therefore, that need to be addressed here are: How do we reshape the regulatory framework for the financial system to ensure compliance with these *Sharīᶜah* standards? The authors firmly believe that the standard of care imposed by the *Sharīᶜah* on both the providers and seekers of credit is considerably higher than the standards prevailing in other jurisdictions, which are based on the principles of either *caveat venditor* (let the seller beware) or *caveat emptor* (let the buyer beware). The standard of care in the *Sharīᶜah* is based on ethico-legal principles that link ethical considerations to legal requirements. The following illustrations may help to better explain the Islamic perspective on ethico-legal requirements.

Conventional banks skilfully deploy various marketing tactics to lure customers to seek loans and other debt financing from the bank. It is not uncommon for conventional banks to slash their personal loan rates – for example, during festival seasons – to entice their customers to borrow and spend beyond their means in order to satisfy their impulsive desires while in a festive mood. Such marketing tactics are clearly within the boundaries of legal permissibility; however, they may not conform to Islamic ethico-legal principles. For example, one can observe Islamic banks slashing their personal finance rate during *ramaḍān* to entice customers to borrow beyond their means. Isn't *ramaḍān* the month for *ᶜibādah* and other good deeds? Should Islamic banks skilfully deploy shrewd marketing tactics to entice customers into debt as conventional banks do? Legally, Islamic banks may be entitled to slash the rates whenever they like, but from an Islamic ethico-legal perspective, should Islamic banks 'entrap' customers by skilfully playing upon their impulsive desires?

Unfortunately, the current offering of *Sharīᶜah*-compliant products is focused only on the *ḥalāl* or legal aspects of the transactions, without taking into consideration the ethical dimensions that Islam purposes to achieve. Islamic banks are under a duty of care to educate the customers that, although debt is *ḥalāl*, it should not be simply resorted to in accordance with one's whims and fancies. Like *ṭalāq* (divorce), debt should be resorted to only when there is a genuine necessity and upon due care and consideration. *ṭalāq*, like debt, is also *ḥalāl* but is the most detestable among the things made permissible by *Allah* (*swt*).[3] In this context, the authors firmly believe that debt should be treated similar to *ṭalāq* (divorce) and resorted to only as a last option.

If debt is comparable to *ṭalāq* in terms of scope of permissibility in Islam, should Islamic banks indulge in clever marketing tactics to entice customers to debt? We can't imagine the *Sharīʿah* allowing, for example, divorce lawyers to deploy artful marketing tactics to solicit their legal services for *ṭalāq* at a discounted fee to lure 'disgruntled' spouses into divorce! Surely, from an ethico-legal perspective the lawyers must advise the clients that they should try to make the marriage work, given that *ṭalāq* should only be resorted to as a final option in the *Sharīʿah*. Should Islamic bankers also be required from an Islamic ethico-legal perspective to provide the right advice to the customers instead of deploying clever marketing tactics and fineprint to lure customers into debt?

2.4.1 *The Sellers' Standard of Care*

Unlike conventional banks, Islamic banks need to be clearly mindful of the limited scope of credit in Islam, and as suppliers of credit they need to become more customer-centric. They need to educate customers on the true cost of credit and show them the cost–benefit analysis between 'buy now and pay later' and 'save now and buy later' options. Unfortunately, the current business design of Islamic banks, modelled on conventional banks, is purely product-centric. Given that banks (both Islamic and conventional) make more profit on selling credit products, they often have no incentive to become customer-centric. This is not to say that Islamic banks should not pursue profits. However, unlike conventional banks, Islamic banks should not make profits at the expense of or to the detriment of customers. Such a practice would be contrary to Islamic ethico-legal principles. But, one may well wonder, doesn't the bank always make profit at the expense of the customer in a debt-based product? The answer is no, if banks become customer-centric and educate them about the status of debt in Islam, the true cost of borrowing (like annual percentage rate (APR)) and the cost–benefit analysis between debt and savings, and genuinely offer them saving schemes as alternatives to debt so that customers can 'save now and buy later' if they desire. If an Islamic bank provides all of the above services and the customer chooses the debt option with full knowledge, then that bank will not be seen as exploiting the customer.

Furthermore, Islamic banks also lack transparency when offering their products. Like conventional product offerings, Islamic banks also often end up showing only the exciting product highlights to capture the customers and artfully obscuring the less exciting and onerous terms under 'other terms and conditions apply', appearing always as footnotes, and that, too often, in fine print. Although such an offering is legally permissible, given that the Islamic banks set out all the onerous terms in the legal agreement, in reality not many customers actually understand or even read the legalese agreement. Such practice is evidently unacceptable from an Islamic ethico-legal perspective.

The following ethical considerations with regard to sale contracts, as highlighted by al-Zuhayli (2003: 7–8), may shed some light on the scope of the seller's standard of care in Islam:

(i) The avoidance of excessive profits: Islam, as well as all other religions, prohibits 'excessive profit and taking advantage of buyers'.

(ii) Truthful and complete disclosure of information: The seller is required to provide full and truthful information about the product, its type, origin and cost. Al-Tirmidhi reported a *ḥadīth* on the authority of Rifāʿah: 'All merchants will be resurrected on the Day of Judgment as sinners, except for those who feared *Allah*, treated their customers well and were truthful' (cited in Al-Zuhayli, 2003: 7). The buyer's knowledge of the subject matter of the sale contract is considered one of the conditions for the validity of the contract (Al-Zuhayli, 2003: 33).

(iii) Ease of conduct: Islam also requires both seller and buyer to be reasonable when setting the terms and condition of the contract. Jābir quoted *Allah*'s Messenger (*pbuh*) as saying, '*Allah* is merciful to the man who is easygoing when he sells, when he buys, and when he collects his loans' (Al-Bukhari cited in Al-Zuhayli, 2003: 7).

(iv) Documentation and witnessing of all debts: All contracts and loans should be written and witnessed as prescribed in the *Qur'ān* (2: 282).

The discussion above leads us to conclude that Islam calls for justice, fairness, cooperation and shared responsibility in commercial transactions. With regard to debt transactions, Islam imposes a much higher standard of care, as elaborated above. This then implies that debt-based Islamic financial products should not only be *Sharīʿah*-compliant or *ḥalāl* but also '*ṭayyiban*' (wholesome, good). What does *ṭayyiban* really mean in the context of debt-based contracts?

Allah (*swt*) mentions at several places in the *Qur'an* that He has provided us with sustenance that is '*ḥalālan ṭayyiban*' (that is, lawful and good). See, for example: 2:168; 5:88; 8:69 and 16:114. These verses imply that the sustenance that *Allah* (*swt*) has provided for us is not only *ḥalāl* in nature but it is also *ṭayyiban* (wholesome, good) for us. We should apply the same principle to financial instruments; not only should they be *Sharīʿah*-compliant (that is, *ḥalāl*) but also they should be *ṭayyiban* (wholesome, good) in nature. This means that the products should, among other things, be just to both seller (creditor) and buyer (debtor).

In reality, what Islamic banks have done in the past three or more decades is focus all their resources on making their products *ḥalāl* from a purely legal perspective. The Islamic finance industry has, unfortunately, failed to take into consideration the ethico-legal dimensions discussed above. What we have now is comparable to the *ḥalāl* McDonald's food chain existing in some Muslim countries. From a purely legal perspective, the Muslim 'McDonald's' food is *ḥalāl* and may share the same economics in terms of pricing with a non-*ḥalāl* McDonalds' in the United States. But the McDonald's food would not become wholesome or healthy merely by being served as *ḥalāl*. What we need, from an ethico-legal perspective is to transform the *ḥalāl* food to become *ṭayyiban*. This 'wholesome' food revolution is already happening in the developed world. McDonald's is transforming itself to become more customer-centric by disclosing the amount of fat, calories and other contents in its food and giving the consumer the choice between high-calorie fast-food and healthier wholesome food. What we need to see now is a similar transformation in the Islamic finance industry. In other words, we need the Islamic finance industry to evolve from the mere *ḥalāl* stage to the '*ḥalālan ṭayyiban*' stage.

Given that Islamic banks, as suppliers of credit, are subject to a higher standard of care, as discussed above, it is only reasonable to impose a similar high standard of care on conventional banks as well. If only Islamic banks are subject to a higher standard, they will become less competitive in the market. It is now incumbent upon Islamic banks to expand their scope and take the lead to reshape the financial system based on the higher objectives of the *Sharīʿah*. It is quite evident that Islamic banks will clearly fail in their efforts to reshape the Islamic banking system unless they push for a total reform of the conventional financial system.

Fortunately, the recent global financial crisis has given birth to various initiatives to reform the conventional financial system. Warren and Tyagi (2009) believe that there is a dire need for the establishment of a Consumer Credit Safety Commission (CCSC). This commission would be similar to the Consumer Product Safety Commission (CPSC), which ensures that all the products sold in the United States meet basic safety requirements. The main objective of the CCSC would be to make sure that financial products are more transparent and free from any tricks and traps, which would in turn help consumers to make prudent financial decisions. 'Shorter contracts and clearer terms,' Warren and Tyagi (2009: 22) argue, 'could replace lenders' current race to the bottom with a race to the top, based on consumer friendliness and fairness' (see also Roubini, 2008: 44). Even President Obama showed his support for the establishment of an independent agency that would protect consumers against lending abuses that contributed to the financial crisis (Calmes and Chan, 2010).

The chairman of the Federal Reserve, Bernanke (2009), shares the view that consumer protection will bring about financial stability:

> Protecting consumers also contributes to financial stability. The increased complexity of many consumer products, as well as their sale by a range of financial institutions to a larger segment of the public, is arguably one of the causes of the current crisis. In the past year or so, the Board has developed extensive new disclosures for a variety of financial products, most notably credit cards, and we are currently in the midst of a major overhaul of mortgage disclosures. Because even the best disclosures are not always adequate, we also comprehensively overhauled our mortgage and credit card regulations to prohibit certain practices.
>
> Bernanke (2009)

One of the steps necessary for strengthening the resilience of Islamic finance, according to the Governor of Bank Negara Malaysia, Dr Zeti Akhtar Aziz, is the assimilation of *Sharīʿah* values in the realisation of benefits (*maṣāliḥ*) to the relevant stakeholders. As mentioned above, Islam calls for justice, fairness, cooperation and shared responsibility.

The goals of Islamic finance go far beyond monetary indicators and growth; it promotes ethics and market discipline. Thus, there is a need for 'a comprehensive consumer protection framework' (Aziz, 2008; see also OECD, 2009a: 10). Protecting consumers is definitely the right thing to do, but it does not mean that the customers themselves should not be responsible and active. As a buyer (borrower), a Muslim is obliged to repay his or her debts on time and according to the terms agreed with the seller (creditor). Not only that, Islam also requires from him to be thankful and to express gratitude to the seller (creditor) while repaying the debt (Ayub, 2007: 162). Islam teaches us that we need to fulfill our commitments and to act with utmost sincerity and responsibility (see the *Qur'an*, 5:1; 17:34).

2.4.2 The Responsibility of Regulators

Achieving sustainable growth and resilience of the Islamic financial system in particular and the global financial system in general, is a challenging task for the parties involved. Supply (seller) and demand (buyer) sides of the market are but one side of the coin, the other being the regulatory framework together with central banks and governments. In brief, there is a need for an efficient regulatory and supervisory framework that will be ahead of the market and make sure that the market is not overstretching (Aziz, 2008; Mirakhor and Krichene, 2009).

The proposed consumer protection agency can act as a check-and-balance between the seller (creditor) and buyer (debtor). Obama's administration proposed that this agency would have power over banks, credit unions and mortgage brokers, and would oversee products including mortgages, credit cards, loan servicing, consumer-reporting data, debt collection and real estate settlements (Calmes and Chan, 2010). This way, the agency can follow up on financial development and ensure that there are no abuses in the market.

Furthermore, the regulator must ensure that seller's standards, *caveat venditor*, are imposed on all banks, Islamic or conventional. Otherwise, if these standards are imposed on Islamic banks alone, following the law of one price, there will be 'regulatory arbitrage' and conventional banks will have comparative advantage in the market (at least for a period of time). These standards will make sure that the financial products are not only in line with law, but also in line with ethico-legal considerations.

By complying with ethico-legal requirements, the banks will disclose information and educate their customers about their products. This will lead to greater transparency, responsibility and accountability. Responsibility here refers to educating the customers, while accountability means that the banks will be held accountable if they fail to do so.

One good example related to the above discussion is the Credit Card Accountability Responsibility and Disclosure Act of 2009 (CARD Act 2009). Due to space limitations, we cannot discuss it in detail, but in short this Act tries to strike a balance between the sellers of credit cards and the buyers. It aims at protecting the latter by imposing some sort of *caveat venditor* standards.

2.5 Conclusion

The global financial crisis revealed the weaknesses of the global financial architecture on one side and provided an opportunity for Islamic finance to show its inherent strengths and qualities on the other. Although the current financial crisis has been discussed extensively in the last two years, there is still no clear consensus on the main causes and how to avoid similar financial disasters in the future.

This paper offers some possible *Sharīʿah*-based solutions that can help the financial world avoid similar crises in the future. In short, there is an urgent need to revamp the entire financial architecture. All the causes mentioned above result from the inherent flaws and defects in the global financial system, and unless the world takes immediate and wholehearted measures to remedy these flaws, we will inevitably face similar crises in the near future.

These remedial measures are especially important for the Islamic financial industry. As it is still in its infancy stage, the Islamic finance industry has to make sure that it does not repeat the same mistakes made by the conventional financial industry. To avoid them, it needs to change the way it is managing its business, especially when it comes to debt-based products.

On the whole, the global financial crisis provided us with an opportunity to make things better, and the Islamic financial industry should take a leading role in doing so. The paper argues that the industry needs to do two things: One, bearing in mind the limited scope for debt in Islam, it should promote more equity-based products and implement ethico-legal principles when offering debt-oriented products, as discussed above. Second, new standards based on ethico-legal principles should be imposed by regulatory and supervisory bodies on the entire financial services industry, conventional as well as Islamic financial sectors, to ensure that there is no arbitrage between conventional and Islamic financial sectors.

Notes

1. The italics here are ours, added for emphasis.
2. In an authentic *ḥadīth* on the issue, Salamah ibn al-Akwā related that a deceased man was brought to the Prophet (*pbuh*), who asked, 'Is there any debt on him?' [The companions] replied, 'Yes.' He asked, 'Has he left anything [behind to repay the debt]?' They replied, 'No.' He said, 'Pray on your companion.' Abu Qatādah said: 'O Messenger of *Allah*, [the debt] is on me.' Then only did the Prophet (*pbuh*) pray on the deceased (Al-Bayhaqi, 1994b: 73; n.d.: 96).
3. Ibn ʿUmar (may *Allah* be pleased with him and his father) narrated that the Prophet (*pbuh*) said: '*The most detestable ḥalāl (lawful thing) to Allah is ṭalāq (divorce)*' (Al-Bayhaqi,

1994a: 322, *ḥadīth*, no. 14,671). This *ḥadīth* was also reported by Abu Dāwud (2/255, no. 2,178); Ibn Mājah (1/650, no. 2,018); al-Ḥakim (2/214, no. 2,794), who stated that its chain of narrators (*sanad*) is *Sāḥīḥ*; Ibn Baja (6/461), and al-Tabari.

References

Ahmed, H. (2009). 'Financial crisis risks and lessons for Islamic finance', *ISRA International Journal of Islamic Finance* 1(1): 7–32.

Al-Bayhaqi (1994a). *Al-Sunan Al-Kubrā*. Vol. 7. Makkah al-Mukarramah: Dar al-Bāz.

Al-Bayhaqi (1994b). *Al-Sunan al-Kubrā*. Vol. 6. Makkah al-Mukarramah: Dar al-Bāz.

Al-Bayhaqi (1994c). *Al-Sunan al-Kubrā*. Vol. 4. Makkah al-Mukarramah: Dar al-Bāz.

Al-Bayhaqi (n.d.). *Maᶜarifah al-Sunan wa al-Āthāri*. Vol. 10, Makkah al-Mukarramah: Dar al-Bāz.

Al-Bukhari (1987a [1407]). *Al-Jāmiᶜ al-Saḥīḥ al-Mukhtasar [Saḥīḥ Al-Bukhāri]*. Vol. 1. Beirut: Dār Ibn Kathīr.

Al-Bukhari (1987b [1407]). *Saḥīḥ al-Bukhārī*. Vol. 2. Beirut: Dār Ibn Kathīr.

Al-Nasa'i (1420). *Sunan al-Nasāᵓī bi Sharh al-Suyūtī wa Hashiyah al-Sanad*. 5th edn. Vol. 8. Beirut: Dār al-Maᶜarifah.

Al-Sa'adi, A.-R. b. N. (2000 [1420]). *Taysīr al-Karīm al-Rahmān Fī Tafsīr Kalām al-Mannān*. Beirut: Mu'assisah al-Risālah.

Al-Tabari, M. i. J. (2000 [1420]). *Jāmiᶜ al-Bayān Fī Ta'wīl al-Qur'an*. 1st edn. Vol. 6. Beirut: Mu'assisah al-Risālah.

Al-Zuhayli, W. (2003). *Financial Transactions in Islamic Jurisprudence*. Vol. 1. Trans. M. A. El-Gamal. Damascus: Dar al-Fikr.

Allen, F. and Carletti, E. (2008). *The Role of Liquidity in Financial Crises*, Paper presented at the Federal Reserve Bank of Kansas City's Symposium: Maintaining Stability in a Changing Financial System, September. Available at: www.kansascityfed.org/publicat/sympos/2008/AllenandCarletti.09.14.08.pdf, last accessed 18 January 2010.

Ayub, M. (2007). *Understanding Islamic Finance*. Chichester: John Wiley and Sons.

Aziz, Z. A. (2008). *Enhancing the Resilience and Stability of the Islamic Financial system*, Paper presented at the Islamic Financial Services Board and Institute of International Finance Conference: Enhancing the Resilience and Stability of the Islamic Financial System, 20 November 2008, Kuala Lumpur. Available at: www.bis.org/review/r081126c.pdf.

Basel Committee on Banking Supervision (2008). *Principles for Sound Liquidity Risk Management and Supervision*. Basel: Bank for International Settlements.

Bernanke, B. S. (2008a). *Addressing Weaknesses in the Global Financial Markets: The Report of the President's Working Group on Financial Markets*, Speech delivered at the World Affairs Council of Greater Richmond's Virginia Global Ambassador Award Luncheon, Richmond, Va.,10 April 2008. Available at: www.federalreserve.gov/newsevents/speech/bernanke20080410a.htm, last accessed 16 January 2010.

Bernanke, B. S. (2008b). *Risk Management in Financial Institutions*, Speech delivered at the Federal Reserve Bank of Chicago's Annual Conference on Bank Structure and Competition, Chicago, 15 May 2008. Available at:www.federalreserve.gov/newsevents/speech/bernanke20080515a.htm, last accessed 16 January 2010.

Bernanke, B. S. (2009). *Lessons of the Financial Crisis for Banking Supervision*, Speech delivered at the Federal Reserve Bank of Chicago Conference on Bank Structure and Competition, Chicago, Illinois (via satellite), 7 May 2009, www.federalreserve.gov/newsevents/speech/bernanke20090507a.htm [last accessed 10 January 2010].

BIS (2008). *78th Annual Report*. Basel: Bank for International Settlements.

Bordo, M. D. (2008). *An Historical Perspective on the Crisis of 2007–2008*, Paper presented at the Central Bank of Chile Twelfth Annual Conference: Financial Stability, Monetary Policy and Central Banking, Santiago, Chile, 6–7 November.

Calmes, J. and Chan, S. (2010). 'Obama pressing for protections against lenders', *The New York Times* (online edition), 20 January. Available at: www.nytimes.com/2010/01/20/us/politics/20regulate.html, last accessed 24 February 2010.

CARD Act (2009). S. 414 – 111th Congress: *Credit Card Accountability Responsibility and Disclosure Act of 2009*, 7 February 2010,, from GovTrack.us (database of federal legislation). Available at: www.govtrack.us/congress/bill.xpd?bill=s111-414, last accessed 24 February 2010.

Chapra, M. U. (2008). *The Global Financial Crisis: Can Islamic Finance Help Minimize the Severity and Frequency of Such a Crisis in the Future?*, Paper presented at the Forum on the Global Financial Crisis, Jeddah, Islamic Development Bank.

Cooper, G. (2008). *The Origin of Financial Crises: Central Banks, Credit Bubles and the Efficient Market Fallacy*. Hampshire: Harriman House.

Dusuki, A. W. (2009). *Challenges of Realizing Maqasid al-Shariah (Objectives of Shariah) in Islamic Capital Market: Special Focus on Equity-Based Sukuk*, Paper presented at the Keynote Address at the 3rd USM–ISDEV International Islamic Management Conference on Islamic Capital Market.

European Central Bank (ECB) (2010). *Glossary*. Available at: /www.ecb.eu/home/glossary/html/glossl.en.html, last accessed 18 January 2010.

Financial Stability Forum (2008). *Report of the Financial Stability Forum on Enhancing Market and Institutional Resilience*. Basel: Financial Stability Forum, 7 April 2008.

FSF (2008). *Report of the Financial Stability Forum on Enhancing Market and Institutional Resilience*. Basel: Financial Stability Forum, 7 April 2008.

Jones, C. I. (2009). *The Global Financial Crisis: Overview*. Available at: www.econ.iastate.edu/classes/econ502/tesfatsion/GlobalFinancialCrisisOverview.2009.CJones.pdf, last accessed 1 February 2010.

Jordan, C. and Jain, A. (2009). *Diversity and Resilience: Lessons from the Financial Crisis*, Paper presented at the Canadian Law and Economics Association Meeting, University of Toronto, Canada, October.

Karuvelil, K. Z. (2000). *Islamic Finance: Sustaining success*, Proceedings of the Third Harvard University Forum on Islamic Finance. Cambridge, MA: Center for Middle Eastern Studies, Harvard University.

Kashyap, A. K., Rajan, R. and Stein, J. (2008). *The Global Roots of the Current Financial Crisis and its Implications for Regulation*, Paper presented at the 5th ECB Central Banking Conference, November. Available at: www.ecb.int/events/pdf/conferences/cbc5/Rajan.pdf?17bea4624be62b27d96a6a290c65da52, last accessed 18 January 2010.

Mersch, Y. (2009). *About the Role of Central Bank in Financial Stability and Prudential Liquidity Supervision, and the Attractiveness of Islamic Finance*, IFSB 2nd Public Lecture on Financial Policy and Stability, Kuala Lumpur, Islamic Financial Services Board.

Minsky, Hyman (2008). *Stabilizing an Unstable Economy*. New York: McGraw-Hill Professional.

Mirakhor, A. and Krichene, N. (2009). *The Recent Crisis: Lessons for Islamic finance*, IFSB 2nd Public Lecture on Financial Policy and Stability, Kuala Lumpur, Islamic Financial Services Board.

Mishkin, F. (1997). 'The causes and propagation of financial instability: Lessons for policy-makers', in Federal Reserve Bank of Kansas City (ed.), *Maintaining Financial Stability in a Global Economy*. Kansas City, Wyoming: Federal Reserve Bank of Kansas City, pp. 55–96.

Mizen, P. (2008). 'The credit crunch of 2007–2008: A discussion of the background, market reactions, and policy responses', *Federal Reserve Bank of St. Louis Review* 90(5): 531–67.

Nier, E. W. (2009). *Financial Stability Frameworks and the Role of Central Banks: Lessons from the crisis*, IMF Working Paper 09/70. Available at: www.imf.org/external/pubs/ft/wp/2009/wp0970.pdf, last accessed 27 January 2010.

Nonomiya, L. and Lanman, S. (2008). *Greenspan Says Credit Crisis Is Worst in 50 Years* (Update 2), Bloomberg.Available at: www.bloomberg.com/apps/news?pid=2060108 7&sid=aclMlgBb3taQ&refer=home#, last accessed 18 January 2010.

The New York Times (2010). 'Credit crisis – the essentials', *The New York Times* (online edition). Available at: http://topics.nytimes.com/top/reference/timestopics/subjects/c/credit_crisis/index.html, last accessed 12 January 2010.

OECD (2009a). *The Financial Crisis: Reform and Exit Strategies*. Paris: Organization for Economic Co-operation and Development.

OECD (2009b). *OECD Economic Outlook*. Preliminary edn. Vol. 2. Paris: Organization for Economic Co-operation and Development.

Robbins, L. (1952). *The Theory of Economic Policy in English Classical Economics*. London: Allen and Unwin.

Robertson, J. (1990). *Future Wealth: A New Economics for the 21ˢᵗ Century*. London: Cassell Publications.

Roubini, N. (2008). 'Financial crises, financial stability, and reform: Supervision and regulation of financial systems in a world of financial globalization', in *The Financial Development Report 2008*, New York: World Economic Forum, pp. 3–26.

Sarkar, A. (2009). *Liquidity Risk, Credit Risk, and the Federal Reserve's Responses to the Crisis*, Federal Reserve Bank of New York Staff Reports, No. 389, September.

Taylor, J. B. (2008). *The Financial Crisis and the Policy Responses: An Empirical Analysis of What Went Wrong*, Stanford University Working Paper, November. Available at: www. stanford.edu/~johntayl/FCPR.pdf, last accessed 18 January 2010.

Trichet, J. C. (2009). *What Lessons can be Learned from the Economic and Financial Crisis?*, Speech delivered at the '5e Rencontres de l'Entreprise Européenne' organised by La Tribune, Roland Berger and HEC Paris, 17 March 2009. Available at: www.ecb.int/press/key/date/2009/html/sp090317.en.html, last accessed 10 January 2010.

Truman, E. M. (2009a). *The Global Financial Crisis: Lessons Learned and Challenges for Developing Countries*, Remarks at the Eighteenth Cycle of Economics Lectures, Banco de Guatemala, 16 June 2009. Available at: www.iie.com/publications/papers/paper. cfm?ResearchID=1240, last accessed 10 January 2010.

Truman, E. M. (2009b). *Lessons from the Global Economic and Financial Crisis*, Keynote address at the conference 'G-20 Reform Initiatives: Implications for the Future of Regulation,' cohosted by the Institute for Global Economics and the International Monetary Fund, Seoul, Korea, 11 November 2009. Available at: www.iie.com/publications/papers/truman0911.pdf, last accessed 10 January 2010]

Usmani, M. T. (2010a). *Post-Crisis Reforms: Some Points to Ponder*, World Economic Forum. Available at: www.weforum.org/pdf/faith/UsmaniPostCrisisReforms.pdf, last accessed 7 February 2010.

Usmani, M. T. (2010b). 'Post-crisis reforms: Some points to ponder', in World Economic Forum (ed.), *Faith and the Global Agenda: Values for the post-crisis economy*. Geneva: World Economic Forum, pp. 51–54.

Volcker, P. (2010). 'How to reform our financial system,' *The New York Times* (online edition), 31 January 2010. Available at: www.nytimes.com/2010/01/31/opinion/31volcker. html, last accessed 18 January 2010.

Warren, E. and Tyagi, A. (2009). 'Consumer safety for consumer credit', *Harvard Business Review* 87(2): 22.

Yellen, J. L. (2009). *A Minsky Meltdown: Lessons for central bankers*, FRBSF Economic Letter No. 2009-15 May 1. Available at: www.frbsf.org/publications/economics/letter/2009/el2009-15.pdf, last accessed 1 February 2010.

3

ASSESSING THE RESILIENCE OF ISLAMIC BANKS: AN EMPIRICAL ANALYSIS

Rania Abdelfattah Salem and Ahmed Mohamed Badreldin

3.1 Introduction

Due to the sub-prime financial crisis, and with banks being one of its major players, many countries have begun to look for more prudent, more transparent banking models in order to overcome the critical flaws of the conventional and current banking system, especially after some of its major defects have become apparent (Newman, 2009). One of the banking models currently being examined by a number of countries, such as the United Kingdom (FSA, 2009) and France (Kamel, 2009), is the Islamic banking model, which emphasises transparency and value creation in its dealings, and shuns greed and profit-only oriented transactions. While the net profits of the world's largest conventional banks were highly affected by the crisis, Islamic banks witnessed relatively stable returns. For instance, the United Bank of Switzerland (UBS) reported net losses from 2007 to 2009, while Citibank reported a considerable decline in net profits during 2007 reaching a negative figure in 2008. On the other hand, none of the largest Islamic banks reported losses on those years (Islamic Finance and Global Stability Report, 2010). Nevertheless, it should be noted that the aggregate total assets of Islamic banks worldwide account for only 26 per cent of UBS's total assets, which is the world's largest bank by total assets as of 2008 (BankScope, 2010).

Excessive risk taking and the use of innovative complex products have been among the identified elements of the crisis. On the one hand, Islamic banks do not, at least to date, engage in such activities due to *Sharīʿah* considerations. On the other hand, Islamic banking operations are not isolated from the global financial system, and accordingly one would expect to see Islamic banks influenced to an extent by crises in the global financial system (*Shirkah*, 2009). Hence, an analysis of the performance of Islamic banks proves essential to test the true grounds of the resilience of Islamic banks. Yet, due to the newness of the system and the absence of universally regulating bodies for financial reporting or supervision, current Islamic banks are using diverse performance measures and representation methods. This creates numerous difficulties in measuring their performance, let alone comparing it across the Islamic banking sector or across countries. Therefore, it becomes important to use adapted performance measures rather than those typically used to measure the performance of conventional banks.

One such tool specifically adapted to Islamic banks is the Adapted Return on Equity (*ROE*) Analysis Scheme (Badreldin, 2009).

Since operational mechanisms and instruments of Islamic and conventional banks are different, comparing them would not be appropriate or even fair, at least at an abstract level. This paper aims at assessing the performance of Islamic banks with regard to the banks' employed risks. The world's largest Islamic banks by total assets at the time of publication are analysed, excluding those operating solely in a completely Islamic financial system since these are not expected to be affected by the financial crisis and will tend to bias the sample. The banks' available and published financial statements were used to analyse their performance from 2003 to 2009, by applying an Islamic bank-specific *ROE* model.

The next section provides a background on the status of Islamic banks and the current financial crisis. Section Three explains the data collection and the methodology used to analyse the selected sample of Islamic banks. The analysis is presented in Section Four of this paper, whereas the last section presents the conclusion.

3.2 Background

After the crisis Islamic banks were perceived as a possible alternative to conventional banks since, in some views, Islamic banks were not affected by the crisis, compared to the conventional banks (*Shirkah*, 2009). However, others acknowledge that Islamic banks, because they are part of the international financial system, cannot be exceptionally excluded from being affected. Usmani (2010) and Chapra (2009) consent with this latter view; they refer to the fact that Islamic financial institutions, being in their infancy, are operating in a conventional-dominant financial system and thus are forced to participate in the existing market risks. Hence, Islamic banks and financial institutions are affected, but appear to be more stable than their conventional counterparts due to engaging in *Sharīʿah*-compliant activities. The Islamic Finance and Global Stability Report (2010) stated that, amid the crisis, Islamic banks in the gulf area witnessed 38.2 per cent asset growth rate and 20.1 per cent profit growth rate compared to 16.3 per cent and -6.1 per cent, respectively, for their conventional counterparts, as of 2007–8.

In general, Islamic banks are a possible alternative to meet the demands of society for mobilising savings across economic units. In Islamic banking, these savings are mobilised according to the prevailing opportunities and economic conditions on the basis of profit and loss sharing rather than interest payments. This allows a fairer distribution of wealth, as well as meeting the religious demands of Muslims, while at the same time creating and encouraging economic growth in the country. The presence of such an alternative banking system ensures further freedom of choice for people and therefore higher social welfare, human rights and democracy (Kahf, 2007: 283).

The crisis affected the global economy and caused major bailouts of a number of the world's largest banks and financial institutions. Banks that were not highly involved in the complex conventional banking practices were less affected by the turmoil, yet these were few in number. Similarly, Islamic banks were able to avoid the greater impacts and negative effects of the crisis (IDB, 2007: 18). It is perhaps under such circumstances that thoughts about alternative banks began to emerge. This is not to suggest that the Islamic Financial System is or will be immune to crises, and even Islamic banking scholars admit that their industry is still young and that they are continuously learning from the experience and mistakes of the conventional banking system, and that the learning curve is still quite steep even after four decades of Islamic banking (KPMG, 2007: 19; Khan and Bhatti, 2008: 709; Hassan and Lewis, 2007:16).

To analyse whether the Islamic banking system is able or not to provide an alternative system that curbs financial crises, the primary causes of the recent sub-prime crisis need to be discussed. According to Chapra (2009), the crisis started as a result of excessive lending behaviour and high-leverage activity that was extended by the unwillingness of banks to share in excessive risks (Ebrahim, 2008). Banks created Special Purpose Vehicles (SPVs) as a method to transfer out the underlying risks associated with the sub-prime lending. Other scholars suggest that the crisis emerged as a consequence to financial deregulation and lack of transparency, among other factors (Rudolph and Scholz, 2008). Another view suggests that engaging in complex derivative instruments and securitisation were among the factors that highly contributed to the crisis (Ahmed, 2009).

Hence, it can be, theoretically, inferred that based on the *Sharīʿah* constraints imposed on Islamic banking operations, the primary causes of the crisis can be avoided. For instance, the prohibition of *ribā* and *gharar* (*Shirkah*, 2009; Ariff, 2007; Zaher and Hassan, 2001) will control excessive lending and enforce transparency into the market. Moreover, knowing that earning profits must be accompanied by a sharing of risks (Iqbal and Molyneux, 2005), the behaviour of solely taking on excessive risk will be avoided by financial institutions. Moreover, the need to come up with ways to get rid of the higher-risk burden through SPVs or other methods will not be necessary. On the other hand, Ahmed (2009) suggests that the above-mentioned three key factors of the crisis can evolve in the Islamic financial sector as well. This view is supported by the existing limitations that hinder a full application of Islamic banking. Such limitations include the lack of legal support for Islamic contracts in many countries, the undergoing development of risk management and accounting standards, and the absence of an Islamic secondary market, short-term money market and inter-bank market (Akkizidis and Khandelwal, 2008: 5, 6; Brown et al., 2007: 104, 107, 108). However, as long as Islamic banks stay away from replicating the toxic assets that were the primary cause of the crisis, the crisis episode appears far from the Islamic banking industry.

The lack of legal support for Islamic contracts as well as market forces causes Islamic banks to deviate in practice from theory in some aspects. The most recognised aspect is the claim that Islamic banks do not engage in PLS financing activities (Metwally 1997: 93; Hassan and Bashir 2000: 10–11), where on average, only 6.34 per cent of their total financing activities is directed towards PLS instruments (Khan and Bhatti, 2008). Yet, the degree of divergence, from theory to practice, cannot be generalised since it depends on the product, bank and country. At the end of the spectrum, Islamic and conventional banks may only vary as far as the terminology is concerned (Errico and Farahbakash, 1998). This adds to the risk of having an inconsistent Islamic banking model, which consequently affects financial reporting and disclosures, despite the efforts of the Accounting and Auditing Organization for Islamic Financial Institutions (AAOIFI). The AAOIFI developed accounting standards for Islamic financial institutions complementary to the International Accounting Standards (IAS), but the majority of Islamic banks do not yet follow the standardised reporting system. Such a fact contributes to the difficulty of analysing the performance of Islamic banks.

Moreover, Islamic banks have underdeveloped risk and liquidity management systems. Islamic banks have been criticised as being institutions with a high degree of financial risk because of the lack of guarantees and collaterals in its products and investments. Hence, Islamic banks undertake riskier operations as compared to their peers in conventional banks to be able to achieve a comparable return for their shareholders (Bashir, 2001: 5). Additionally, some risks develop as a result of applying the Islamic banking model, such as displaced commercial risk, equity risk and *Sharī^cah* risk. Furthermore, the lack of liquid assets and interbank activities hold back an appropriate management of liquidity in Islamic banks. Such factors appear to broaden the risk profile of Islamic banks. Accordingly, it is difficult to determine the true grounds of the resilience of Islamic banks amid a financial crisis without analysing the financial performance of these banks.

Many studies analysed the performance of Islamic banks per se (Bashir, 2001: 2; Ahmad, 1998: 57–8; Ahmed, 2006; Zoubi and Al-Khazali, 2007: 504, 508; CIBAFI, 2006: 7). Yet, such an analysis has been hindered by the lack of common accounting standards and reporting methods, the scarcity of data and the lack of appropriate measures (Brown, Hassan and Skully 2007: 99, 101, 102). Other studies have attempted to compare the performance of both Islamic and conventional banks despite the difficulty of conducting such a comparison due to the existing discrepancies in financial accounting and reporting standards (Kazarian, 1993; Samad and Hassan 1999; Hassan and Bashir, 2000). Studies conducted by Brown et al. (2007–2), Rosly and Abu Bakar (2003), Hassan and Bashir (2000), Ahmed (2006) and Bashir (2001) concluded that, based on the Return on Equity (*ROE*) and Return on Assets (*ROA*) measures, Islamic banks have outperformed conventional banks. This is sometimes attributed to what is termed the 'equity premium puzzle' in Islamic banks, where *ROE* is higher than explainable by risk-premium logic. Yet, Ahmad (1998) suggests that the outcomes of Islamic and conventional banks should not be subject to comparisons since the two types of banks follow different operational modes. Both banking systems operate in a dual-financial system that is dominated by the conventional financial system, but each of the banking systems has a different operating model. This study provides an analysis of Islamic banks amid the recent sub-prime crisis with highlights on risk management.

3.3 Data and Methodology

In order to test the performance of Islamic banks using the Adapted *ROE* Scheme, data was collected from the annual reports of Islamic banks in different regions of the world, based on their rank by total assets. The income statement, statement of changes in stockholders' equity, balance sheet, statement of cash flows and the notes to the financial statements were obtained from the annual report of each bank. In the selection of the period of analysis, a crucial issue was the availability of data. Furthermore, exclusions were made for those banks that were operating in a strictly Islamic financial environment since these would tend to bias the sample and remove effects of the sub-prime crisis on interbank dealings. We were able to obtain data for six banks covering the years from 2003 to 2009 (Zoubi and Al-Khazali, 2007). The initial list of the top eighteen Islamic banks is provided in Table 3.1. However, after excluding Islamic banks operating in a sole Islamic financial industry and those who have no accessible data or

Table 3.1 Top Islamic Banks by Total Assets

Bank	Country	Total Assets in Mill USD
Al Rajhi Banking & Investment Corporation	Saudi Arabia	45,528
Bank Mellat*	Iran	42,484
Bank Saderat Iran*	Iran	41,131
Kuwait Finance House	Kuwait	39,368
Bank Tejarat*	Iran	34,546
Bank Sepah*	Iran	25,007
Dubai Islamic bank	United Arab Emirates	22,956
Bank Maskan*	Iran	19,311
Agricultural Bank of Iran*	Iran	17,808
Abu Dhabi Islamic bank	United Arab Emirates	17,450
AlBaraka Banking Group	Bahrain	13,166
Islamic Development Bank**	Saudi Arabia	11,521
Qatar Islamic bank	Qatar	10,789
Maybank Islamic Berhad***	Malaysia	9,660
Asya Katilim Bankasi***	Turkey	7,873
Bank Islam Malaysia Berhad***	Malaysia	7,804
Emirates Islamic bank***	United Arab Emirates	6,886
Masraf Al Rayan***	Qatar	6,627

* Islamic banks excluded because of operating in a completely Islamic financial industry
** Excluded because it does not represent an Islamic bank in its traditional form
*** Islamic banks that were excluded because of the non-availability of data
Source: https://bankscope2.bvdep.com, 2010

Table 3.2 Ratios and Abbreviations Used in the Adapted *ROE* Scheme

Ratio	Abbreviation Used	Ratio	Abbreviation Used
Financing margin	*FM*	Gross Profit Margin	*GPM*
Fee-based Margin	*FBM*	Risk Provision Margin	*RPM*
Investment Margin	*IM*	Return on Assets	*ROA*
Extraordinary and Other Income Margin	*EXOT*	Equity Rato	*ER*
		Return on Equity (Pre-tax)	*ROE*
Gross Income Margin	*GIM*	Cost–Income Ratio	*CIR*
Operating Expenditure Margin	*OEM*	Risk Provision Ratio	*RPR*

Source: Badreldin (2009)

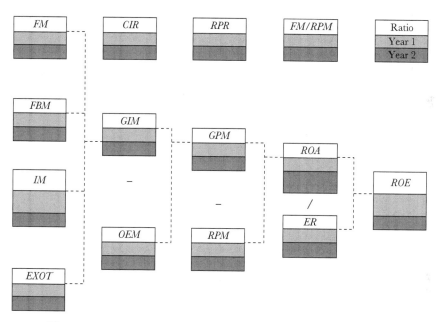

Figure 3.1 The Tracing Procedure of the Adapted *ROE* Scheme

Source: Badreldin (2009)

incomplete data for the required time period, the final sample is represented by six Islamic banks.

Agreeing that financial performance measures of conventional banks cannot be used on Islamic banks without significant adaptations and modifications, it becomes critical to identify how such an adaptation can be made to reflect fairly the same meaning intended but using the appropriate accounts, terms and concepts. Table 3.2 and Figure 3.1 show the Adapted *ROE* Scheme as suggested to be used for Islamic banks. The actual adaptation of each component is discussed below.

The same concept used in the conventional *ROE* Scheme of dividing all components by the total assets of the bank to create margin ratios is used in the Adapted *ROE* Scheme. Creating margin ratios helps in comparing them to industry benchmarks or other banks as well as across years (Greuning and Iqbal, 2008: 7, 16). The *ROE* Scheme can then be traced back to its elements, which are the Return on Assets (*ROA*) as well as the Financial Leverage Multiplier (*FLM*), which is the reciprocal of the equity ratio. These items are related by the following equation (Kalhoefer and Salem, 2008):

$$ROE = ROA \times FLM$$

$$= \frac{Net\ Profit}{Total\ Assets} \times \frac{Total\ Assets}{Equity}$$

$$= \frac{Net\ Profit}{Equity}$$

According to Badreldin (2009), the components of the Islamic bank Adapted *ROE* Scheme initially include financing income that is generated from the bank's core role as intermediary in the economy. This is composed of income generated from sales-based and equity-based products. In general it should include all financing income generated from shareholders' funds, investment deposits and savings accounts net of any financing expenses such as profit returns shared among shareholders and depositors. This is equivalent in function to conventional banks' interest income net of any interest expense – represented in Islamic banks as distributed profits among investment account holders and shareholders, as well as profit on rent from leasing.

The next component of income is fee-based income, which is derived from clients for conducted transactions, intermediary, brokerage or fund management services whether generated from shareholders' funds, profit-and-loss investment accounts or other deposits (Greuning and Iqbal, 2008: 4, 5). In general it includes all income from fee-generating activities and is similar to conventional banks' fees and commissions income (IFSB, 2007: 67). Investment income is composed of returns whether realised or unrealised from the difference between purchases and sales prices when trading financial instruments and securities. These include trade in *sukuk* and shares as well as any profit not included in financing income that represents profits on non-financing investments generated from shareholders' or depositors' funds. It includes investments held for trading or for investment and excludes sale of equity in associates. This component is similar to conventional banks' gains on financial instruments or trading income while taking into consideration that all instruments are *Sharīʿah*-compliant.

The final component of income is the extraordinary and other income that includes all other net income not included in the previous three elements. This is more or less general and does not have a specific alternative in conventional banks except generally other income. As for the operating expenses, they include all personnel, administrative and other overhead expenses directly related to operating the bank. Any non-operating and other expenses are included in the extraordinary and other income as expenses. Provisions for loan losses in conventional banks are substituted by Provisions for Doubtful Financing and Impairment since no loans exist in Islamic banks (IFSB, 2007: 67, 68). These are provisions against the default of payments from Islamic bank clients for products involving PLS that usually represent a large portion of Islamic bank activity and therefore are suggested to similarly reflect and represent the credit risk component for Islamic banks.

Thus it is possible to categorise the different income and expense components of Islamic banks based on more or less the same conditions of conventional bank while taking into consideration their significant differences in types of instruments, deposits and accounts. By taking these changes into consideration it becomes possible to use the Adapted *ROE* Scheme to measure performance of Islamic banks fairly and accurately without any loss of information, discrepancies in intended meaning or incorrect categorisation of funds, deposits or income. This is considered a much more efficient tool to use rather than adapting the financial statements themselves as was done in much research by fitting them into conventional measures. The Adapted *ROE* Scheme can be used on most, if not all, Islamic banks and allows the comparison and evaluation of management decisions.

3.4 Analysis

In general, our analysis reveals that all sample Islamic banks hold sustainable profitability ratios amid the financial crisis as shown by the Pre-Tax Return on Equity (ROE_{bt}) (Figure 3.2). However, Kuwait Finance House (KFH) and Abu Dhabi Islamic Bank (ADIB) witnessed a considerable decline in ROE_{bt} from 2008 to 2009, where it declined by 66 per cent and 91 per cent, respectively. This is also confirmed by the aggregate consolidation of data across the aggregate *ROE* and *ROA* figures for the years analysed, where the *ROE* is maintained at 19 per cent, despite a drop of 32 per cent in the aggregate *ROE* from 2006 until 2009 (see Figure 3.3). In no manner were the figures similar to the major drops witnessed by conventional banks for the same period. In general, all figures remained positive, which was not the same case in many conventional banks during the same period. This shows that Islamic banks to date appear to remain resilient towards deteriorating market conditions. On the other hand, the capital structure of Islamic banks have been slightly affected where the Financial Leverage

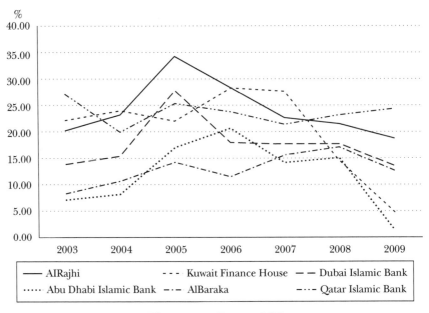

Figure 3.2 Pre-tax *ROE*

Source: Banks' annual reports; own calculation

Multiplier *(FLM)* witnessed an increase of 11 per cent compared to a decrease in the equity ratio *(ER)* of 13 per cent, on the aggregate level from 2006 to 2009. Key figures of the sample banks are shown in Tables 3.3 and 3.4. Tracing back along the figures can reveal that one of the reasons for a decrease in *ROA* was due to higher-risk provision margins as well as operating expenditures.

The cost–income ratio *(CIR)* that provides an indicator of banks' profitability before deducting impairment provisions affirms the positive performance of Islamic banks. However, the effect of the crisis is clear through the risk provision ratio *(RPR)*, which shows the amount of gross profit that has been dedicated for impairment and bad debt provisions (see Table 3.4). The sample banks show an increase in their *RPR* in 2007, 2008 and 2009 (doubled on the aggregate level), with the exception of Qatar Islamic Bank (QIB) that reveals a negative figure of *RPR* in 2008. The *RPR* generally provides an indicator of the quality of a bank's financing activity; however, under the sub-prime crisis an increase in *RPR* can be attributed to the financial turmoil since banks' management would expect an increase in impaired obligations as a result of the economic downturn. Hence, this indicates the degree of integration of Islamic banks into the global financial system. It is worth noting that ADIB appear with the highest increase in *RPR*, reaching 95 per cent in 2009. Moreover, the sample banks are viewed to be fairly capitalised with an equity ratio varying from 9per cent to 20per cent. Yet, further

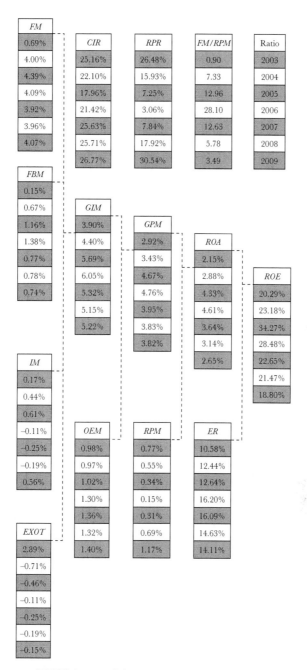

Figure 3.3 *ROE* Scheme of Aggregated Averages for Entire Sample of
Islamic Banks

Source: Banks' annual reports; own calculation

risk analysis is required in order to determine if the capital assigned per bank is sufficient in accordance with the associated risky assets.

Furthermore, from the analysis it can be seen that Islamic banks do not follow a common management strategy in terms of their financing activities and provided investment deposits. For instance, KFH, DIB and ADIB follow the same strategy of maintaining a higher financing margin as compared to the deposits margin. On the other hand, the deposits margin of QIB, AlRajhi and AlBaraka is greater than their financing margin (see Figure 3.4).

As a result of the perceived resilience, deposits in Islamic banks are expected to increase, backed by the positive increase in returns, while the cost of financing remains high for providing financing activities. This may leave Islamic banks in a liquidity management dilemma where there is a flow of funds on one side (deposits) and limited sources of financing and/or investments on the other side (assets). If Islamic banks are able to adequately manage the promised liquidity, the industry is expected to witness further growth than was expected before the crisis occurred.

When analysing the components of the Gross Income Margin as categorised by Badreldin (2009) into four categories, it is noticed that on the aggregate level the financing income contributes as the major source of income for the sample banks, representing more than 70 per cent of gross income margin in almost all the years under analysis. It is worth noting that the financing income margin includes the core products of the bank represented in sale-based and equity-

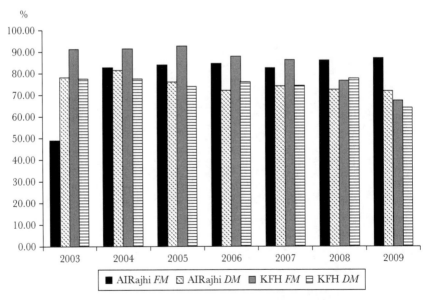

Figure 3.4 Financing Margin (*FM*) vs Deposit Margin (*DM*)

Source: Banks' annual reports; own calculation

Table 3.3 Key Figures – *ROE* and *FLM*

Ratio	Al-Rajhi		KFH		DIB		ADIB		Al-Baraka		QIB	
	ROE	*FLM*	*ROE*	*FLM*	*ROE*	*FLM*	*ROE*	*FLM*	*ROE*	*FLM*	*ROE*	*FLM*
2003	23.88%	9.12	22.18%	10.71	13.96%	13.41	7.18%	6.58	8.38%	8.39	27.08%	9.98
2004	28.83%	7.64	23.93%	10.61	15.44%	10.25	8.16%	8.43	10.62%	8.94	19.89%	5.08
2005	41.82%	7.06	22.00%	7.80	27.78%	11.20	17.10%	11.01	14.25%	8.22	25.33%	4.44
2006	36.18%	5.21	28.21%	8.99	17.95%	7.30	20.65%	13.10	11.53%	6.30	23.76%	3.44
2007	27.32%	5.29	27.68%	7.27	17.64%	7.91	14.19%	8.12	15.64%	6.44	21.41%	4.49
2008	24.14%	6.04	14.52%	8.50	17.72%	9.53	15.10%	9.09	17.10%	7.04	23.13%	4.55
2009	23.55%	5.94	4.90%	7.21	13.57%	9.39	1.38%	11.37	12.70%	7.58	24.35%	5.33

Source: Banks' annual reports; own calculation

Table 3.4 Key figures – *CIR* and *RPR*

Ratio	Al-Rajhi		KFH		DIB		ADIB		Al-Baraka		QIB	
	CIR	*RPR*	*CIR*	*RPR*	*CIR*	*RPR*	*CIR*	*RPR*	*CIR*	*RPR*	*CIR*	*RPR*
2003	17.81%	29.80%	34.95%	5.97%	61.93%	−22.80%	53.57%	3.85%	32.45%	56.32%	21.35%	30.13%
2004	15.80%	15.67%	29.77%	15.22%	39.80%	16.03%	45.66%	34.57%	39.39%	25.89%	18.16%	5.37%
2005	11.92%	3.82%	35.00%	21.89%	32.71%	10.88%	31.71%	30.78%	34.46%	22.76%	11.82%	6.27%
2006	13.18%	1.09%	44.03%	12.00%	41.11%	4.40%	37.45%	9.50%	34.60%	19.12%	9.77%	6.23%
2007	17.45%	6.23%	36.56%	10.19%	40.22%	13.79%	38.36%	13.22%	31.90%	8.94%	15.39%	0.14%
2008	17.56%	15.83%	41.38%	53.92%	40.67%	25.14%	40.38%	35.04%	33.11%	15.44%	14.43%	−2.88%
2009	19.34%	20.65%	51.10%	72.76%	39.98%	40.16	39.42%	94.89	35.63%	32.07%	19.85%	6.79%

Source: Banks' annual reports; own calculation

based financing instruments. Likewise, fee-based income, representing commissions and other brokerage fees, provides a significant positive contribution to the gross income. On the other hand, the investment margin, which represents income generated from trading in securities and other investments other than those in the financing income, shows slightly negative figures for 2006 through 2008 and rebounds in 2009. This reflects the incurred losses from trading activities for banks worldwide, thus once again showing that Islamic banks are affected by global events and financial changes. Finally, the other income margin (*EXOT*) reflects negative contributions to the gross income margin. The percentage of contribution of each source of income to the gross income can be seen in Figure 3.5.

In addition, it is worth noting that Islamic banks should work on transparency and financial disclosure issues. No disclosures of *PER* (profit equalisation reserve) or *IRR* (investment risk reserve) were revealed in any of the financial statements. Both measures would considerably affect the decisions of investment account holders (depositors) and shareholders. Furthermore, banks should provide a wider explanation of the underlying risks and the methods utilised to quantify and manage them. This should help regulators and supervisors in identifying problem banks and avoiding systemic risks.

3.5 Conclusion

Analysis of Islamic banks proves their resilience, in terms of the different performance measures, towards the financial crisis to date. The analysis shows that the profitability of Islamic banks has been relatively stable while impairment provisions have significantly increased. The increase in impairment provisions is a response towards the sub-prime crisis that confirms the fact that Islamic banks are part of the global financial system. Thus, Islamic banks are affected, even if mildly, by surrounding activities and investment morale changes.

The Islamic banking industry faces many challenges as regards to regulation, standardisation, risk management and liquidity management. Transparency and adequate financial reporting should be standardised and imposed by Islamic banks worldwide to avoid the recurrence of a similar crisis. Looking back to the lessons learned from the crisis, Islamic banks should be aware of the risks underlying the Islamic banking model and be prepared for appropriate management. Liquidity management is another major challenge that endangers the stability of the industry. Finding adequate *Sharīᶜah*-compliant liquidity management tools is inevitable if the industry expects to reap the benefits of their proven resilience.

Finally, since Islamic banks by definition avoid 'toxic assets', which imposes excessive risk-taking behaviour, this has contributed to their resilience against financial crisis. Hence, involving the industry in the so-called innovative *Sharīᶜah*-compliant products should be extensively examined and regulated to avoid similar episodes within the Islamic banking industry. Whether Islamic

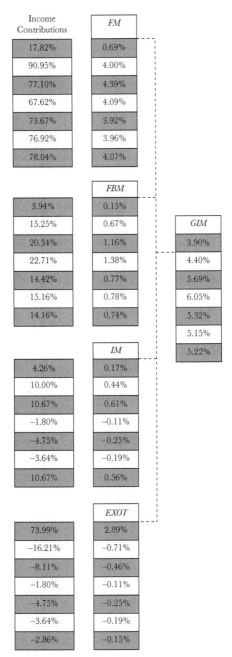

Figure 3.5 Percentage Contribution of Each Income Component to the Gross
Income Margin

Source: Banks' annual reports; own calculation

banks will remain profitable and away from turbulences is yet to be further analysed as time proceeds.

Bibliography

Ahmad, I. U. (1998). 'Comments on Turen, S.'s performance and risk analysis of Islamic banks: The case of Bahrain Islamic bank', *Journal of King Abdulaziz University: Islamic Economics* 10: 57–9.

Ahmed, H. (2006). *Using RAROC in Islamic banks: Value creation and risk management.* Paper presented at the Second International Conference on Islamic Banking, Kuala Lumpur, 7–8 February 2006.

Ahmed, H. (2009). *Financial Crisis, Risks and Lessons for Islamic Finance,* Paper presented as part of the Harvard-LSE Workshop on Risk Management: Islamic Economic and Islamic Ethico-Legal Perspectives on the Current Financial Crisis, London School of Economics, 2009.

Akkizidis, I. and Khandelwal, S. (2008). *Financial Risk Management for Islamic Banking and Finance.* London: Palgrave Macmillan.

Ariff, M. (2007). 'Islamic banking: A variation of conventional banking?', *Monash Business Review* 3(1): 1–8.

Badreldin, A. (2009). *Measuring the Performance of Islamic Banks by Adapting Conventional Ratios,* German University in Cairo Working Paper Series. Available at: http://ideas.repec. org/p/guc/wpaper/16.html, last accessed 18 January 2010.

Bashir, A. M. (2001). *Assessing the Performance of Islamic Banks: Some Evidence from the Middle East,* presented at ERF Annual Meeting, Amman Jordan, 26–9 October 2000. Available at: www.mafhoum.com/press/48E1.htm, last accessed 1 April 2009.

Brown, K., Hassan, M. K. and Skully, M. (2007). 'Operational efficiency and performance', in. K. Hassan and M. Lewis (eds), *Handbook of Islamic Banking.* Cheltenham: Edward Elgar, pp. 96–115.

Brown, M. and Skully, K. (2003). *A Cross-Country Analysis of Islamic Bank Performance,* Paper presented at the International Banking Conference on From Money Lender to Banker: Evolutions of Islamic Banking in Relation to Judeo-Christian and Oriental Traditions, organized by Monash University Malaysia, Prato, Italy, 9–10 September 2003.

Chapra, U. (2009). *The Global Financial Crisis: Some Suggestions for Reform of the Global Financial Architecture in the Light of Islamic Finance.* Research Center for Islamic Area Studies, Center of Islamic Area Studies (KIAS), Kyoto University, Kyoto, Japan.

Ebrahim, M. S. (2008). 'The financial crisis: Comments from Islamic perspectives, discussion paper', *IIUM Journal of Economics and Management* 16(2): 111–38.

Errico, L. and Farahbaksh, M. (1998). *Issues in Prudential Regulations and Supervision of Islamic Banks,* IMF Working Papers, WP/98/30, Washington, DC.

Financial Services Authority (FSA) (2009). *Islamic Banking in the U.K.* Available at: www.fsa. gov.uk/pages/About/Media/notes/bn016.shtml, last accessed 1 April 2009.

General Council for Islamic Banks and Financial Institutions (CIBAFI) (2006). *CIBAFI Performance Indicators.* Available at: www.cibafi.org/engcorporat/CouncilAchive. aspx?Page=2, last accessed 1 April 2009.

Greuning, H. V. and Iqbal, Z. (2008). *Risk Analysis for Islamic Banks.* Washington, DC: The World Bank Group.

Hassan, M. K. and Bashir, A. M. (2000). *Determinants of Islamic Banking Profitability,* presented at ERF Annual Meeting, Amman Jordan, 26–29 October 2000. Available at: www.erf.org.eg/CMS/getFile.php?id=636, last accessed 1 April 2009.

Hassan, M. K. and Lewis M. (2007). 'Islamic banking: An introduction and overview', in

K. Hassan and M. Lewis (eds), *Handbook of Islamic Banking*. Cheltenham: Edward Elgar, pp. 1–17.

Hassan, M. K. (2003). *Cost, Profit and X-Efficiency of Islamic Banks in Pakistan, Iran and Sudan*, Paper presented at the International Conference on Islamic banking: Risk Management, Regulation and Supervision, organised by Bank Indonesia, Indonesia Ministry of Finance and IRTI–Islamic Development Bank, Jakarta, Indonesia, 30 September–2 October 2003.

Islamic Development Bank (IDB) (2007). *Annual Report 1428*. Jeddah: IDB.

Islamic Finance and Global Financial Stability Report (2010). Islamic Financial Services Board (IFSB); Islamic Development Bank (IDB); Islamic Research and Training Institute (IRTI).

Islamic Financial Services Board (IFSB) (2007). *Compilation Guide on Prudential and Structural Islamic Finance Indicators*. Available at: www.ifsb.org/docs/compilation_guide.pdf, last accessed 1 April 2009.

Iqbal, M. and Molyneux, P. (2005). *Thirty Years of Islamic Banking: History, Performance and Prospects*. London: Palgrave Macmillan.

Kahf, M. (2007). 'Islamic banks and economic development', in K. Hassan and M. Lewis (eds), *Handbook of Islamic Banking*, Cheltenham: Edward Elgar, pp. 277–84.

Kalhoefer, C. and Salem, R. (2008). *Profitability Analysis in the Egyptian Banking Sector*, German University in Cairo Working Paper Series. Available at: http://ideas.repec.org/p/guc/wpaper/7.html, last accessed 18 January 2010.

Kamel, S. (2009). *10 Years of Convincing for Islamic Banks to Enter France*. Available at: www.asharqalawsat.com/details.asp?section=58andarticle=511227andfeature=1andissueno=11067 (self-translated), last accessed 1 April 2009.

Kazarian, E. G. (1993). *Islamic Versus Traditional Banking: Financial innovation in Egypt*. Boulder, CO: Westview Press.

Khan, M. M. and Bhatti, M. I. (2008). 'Islamic banking and finance: On its way to globalization', *Managerial Finance 24(10)*: 708–25.

KPMG (2007). *Growth and Diversification in Islamic Finance*. Available at: www.kpmg.co.id/kpmg/pdf/Growth%20and%20Diversification%20in%20Islamic%20Finance%20 2007.pdf, last accessed 1 April 2009.

Mokhtar, H. S., Abdullah, N. and Al-Habshi, S. (2006). 'Efficiency of Islamic banking in Malaysia: A stochastic frontier approach', *Journal of Economic Cooperation 27(2)*: 37–70.

Metwally, M. M. (1997). 'Differences between the financial characteristics of interest-free banks and conventional banks', *European Business Review 97(2)*: 92–8.

Newman, M. (2009). *EU's Kroes Seeks More 'Prudent' Banks under Restructuring Plans*. Available at: www.bloomberg.com/apps/news?pid=20601100andsid=aWYj5ZxjDuhwandrefer=germany, last accessed 1 April 2009.

Rosly, S. A. and Abu Bakar, M. A. (2003). 'Performance of Islamic and mainstream banks in Malaysia', *International Journal of Social Economics 30(12)*: 1249–65.

Rudolph, B. and Scholz, J. (2008). *Driving Factors of the Subprime Crisis and Some Reform Proposals*, CESifo DICE Report 3/2008.

Samad, A. and Hassan, M. K. (1999). 'The performance of Malaysian Islamic bank during 1984–1997: An exploratory study', *International Journal of Islamic Financial Services 1(3)*: 3–12.

Shirkah (2009). *Shirkah Magazine: The first Swiss magazine of Islamic banking and finance*, Year 3, Issue 10. Available at: www.shirkah-finance.com/Shirkah%20n%2010.pdf, last accessed 25 February 2012.

Sulaeiman, M. N. (2005). *Corporate Governance in Islamic banks*. Available at: www.al-bab.com/arab/econ/nsbanks.htm, last accessed 1 April 2009.

Usmani, M. T. (2010). *Post Crisis Reforms: Some Points to Ponder*, presented at the World Economic Forum, Davos, Switzerland, January 2010.

Zaher, T. S. and Hassan, M. K. (2001). 'A comparative literature survey of Islamic finance and banking', *Financial Markets, Institutions & Instruments* 10(4): 155–99.

Zoubi, T. A. and Al-Khazali, O. (2007). 'Empirical testing of the loss provisions of banks in the GCC region', *Managerial Finance* 33(7): 500–11.

4

STABILITY OF ISLAMIC BANKS: A COMPARISON OF CONVENTIONAL AND ISLAMIC BANKS

Matthias Verbeet

4.1 Introduction

The recent credit crisis did not only raise questions about the instruments and institutions involved but about the financial system as a whole. When debating alternative ways of banking and finance, any media-led discussion will sooner or later reach the topic of Islamic banking. Key phrases like 'interest-free', 'ethical investments' and 'profit and loss sharing' make the concept of Islamic banking appear even more attractive to the half-informed audience of these discussions. Yet there is an ongoing debate about Islamic banking from many perspectives. But, with regard to the current crisis, the question to be asked would be, 'Is it more stable?'

As the literature about the stability of Islamic banks is surprisingly narrow, this chapter focuses on the published annual reports of Islamic and conventional Banks of Malaysia. On the one hand, this chapter will contribute to the relatively undeveloped field of financial stability and Islamic banking; on the other hand it will enhance the literature of comparisons between Islamic and conventional banks by offering an additional perspective.

For this purpose it seems adequate to examine the concept of stability first. Hence the first section will review relevant literature on financial stability in general, and the risks banks, especially Islamic banks, are exposed to. The second section will introduce the methodology chosen for this research. Conceptually, stability will be tested by financial ratio analysis from three perspectives that are connected to liquidity, performance and risk; this will be followed by the fourth section describing the sample selected for analysis.

Sections five and six are the main body of this research and contain the descriptive analysis and its interpretation. In the first two parts the example of two British banks is used to illustrate how ratio analysis can be used to assess financial stability. In a third part trends and developments of the financial ratios of the Malaysian banks will be summarised and important points identified, which are discussed in section six. The finding will be discussed and their underlying factors explained if possible. From these findings three propositions about stability and Islamic banking could be derived and supported as far as this study is concerned. Finally section seven will summarise the research, findings and results in concluding remarks and will suggest topics for additional research.

4.2 Framework

4.2.1 Reflections on Stability

Since their business is to trade in risks of different levels, banks must be considered fragile by definition. The question is when does this fragility turn into instability, endangering the bank and its clients? By reviewing relevant literature the following section will give a brief introduction of stability in order to answer the above question. The section thereafter will introduce the specific risk of Islamic banks in order to draw conclusions about their general stability.

Despite a general understanding about what 'stability' or 'instability' means in the banking sector, there seems to be no widely accepted definition of either term. Whether describing stability or instability, the focus of publications lies on two aspects: macro-economic effects and effects on the banking level. Works on the importance of stability for the economy as a whole are much more frequent. Allen and Wood (2006: 160) provide the only attempt to define 'financial stability' as 'a state of affairs in which episodes of instability are unlikely to occur'. The authors do not suggest an adequate definition themselves, which must be considered as the weakest point of their paper. Furthermore, the phrase 'a state of affairs' remains very vague; in other words, they simply define stability as the absence of instability. However, they do mention that in physics 'stability' is described as a property of a system, not as a state of affairs (Allen and Wood, 2006: 160). This point is interesting as far as we accept the economy as a complex system and view each bank operating within it to be a (sub-)system as well.

In their literature review Allen and Wood (2006) further quote a number of interesting ideas to outline stability: Mishkin (1991 cited by Allen and Wood, 2006: 156) defines stability as 'the prevalence of a financial system which is able to ensure in a lasting way and without major disruptions, an efficient allocation of savings to investment opportunities'. The European Central Bank (2005 cited by Allen and Wood, 2006) provided a similar definition describing the purpose of financial stability in 'maintaining the smooth functioning of the financial system and its ability to facilitate and support the efficient functioning and performance of the economy'. Instability, on the other hand, was defined by Haldane *et al.* (2004 cited by Allen and Wood, 2006: 159) as 'any deviation from the optimal saving-investment plan of the economy that is due imperfections in the financial sector'.

All of the above definitions, including the one provided by Allen and Wood (2006), share some common traits: They all see instability as the disturbance of the desired normal way of business, which is found at an economic equilibrium providing the highest possible amount of welfare. Hence stability could be defined as the absence of volatility, which causes this disturbance.

The consideration of Allen and Wood (2006) is given so much space here since it illustrates the problems one meets by trying to define 'stability'. From this paper we can learn that stability is more to be outlined than to be clearly defined and that the literature prefers to see it as a macro-economic phenomenon rather than to assess it on a company level. Hence, outlining different aspects of stability and volatile effects seems the best way to find out about its relevance for the economy and financial institutions. The following sections will consider a number of factors causing volatility and its effects on financial institutions and the economy as a whole.

Why is banking stability so important at all? The answer is the potential cost of instability. This is not only the cost of bankruptcy of a financial institution but the costs for the economy resulting from the key position the banking-system has within this economy. Hoggarth, Reis and Saporta (2002) identify the cost of bank-instability as direct costs for governments and further costs for the society as welfare loss. The authors point out the importance of bank-credit for the economy of developed and developing countries; any economic shock affecting the banking-system would negatively affect the credit availability for this economy and cause recession. They further examine that these costs in the form of welfare loss would be as high (or even higher) for developed countries than for developing economies, and that emerging economies only suffer higher costs if a banking crisis is accompanied by a currency crisis (Hoggarth et al., 2002). These findings emphasise the importance the banking sector gains with the increasing complexity of the overall economic development, and hence the importance of financial stability for these economies.

De Graeve, Kitck and Koetler (2008) examine a trade-off between monetary and financial stability. They found out that any unexpected tightening of monetary policy increases the probability of distress. To identify a stricter monetary policy as an asset-shock sounds reasonable, as it directly affects the bank's ability to lend money. The recent credit crisis quickly drew the focus on credit-derivatives, a financial instrument that is suspected to have initiated the turmoil. This was criticised by White (2008), who pointed out that not only are innovative products responsible for a crisis, but fundamental problems within the financial system such as inadequate risk management and credit policy are also partly responsible. Credit growth on this basis would lead to unsustainable consumption and investment decisions and increased asset prices (White, 2008). His paper suggests two directions for stability: the importance of credit-risk assessment and the adequate pricing of assets.

The stressed credit-derivatives have originally been welcomed pre-credit-crunch as an instrument that would permit the transfer of credit risk from banks to non-banks. Wagner and Marsh (2006) appreciate the opportunities to increase stability within the financial system by moving a part of the fragility of banks out of the banking sector via credit risk transfer (CRT), but they also emphasise that a lot of this CRT takes place within this very sector. Hereby the positive effect of CRT is off-set. Even worse, since risk has been partially traded away, banks are tempted to take in new risks, thus increasing the level of instability again (Wagner and Marsh, 2006). Wagner and Marsh (2006) point out the importance of credit risk management for the stability of a bank and that this stability could be improved by transferring this risk from the financial institution to non-banks. This transfer of risks will be picked up again in the second section, where the specific risks of Islamic banks will be considered.

Instability of the banking system cannot only be caused by the attitude of financial institutions towards the risks they carry but by consolidation as well as by regulation. Uhde and Heimshoff (2009) found out that any concentration of the banking sector that would cause a reduction of competitive pressure, as well as any increased governmental intervention within this sector, would result in an increased risk of instability for this sector. Governmental intervention is excluded from capital regulation, which is considered to enhance stability (Uhde and Heimshoff, 2009). Nier (2005) considered a limit to regulatory requirements such as transparency, which would allow depositors and investors to assess the level of risk a financial institution is taking and hence how far it would be exposed to any kind of shock. He also acknowledges that by this transparency would lead to a higher sector discipline and that the benefits of transparency would generally outweigh its costs. But he also considers that to a bank under pressure after occurrence of a macro-economic shock transparency may lead to further destabilisation and may therefore enhance the crisis (Nier, 2005). A deregulation of the banking sector on the other hand could lead to crisis as well, since it could lead to inadequate credit growth as described as cause for the Nordic banking crisis (Peter, 2009).

The shock most likely to hit any kind of bank would be a sudden change of asset prices. Peter (2009) emphasises that banks are even exposed to changes in asset prices if they do not hold the affected assets themselves but their borrowers do. He concludes that financial stability depends on the bank's behaviour towards falling asset prices and the relocation of the risks involved (Peter, 2009). Adequate risk management hence is a way of preventing any shocks to the assets that a bank holds (direct or indirect). Such shocks can be provoked by the asset holders themselves when asymmetric information and herding behaviour cause a price-bubble (Holt, 2009). Holt's finding is of particular interest if one considers developments in emerging markets, where a high level of information cannot be presumed.

Not only the exposure of assets to risks can cause instability for the bank holding them, but so can an increased liquidity of bank assets as emphasised by Wagner (2007). He stresses that, once banks have the ability to trade away credit risk, they will be more strongly invested in riskier assets. Hence, an increased liquidity of bank assets will reduce banking stability. However, Wagner (2007) well notices that the illiquidity of bank assets is a source of fragility as well. He further suggests increased capital requirements to encounter the negative effects of enhanced risk-taking but limits this method as its effectiveness will fade with the growing liquidity of assets (Wagner, 2007). According to Wagner's paper, stability would be found at a balance point between the ability to liquidise assets if necessary and the avoidance of doing so if possible. This balance point is further influenced by the company's ability to assess the risk of the assets it holds correctly.

This fact leads to the last paper introduced in this section, which will deal with risk management. Daníelsson (2008) wrote about the reliability of statistical models to capture risk. He found out that the reliability of any model declines with the increasing complexity of the financial system while at the same time the demand for models assessing risk increases with the increasing complexity of the financial system. Increased use of models will lead to instability once investment decisions are based on them if either the model contains an error right from the beginning or the expectations about what the model would explain and which risks it captures are unrealistic. Daníelsson does not challenge the general use of statistical models or the level of sophistication of these models, but the quality of the underlying assumptions and the grade of application of models. Finally, he points out that models are not as stable as physical laws and that no model can replace the understanding of a financial product (Daníelsson, 2008).

Daníelsson's (2008) last statement directly points in the direction of the importance of sound management. Podpiera and Weill (2008) found that banking failures in emerging and transition countries are directly linked to management failures, arguing that bad management not only leads to low-cost efficiency but also affects the risk assessment of the company and their credit policy. In an unfortunate combination this could lead to a high amount of non-performing loans in the bank's portfolio and would probably result in distress. They conclude that poor management significantly increases the risk of banking failure, especially in emerging and transition countries (Podpiera and Weill, 2008).

Instability on the bank level can appear from within the financial sector itself as well as it can be caused by circumstances affecting the financial sector. Its economic effects could work in both directions – a macro-economic shock influencing financial institutions or a general instability among the banking sector resulting in an economic crisis.

Important aspects of stability can be drawn from the literature presented on three levels: On a macro-economic level there would be the ability to take a shock. A system that is sustainably stable should be able to absorb the shock and recover with a minimum of damage. A sudden change of asset prices has frequently been mentioned to be a great threat to financial stability and hence a connection between asset-price stability and bank stability is suggested. The concept of price stability will not be developed any further here but it should be mentioned that asset-price stability would require a stable economic and political environment and further more would require access to informational efficient markets.

On the financial sector level the structure of the sector itself would determine stability. Sector structure includes the concentration of financial institutions and the competitive pressure among them as well as potential political interference and regulation. Competition has been shown to be necessary for bank stability, and so is regulation; capital requirements in particular can guarantee stability to some extent.

On the company level, risk management and credit policy are the most important factors creating stability. Poor risk management, especially in the assessment
of credit risk or the provision of a careless credit policy, are certainly causing
instability and are likely to be the most important factors leading to banking
failure while the ability to assess risk correctly and the possibility to shift risks
generally are factors creating stability.

On the company and sector level, stability can be influenced by the financial
institutions, with sound risk management and adequate capital structure being
the most important factors.

4.2.2 Risk and Stability for Islamic Banks

Islamic Finance is a relatively young industry. Although some very enthusiastic
supporters would claim it to date back to the 7th century, the beginnings of
modern Islamic banking are not earlier than the 1970s, with financial services
such as insurances joining the field in the 1990s and the creation of regulatory
standards in the first decade of the new millennium. Islamic Finance is an emerging industry, but given the lack of well-functioning secondary markets and the
overall small scale of the sector it must be mentioned that Islamic finance is an
industry still under construction.

In their textbook about financial institutions management, Saunders and
Cornett (2006) identify no less than eight different risk categories to which
banks are exposed: interest rate risk, market risk, credit risk, off-balance sheet
risk, operational risk, currency risk (FX-Risk), sovereign risk and liquidity risk.
Islamic banks in their role as financial institutions are exposed to all these risks;
in addition, they are also exposed to compliance risk, the risk that a transaction, project or investment, is rejected by the Sharīᶜah Supervisory Council
(Akkizidis and Khandelwal 2008: 41). This could be seen as a special form
of Operational Risk. Even though they do neither charge nor pay interest,
Islamic banks are indirectly exposed to Interest Change Risk as they frequently
use interest rates as benchmarks; if interest rates change, consumer and investor behaviour becomes affected, as reported by Bank Islam Malaysia (BIMB
2006: 16).

According to Haron and Hock (2007), Islamic banks are especially exposed to
credit risk and market risk. The authors provide a short overview about the risks
inherent to Islamic financing products,[1] which in summary are various types of a
risk of default. A specific market risk arises from asset-based transactions, which
are very frequently used as a result of the ownership concept in Islamic banking
(Haron and Hock, 2007). Although Islamic banks are expected to carry very low
risks due to their theoretical conception, in practice, however, they tend mostly
to engage with short-term asset sales and thus they are very reluctant towards real
profit-loss-sharing contracts (Greuning and Iqbal, 2007).

The risk that Islamic banks are exposed to as well as currently available means
of risk management are exhaustively examined and explained in the books on

risk analysis by Greuning and Iqbal (2008) and on risk management by Akkizidis and Khandelwal (2008). The problems of risk management, especially the need to develop new methods to assess risks, as well as the lack of quantitative methods, have been examined by Sundararajan (2007) and by Kulathunga and Grais (2007).

Literature regarding the stability of Islamic banks is surprisingly rare. It is usually mentioned in works about the theoretical concepts of Islamic banking, such as the paper of el-Hawary, Grais and Iqbal: '[I]n the theoretical version, Islamic banks would at face value be less susceptible to instability than their conventional counterpart . . . rooted in the risk sharing feature' (el-Hawary, Grais and Iqbal, 2006). el-Hawary, Grais and Iqbal further point out that this advantage of Islamic banks is neutralised by their practical policies to pay out profits (el-Hawary, Grais and Iqbal, 2006). Marston and Sundararajan (2006) point out that supervision and surveillance by a regulatory body would be essential for maintaining stability in the financial sector. Hence they emphasise the creation of legal and regulatory frameworks that would not only provide a financial infrastructure but would allow supervisors to observe the means of risk management taken. The authors finally point out the problem that instruments to minimise or hedge risks are insufficient for Islamic banks as either innovative instruments do not exist or financial markets for them are not developed yet (Marston and Sundararajan, 2006). The absence of a bond market was negatively noted by Abdul Majid 2006).

The only work expressively on Islamic banks and financial stability is a recent International Monetary Fund (IMF) working paper by Čihák and Hesse (2008). They found that Islamic banks carry an overall higher risk than conventional banks, but that small Islamic institutions are more stable than conventional institutions of comparable size. The situation turns once large institutions are considered (Čihák and Hesse, 2008).

4.2.3 Summary on Stability

In the previous section three levels have been identified by which stability can be affected. The macro-economic environment does affect Islamic and conventional banks likewise, but most countries in which Islamic banks operate are developing or emerging countries which are more likely to suffer from unstable political systems (like Sudan) or economic isolation (like Iran). Neither can take access to sound-functioning capital markets for granted.

At the sector and bank level there are structural differences between the risk management requirements of Islamic- and conventional banks. The specific business of Islamic banks offers several opportunities of shifting risks. Risk sharing in the form of profit and loss sharing contracts is a basic concept of Islamic banking. In theory risks should be carried by all investors. For the banking business this means that depositors take a share in the overall risk of the bank and the bank takes a share in the risks their borrowers are taking.

4.3 Methodology

The study utilises ratio analysis based on the annual reports of a sample of Malaysian conventional and Islamic banks and two British conventional banks. Annual reports have been chosen as the source for this study; they are easy available to everyone, and so is the ratio analysis based on them. No internal data would be required to give conclusions about the stability of the companies mentioned here. This is interesting for potential customers and small private investors who would not be able to gain access to data beyond officially published documents anyway, but who obviously have an interest in the question of whether a certain banking model can be considered to be more stable than the other.

By using a descriptive approach, this study seeks to discover if there is any pattern of stability in Islamic banks during the recent financial crisis. For this study, three types of ratios, liquidity, performance and capital adequacy, have been considered to measure stability on three levels: inflow and outflow of capital as well as risk of the banks. The ratios used in this study are based on the textbook on financial reporting by Gibson (2009).

1) *Liquidity* functions as the backbone of a financial institution and in two ways becomes very relevant in the time of crisis. i) If a high number of credit defaults appear then the bank would be forced to pay current liabilities from reserves or assets that could be easily liquidised. ii) If it comes to a bank-run, depositors demand to be paid out immediately, which creates stress on the liquidity position of a bank. If the bank's liquidity is insufficient in either scenario, the bank may be forced to sell assets held for long-term investments at a discount and suffer a loss by this ('fire-sale'). The bank risks distress and insolvency in the worst case.

Equity Capital to Total Assets defined as per cent

For this ratio it is assumed that ownership can be used as a cushion against risk. A higher number would indicate more security, but would probably affect performance.

Loans to Deposits defined as per cent

This ratio shows how a bank's obligations are covered by assets. A decreasing L/D would imply less risk as more loans are outstanding to meet the demand on deposits.

Deposits times Capital defined as per cent

This ratio measures the relation between deposits and capital to show the debt position of the bank. Again, more capital means more security, while more deposits indicate higher returns.

$ECTA$ and L/D compare elements from the liability and asset side of the bank's balance sheet with each other, looking for a stable balance. D/C measures two liabilities but demands on deposits are more urgent to meet than shareholders' equity and could be met with capital if necessary.

2) This study further considers two *performance* ratios, Return on Assets and Return on Equity, to measure the bank's investment policy. It is assumed for

this study that overall stability can only be achieved by a stable liquidity and investment policy to measure not only the capital flowing into the bank or held by it (liquidity) but also the capital flowing out (investment). Sustainable investment as a stability issue cannot directly be assessed from the financial reports but indirectly concluded by monitoring performance.

Return on Assets defined as per cent

Return on Equity defined as per cent

ROE measures the return on stockholders' investment while *ROA* measures the general ability of a company to create profit.

3) In addition, this study will take **capital adequacy** ratios into account. Those have not been calculated as they are given in the relevant annual reports. A Core Capital Ratio (*CCR*) and a Risk Weighted Capital Ratio (*RWCR*) is reported for the Malaysian institutions and Tier 1 Capital Ratio (*Tier-I*) and Total Capital Ratio (*TCR*) for the British banks.

Tier 1 Capital Ratio / CCR defined as

Total Capital Ratio / RWCR defined as with Tier 2 not exceeding Tier 1.

Theoretically, *Tier-I* and *CCR* should describe the same ratio as should *TCR* and *RWCR*, but as the methodology used to assess and report risk is subject to local standards (BCBS 2005: 15), the ratios will be commented on separately.

Simplified, Tier 1 describes the book value of equity while Tier 2 can be a variety of secondary capital (Saunders and Cornett 2006: 580).

At least for the 2008 data all ratios are based on the Basel II Accord.

As a benchmark 4 per cent will be used as the minimum requirement for *Tier-I/CCR* and 8 per cent for *TCR/RWCR* (Saunders and Cornett, 2006: 581–2).

4.4 The Sample

Malaysia has applied a dual banking system since 1983, meaning that both conventional and Islamic banks can be found alongside each other. This, together with the high-level financial infrastructure, predetermines Malaysia for any research aiming for a comparison between conventional and Islamic banking. Even though the country is probably the most developed market for Islamic banking worldwide, the market share of conventional banks is much larger than that of Islamic banks. Nevertheless, Bank Negara Malaysia (BNM) lists no less than eighteen Islamic banks, most of which are subsidiaries of conventional financial institutions. As the Islamic banking activity of those will usually not be reported separately, only the two indigenous Islamic banks, Bank Islam Malaysia Berhad (BIMB) and Bank Muamalat Malaysia Berhad (BMMB) could be identified.[2]

Further institutions selected are Hong Leong Bank Berhad (HLB), Alliance Financial Group Berhad (AFG) and Affin Bank Berhad (AB).[3] As a result of the dual system it must be mentioned that all three Malaysian banks operate subsidiaries for Islamic banking or offer Islamic banking services. The profit generated from Islamic banking activities varies from 8 to 16 per cent of their total operating profit. As their main business lies in conventional financial services, these companies have been considered to be conventional banks.

In addition, two UK banks, Hongkong and Shanghai Banking Corporation (HSBC) and Northern Rock (NR) have been selected not only as an international comparison but also as a benchmark for stability. Despite suffering considerable losses during the crisis in 2007, HSBC managed to remain stable and profitable while NR came into distress and avoided bankruptcy only by massive governmental intervention. These banks mark two extreme examples of a stable and an unstable company during a financial crisis, making them valuable as comparisons here.

4.5 Descriptive Analysis

The following sections will describe the data collected, the results from the ratios as well as their interpretation. In a first step, a comparison between HSBC and NR will be used to illustrate the concept of stability. Stability as the absence of volatility or unstable moments must occur on both the liquidity and performance levels.

4.5.1 Finding Instability

HSBC has shown to remain profitable and stable during the recent turmoil and will be used as a stability benchmark while NR suffered from distress and could only be rescued from failure by a massive bailout by the British government. Hence instability is assumed for NR.

Table 4.1 (see Appendix) shows a balance sheet excerpt for both companies (lines 1–6) and ratios as described in the previous chapter (lines 7–13). The ratios' trends can also be observed from the relevant graphics below by following the red line for HSBC and the pink line for NR.

1) In Table 4.1, line 7 we see the *ECTA* ratio for both companies declining since 2006, implying that they both have a tendency towards instability. But while the ratio decreases by 37 per cent for the HSBC comparing 2006 and 2008, it decreases rapidly by 81 per cent for Northern Rock over the same period.

Furthermore, the 2008 *ECTA* of HSBC (lowest point observed for the last three years) is still about 25 per cent higher than the 2004 *ECTA* of NR (highest). For 2008 the *ECTA* of HSBC is more than six times higher than the one of NR.

More important for general stability than single numbers seems to be the trend the two companies have been showing since 2004: While HSBC started with a relatively low *ECTA* of 3.22 per cent, they managed to improve this ratio to 5.97 per cent in 2006 right before the crisis and dropped to 4.54 per cent during the crisis. NR at the same time started in 2004 on a comparable *ECTA* of 3.66 per cent but lost continuously ever since until reaching slightly more than 2 per cent in

2006 and below 0,6 per cent in 2008. This implies a trend towards instability that began well in advance of the current crisis, probably creating a structure that was then unable to compensate the effects of the credit crisis as an economic shock.

In line 8, the D/C ratio of NR is almost cut in half from 2006 to 2007 before increasing by almost eight times in 2008. In 2007 it looks better for NR because the deposits are declining much faster than the shareholders' capital. In reality it means that customers are closing their accounts faster than investors would sell their shares. Here the ratio itself does not imply instability, but the underlying factors strongly do as the bank is losing both customers and investors. In 2008 the bank was able to increase deposits to almost two-thirds the level of 2006 but the capital basis of NR must be considered rather poor due to the very high D/C ratio indicating potential instability.

HSBC shows a smooth increase of the D/C ratio, increasing deposits as well as shareholders' equity from 2006 to 2007, but while deposits are increasing further in 2008 shareholders' equity dropped by 27 per cent resulting in deposits being 13.3 times as much as capital. L/D ratio shows the strongest differences between NR and HSBC. If $L/D > 100$ per cent the liability of deposits is more than completely covered by loans outstanding. This makes the business less risky in theory.

We can see that HSBC had their deposits covered by loans 1.17 times in 2006. From then the ratio declined by almost 25 per cent until 2008. This indicates a trend towards instability as HSBC has fewer loans outstanding than it took in deposits. NR covers its deposits by loans 3.1 times in 2006 and 3.6 times in 2008. In 2007 the ratio even jumped to over 8.6 as a result of strongly reduced deposits.

    2) For the performance ratios in lines 12 and 13, ROA shows a slow decline for HSBC until reaching 0.97 per cent in 2007 followed by a sudden drop to 0.27 per cent as a result of the credit crisis. ROE shows a similar picture of decrease in three steps. Beginning in 2004/2005 with approximately 38 per cent and 34 per cent, the ratio dropped to about 17 per cent for 2006/2007 and finally to 5.86 per cent in 2008. For NR the situation looks more severe. ROA are declining from 0.77 per cent to 0.48 per cent from 2004 to 2006 and then turn negative for 2007 (-0.19 per cent) and 2008 (-1.23 per cent). ROE on the other hand looked stable in the beginning with a slight increase between 21.25 per cent in 2004 and 23.62 per cent in 2006, but then sharply dropped to -10.37 per cent for 2007 and to an impressive -207.67 per cent for 2008.

    For both companies the performance ratios indicate a trend towards instability as profit is declining for both of them. But while HSBC could at least remain profitable over the last two years despite the credit crisis NR suffered severe losses.

    3) HSBC shows a slightly growing *Tier-I* ratio from 2004 to 2006 (8.9 per cent to 9.4 per cent). During the credit crisis the ratio decreased to 9.3 per cent in 2007 followed by 8.3 per cent in 2008. For the *TCR* HSBC was able to maintain a slow increase beginning at 12 per cent in 2004

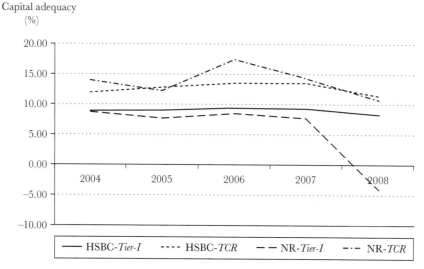

Figure 4.1 Trends of *ECTA*, *D/C* and *L/D*

and reaching 13.6 per cent in 2007, after which the ratio reduced to 11.4 per cent. NR in contrast shows a quite volatile *Tier-I* ratio that moves between 7.7 per cent and 8.7 per cent for the years 2004 to 2007. In 2008, as a result of the situation the bank was in, the ratio became negative (-4 per cent). The *TCR* of NR shows a similarly strong volatility beginning at 14 per cent in 2004, and reaching a peak of 17.5 per cent in 2006 after declining to 12.3 per cent in 2005. Since 2006 the ratio declined over 14.4 per cent in 2007 to 10.8 per cent in 2008.

Figure 4.1 above illustrates the situation.

It is not only the fact that NR's *Tier-I* ratio leaves the area of 'adequately capitalised' that points to instability, but the strong fluctuations of both ratios over the years.

HSBC shows a very smooth, almost steady movement with *Tier-I* and *TCR* keeping approximately the same distance, and only a slow reduction during the crisis years 2007 and 2008, implying overall stability. NR meanwhile has a very unsteady *TCR* combined with strong deviations in the distance between *Tier-I* ratio and *TCR*. This raises questions about their risk management, as risk-weighted assets are the divisor of both ratios; it also questions their capital structure, which seems unbalanced.

4.5.2 Remarks on Instability

The ratios above provide hints about a trend towards instability but not one of them could say where exactly instability would start. Since the ratios, and especially their development over the last three years, look better in the case of HSBC it can be said that this is the more stable company.

There are a few limitations to the ratios themselves, as the L/D ratio ignores the credit risk of defaulting loans and considers the book-value of loans and deposits only. Hence the declining ratio of HSBC implies a trend towards insta-bility, but the continuous increase of deposits over the years means an increase in trust into the company. As trust is an important element in banking this increase of deposits probably points stronger towards stability than the ratio points in the opposite direction. The reduced amounts of loans could be caused by a more careful credit policy after the events of 2007.

The example of HSBC and NR shows that evidence on stability can be found in two ways in all three ratio types: first, a general trend of the ratios towards stability or instability over a longer period and second, rapid changes in the ratios from one year to the next seeming to imply instability.

Changes in the underlying data of certain ratios must be considered as well in order to determine instability, as the 'improvement' in the D/C ratio of NR shows while the company obviously suffered serious problems.

4.5.3 Conventional and Islamic Banks

This section aims for a direct comparison between the two Islamic and the three conventional banks selected for Malaysia under consideration of the findings of the analysis of HSBC and NR on the three levels of stability. The underlying data can be found in Tables 4.2 and 4.3 respectively.

1) Trends of $ECTA$, D/C and L/D can be seen in Figures 4.2, 4.3 and 4.4 below.

The $ECTA$ ratio shows an overall variegated picture.

The first Islamic bank, BIMB, shows a V-shaped graph with a ratio starting at 8.53 per cent in 2004 dropping to 1.49 per cent in 2006, recovering in 2007 to 4.3 per cent and finally reaching 8.1 per cent in 2008 while the other Islamic bank, BMMB, has a very steady ratio that only slightly moves between 5.57 per cent (highest in 2005) and 5.1 per cent (lowest in 2008) with no deviations larger than 0.24 per cent in either direction. Their conventional counterparts show a likewise unsteady picture. The $ECTA$ ratio of HLB is continuously declining from 9 per cent in 2004 to 6.58 per cent in 2008. Except for HLB, only the defaulting NR shows a continuous downturn, but on a much lower level.

The ratio of AFG slightly declines from 7.88 per cent in 2004 to 7.37 per cent in 2006 but then raises to 8.38 per cent in 2007 and 8.99 per cent in 2008, whereas the ratio of AB raises only in 2005 to 8.46 per cent from previously 7.51 per cent but then decreases over the next two years to 7.8 per cent to finally recover to 8.04 per cent in 2008.

It must further be mentioned that the three conventional banks have the overall highest $ECTA$ ratios in this sample, except for 2004 and 2008 where BIMB could reach similar numbers. From the banks examined here only HLB

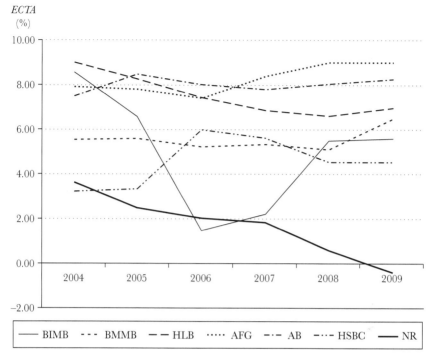

Figure 4.2 Trends of *ECTA*, *D/C* and *L/D*

and BMMB show a steady trend while HSBC and BIMB have the most extreme fluctuations.

D/C ratios appear to be steadier over the entire sample with a few exceptions. Most obvious is the peak in BIMB. The ratio begins at 10.55 times in 2004, increasing to 13.97 times in 2005 and then raising up to 64.74 times in 2006 and falling back to 22.15 times in 2007. In 2008 the ratio reduces further to 11.13 times. A sudden raise of this ratio like this could only be observed for NR in 2008 where the *D/C* ratio increased from 10.76 times to 29.85 times.

BMMB shows the steadiest trend with observations between 16.7 times (lowest in 2005) and 17.64 times (highest in 2007) and the overall highest level.

The conventional AB remains similarly steady with deviations from 8.84 times (lowest in 2005) and 10.83 times (highest in 2007), while HLB shows a steady increase of their *D/C* ratio from 9.08 times in 2004 to 13.35 times in 2008. Only AFG shows significant fluctuations as their *D/C* ratio declines from 9.59 times in 2004 to only 5.11 times in 2005, followed by a slight recovery in 2006 to 5.62 times, an increase to 9.35 times in 2007, and finally a decrease to 9.26 times in 2008. Overall, the Islamic banks have a higher level of *D/C* ratio than the conventional banks.

The *L/D* ratios displayed in figure 4 show almost no extraordinary movements. The ratios of the two Islamic banks are among the lowest observations for

Deposits times capital

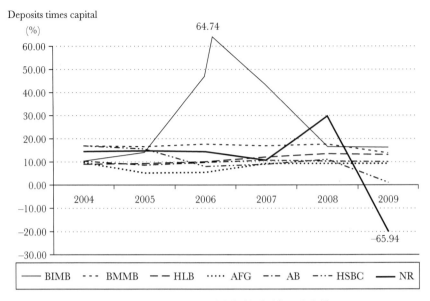

Figure 4.3 Trends of *ECTA*, *D/C* and *L/D*

Loan to deposits

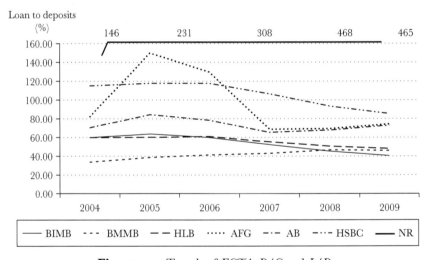

Figure 4.4 Trends of *ECTA*, *D/C* and *L/D*

this sample. BMMB has by far the lowest *L/D* ratio, which is steadily increasing from 33.86 per cent in 2004 to finally 46.27 per cent in 2008. BIMB shows a slow increase in 2005 to 63.53 per cent. The ratio thereafter decreases over 60.33 per cent in 2006, 52.78 per cent in 2007 to 45.5 per cent in 2008. The graph of HLB follows a very similar movement, although their ratio is about 5 per cent higher than the one of BIMB over the last two years.

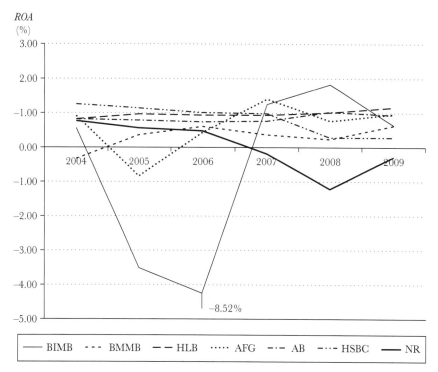

Figure 4.5 Performance Ratios

AFG and AB have the highest level ratio here among the Malaysian banks. But while AB's ratio increases to 84 per cent in 2005 and then declines in 2006 and 2007 to 65.33 per cent and recovers to 67.99 per cent in 2008, the ratio of AFG increases rapidly to 149.86 per cent in 2005, declines to 129.63 per cent in 2006 and then falls to 68.24 per cent in 2007 to maintain approximately this level in 2008 (69.27 per cent).

Overall it can be observed that the Malaysian banks hold a much lower L/D ratio than the British institutions do. While HSBC seems to seek an L/D ratio from approximately 95per cent to 120per cent, most of the Malaysian banks seem to aim for a ratio from approximately 45per cent to 65per cent. The two Islamic banks hold the lowest L/D ratio together with HLB. An interesting observation is the peak of AFG's ratio in 2005 and 2006.

Further interesting is the contrast between most of the banks having a sideways-oriented L/D ratio and the defaulting NR, which has a ratio beginning very high already at approximately 146 per cent but further increasing every year until it reaches approximately 468 per cent in 2008.

2) For the performance ratios displayed in Figures 4.5 (ROA) and 4.6 (ROE), the two Islamic banks score the overall lowest performance in both

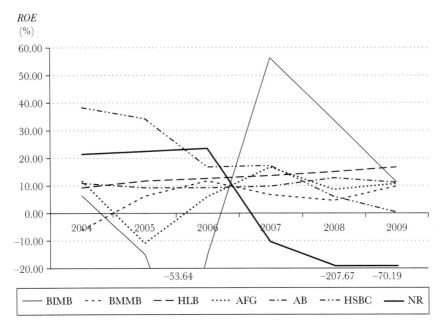

Figure 4.6 Performance Ratios

ratios except for 2007 and 2008 when BIMB becomes extremely profitable. BMMB suffers a loss in 2004, recovers in 2005 with an *ROA* of 0.35
per cent and an *ROE* of 6.33 per cent and reaches a peak in 2006 with
an *ROA* of 0.61 per cent and an *ROE* of 11.69 per cent. BIMB suffered a
period of severe losses in 2005 and 2006, causing an *ROA* in 2006 of -8.52
per cent and an *ROE* of -573.37 per cent.

Among the conventional banks, AFG's ratios show losses in 2005 followed by a recovery in 2006 and a peak in 2007 for both ratios. The *ROA*
of AFG in 2007 is the highest observed (1.41 per cent). In 2008 returns
decline slightly.

Furthermore, it is interesting that all Malaysian conventional banks
managed to increase their performance ratios from 2005 to 2007 and
HLB and AB even for 2008 while the two British institutions decline
over the entire period. From the two Islamic banks, BMMB maintains
profitability on a low level while BIMB, having recovered from three
years of downturn and losses, suddenly outperforms everyone.

3) The last type of ratios consider capital adequacy as a measurement of
how sufficient banks are shielded by capital against the risk they are
taking in.

Among the conventional banks, AB and AFG show an almost parallel steady
CCR movement as displayed in Figure 4.7. Both companies' ratios start slightly

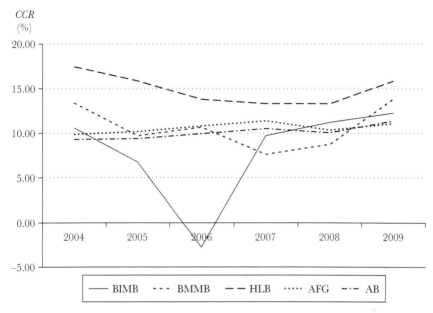

Figure 4.7 Performance Ratios

below 10 per cent, raise until reaching their peak in 2007 from approximately 10.5 per cent to 11.5 per cent, followed by a light decrease in 2008. HLB's *CCR* is the highest in the sample. It starts at 17.49 per cent in 2004, declines strongly to 13.34 per cent and 13.3 per cent in 2007 and 2008.

The two Islamic banks show stronger fluctuations. BIMB's *CCR* shows the V-shape already observed for other ratios. Beginning at 10.6 per cent, the ratio declines to an alarming 6.77 per cent and then declines even further to -2.78 per cent. After that the *CCR* recovers to 9.74 per cent in 2007 and 11.27 per cent in 2008. BMMB's *CCR* declines from 13.4 per cent to 9.7 per cent in 2005, increases slightly to 10.7 per cent in 2006, decreases again in 2007 to 7.6 per cent and finally improves a little in 2008 to 8.8 per cent.

For the *RWCR* (Figure 4.8), again HLB has the highest though declining ratio in the sample. Beginning at 18.99 per cent, the ratio reduces steadily to 16.36 per cent in 2008. The *RWCR* of AFG increases from 14.54 per cent in 2004 to 16.62 per cent in 2006 and then decreases slowly over two years to finally 14.76 per cent in 2008.

The ratio of AB shows the steadiest sideways trend until 2007 moving between 13.51 per cent (lowest observed in 2005) and 14.55 per cent (highest observed in 2004) and then reducing to 13.08 per cent in 2008. For the Islamic banks, BIMB's *RWCR* shows the notorious V-shape with a negative bottom-point of −2.84 per cent in 2006. For 2007 the ratio recovers to 9.74 per cent and reaches 11.27 per cent in 2008. The ratio of BMMB is constantly over 10 per cent but

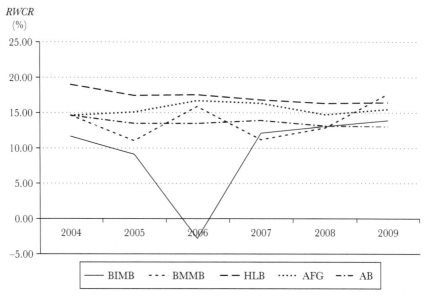

Figure 4.8 Performance Ratios

not less volatile. It falls from 14.6 per cent to 11.1 per cent in 2005, increases
to 15.8 per cent in 2006 to fall again to 11.2 per cent in 2005. Finally, the ratio
reaches 12.9 per cent in 2008. Overall the conventional banks show much less
fluctuations than the Islamic banks and have the higher ratios over the greater
part of the period.

4.6 Discussion of Findings and Propositions

The development of the first type of ratios indicates stability and instability for
the two Islamic banks at the same time. The steady sideway trend of *ECTA*, *D/C*
and *L/D* of BMMB clearly indicates an element of stability. On the other hand,
their *L/D* ratio is the lowest of the sample while their *D/C* ratio is the highest over
time, only occasionally surpassed by the extreme peak of BIMB in 2006 and the
defaulting of NR in 2008. The *ECTA* of BMMB is considerably lower than those
of the conventional Malaysian banks but higher than the ratio of NR and even
higher than the ratio of HSBC for 2004 and 2005. The results for BMMB imply a
risk-avoiding business but this is very likely to affect their performance negatively
as suggested by the definition of the ratios (Gibson, 2009). This can be confirmed
by looking on BMMB's performance ratios. *ROA* shows a loss for the first year
and is lower than the ratio of the conventional banks except for AFG for 2005 to
2006 when they suffered a loss and recovered. *ROE* shows the same development,
except for 2006, when the ratio actually reaches the level of the conventional HLB
and AB. The problem of high liquidity is notorious for Islamic banks. A study on

Middle Eastern banks even found excess liquidity, putting the banks on the edge of business risk. A reason for high liquidity can be seen in underdeveloped financial markets for Islamic financial products (Majid and Rais, 2006).

The loss of 2004 could still be explained as an aftermath of the Asian-crisis of 1997, which lasted until 2002 in Malaysia (Nier, 2005) but the overall low performance raises the question of whether the risk-averse policy will be able to maintain stability or if the bank will lose its competitiveness in the long term.

Considering BIMB, the bank shows an L/D ratio that is slightly higher than the one of BMMB and almost equal to the one of HLB. Nevertheless, there is some explanation needed for the V-shaped (peak) observations in about 2006 in BIMB's $ECTA$ and D/C ratios. For both ratios the development from 2004 to 2006 clearly shows instability. The reasons are non-performing loans as described in the Annual Reports of BIMB. In 2005 the loss caused by non-performing loans summed up to RM 648mio. (BIMB, 2005: 4) and increased to RM 1,48bn in the following year (BIMB, 2006: 5). At this point at the latest, the bank must be considered unstable if not on the edge of distress. The problem of non-performing loans did not appear overnight, as it was mentioned once in the report of 2004 but not further commented on (BIMB 2004: 4). The bank finally reacted by replacing their CEO and other top-management positions during the summer of 2006 but was further in the need of an extensive recapitalisation by two new investors (BIMB: 2006, 9). Even before this a new risk-management framework and a Risk-Management Committee were set up to counter the problem (BIMB, 2005: 9–10). The restructuring did not only affect internal processes but saw also a rebranding of the company. The bank's name stayed the same but a new logo was applied to support a message of change (BIMB, 2007: 26). Overall the restructuring appears to be successful as most of the relevant ratios recovered and surpassed the level of 2004. According to the performance ratios, BIMB is more profitable than any other bank of the sample over the last two years.

The BIMB distress in 2006 had two underlying factors connected with instability. The first was poor credit risk management resulting in a high number of non-performing loans. The second was a probably incompetent senior management not assessing the problem of non-performing loans and unsound credit policy earlier or rather making them possible in the first place. This example fits textbook-like with the findings of Podpiera and Weill (2008) about management failure as a cause of banking distress.

Based on the findings on BIMB and BMMB, the following proposition seems to be justified:

Proposition I: *Islamic banks are not any more stable than conventional banks.*

Overall the ratios of the Islamic banks were inferior to those of their conventional counterparts. This can be explained by the fact that Islamic banks are exposed to almost the same risks as conventional banks but they have less instruments available for them to minimise or diversify the risks that they face (Marston and& Sundararajan, 2006; Sundararajan, 2007). Kulathunga and Grais (2007) supports this position, as does the absence of developed capital markets of various types, which poses a threat to the banks' stability (Majid and Rais, 2006).

The three conventional banks tended to have 1) better liquidity ratios, 2) higher performance ratios and 3) more stable capital adequacy ratios than the Islamic banks. However, capital adequacy is difficult to comment on as Islamic banks do not only have to follow regulatory standards suggested by the Basel Accords but implement suggestions of Islamic Financial Services Board (IFSB) standards as well. Hence it is difficult to determine how their capital adequacy ratios can be compared to those of conventional banks.

Compared to the Islamic banks as well as to the British comparisons AFG, AB and HLB had the highest $ECTA$ ratio over the whole period with only BIMB reaching their level in 2004 and 2008. At the same time their D/C ratio is almost the lowest with only BIMB reaching their level in 2004 and 2008 and HSBC moving on a similar level from 2006 to 2008. As a high $ECTA$ and low D/C may indicate lower returns simply due to risk-averse business a comparison with the performance ratios is necessary. HLB and AB can show a stable ROA at a very high level, outperformed only by HSBC until 2007. In 2007 BIMB and AFG surpass HLB and AB. The combination of high performance and substantial liquidity must be seen as a strong indicator for stability. It must further be mentioned that HLB and AB are the only banks being able to maintain an increasing performance over the whole period while all other banks show a declining performance in 2007 to 2008. The fact that the conventional Malaysian banks do not only have stable liquidity, performance and capital adequacy ratios but a considerable proportion of Islamic Finance among their business activities implies the second proposition.

Proposition II: *Conventional banks can increase their stability by operating significant Islamic windows as part of risk diversification.*

Rapid changes of ratios imply instability. Hence, the volatile period of AFG and of BIMB from 2005 to 2007 must be examined further. Like BIMB, AFG suffered from a huge proportion of non-performing loans. Most of them were older than seven years, which places their origin during the time of the Asian-crisis (AFG, 2006: 11). In addition, both companies mention the strong increase of petrol prices in 2005 to 2006 as a threat to their business (BIMB, 2006: 16; AFG, 2006: 11). AFG further refers to a change in Malaysia's currency policy in 2005, which is appreciated from a general economic view but claimed to create more competitive pressure in the banking sector (AFG, 2006: 6).

AFG finally tackled their problems similar to BIMB by restructuring their debts and applying a new risk management framework, but most importantly by replacing the senior management over the summer of 2005 (AFG, 2006: 9). Hence the following third proposition was formulated:

Proposition III: *Personnel changes among the executive management have a positive effect on the stability of banks in times of distress.*

If we assume management failure to be the major reason of bank failure as suggested (Podpiera and Weill, 2008), the removal of the former management as a source of instability seems only logical. The proposition is further supported by the fact that both banks were able not only to restore their profitability but to improve their ratios of all three types tested to be among the top results of the sample.

4.7 Conclusion

This study examined a sample of seven banks, two Islamic and three conventional banks from Malaysia and two British banks as a further comparison. The purpose of this study was to search for stability by investigating the banks' financial ratios to find out whether Islamic banks are more stable than conventional banks, especially in time of crisis.

Three types of ratios connected with stability (liquidity, performance and capital adequacy) have been selected for this study. Stability as an economic or business concept has been studied initially, revealing that stability could not be clearly defined but several characteristics of stability and instability could be outlined. Comparing the two British banks' instability could clearly be identified in the ratios of Northern Rock. The ratio analysis performed showed several hints and trends towards stability (or instability). Unstable elements could be identified in one of the Islamic and one of the conventional banks, as well as could be the means by which the banks tried to overcome the instability found.

Individually taken, the liquidity ratios of Islamic banks looked stronger than those of conventional banks, but their performance ratios did not. This finding led to the first proposition of this paper, that the stability of Islamic banks is not higher than the stability of conventional banks. Islamic banks may still carry less risk than conventional banks but stability is rather a concept of sustainable business than of risk averseness. This proposition is further supported by theoretical considerations that Islamic banks face the same risks than conventional banks do, even though with different focus.

The fact that Islamic banks share a part of their risks with investors and depositors by their very business model implies that a conventional bank with an Islamic window can use this feature to shift certain risks away from the bank. This idea led to the second proposition, that conventional banks that operate considerably large Islamic windows are more stable than pure Islamic or conventional banks. This proposition is supported by the findings among the ratios for the three conventional Malaysian banks that outperformed the rest of the sample over the larger part of the period. Two of the banks, one Islamic, one conventional, showed significant signs of instability and probably distress. The fact that both of them could overcome these situations and showed very solid ratios of all three types after replacing their senior management led to the third proposition, that a bank in distress can actually improve stability by management change.

Further research will be required to support the third proposition as it is currently only based on the indication by the findings from this study and a further paper on the connection between bank and management failure. The idea of risk diversification through Islamic banking as suggested in Proposition II is an unexplored area as well. If the proposition could be verified it may be useful for banks operating in countries with dual systems like Malaysia, or countries with a significant Muslim population like France or the United Kingdom. For the development of Islamic banking further studies about the effect of the IFSB standards are needed, especially about the comparability of capital adequacy ratios.

Notes

1. For an overview on basic Islamic financial products and underlying concepts see: Usmani (2002) and Vogel and Hayes (1998).
2. Based on a list provided by BNM: www.bnm.gov.my/index.php?ch=13&cat=bankin g&type=IB&fund=0&cu=0
3. Based on a list provided by BNM: www.bnm.gov.my/index.php?ch=13&cat=bankin g&type=CB&fund=0&cu=0

Bibliography

Abdul Majid, Abdul Rais (2006) 'Developing liquidity management instruments: Role of international Islamic financial markets', in T. Khan and D. Muljawan (eds), *Islamic Financial Architecture: Risk Management and Financial Stability*. Jeddah: IRTI, pp. 229–46.

Akkizidis, I. and Khandelwal, S. (2008). *Financial Risk Management for Islamic Banking and Finance*. New York: Palgrave Macmillan.

Allen, W. and Wood. G. (2006). 'Defining and achieving financial stability', *Journal of Financial Stability* 2(2): 152–72.

Alkhan, R. (2006). *Islamic Securitization: A Revolution in the Banking Industry*. Bahrain: Miracle Publishing.

Bank Islam Malaysia Berhat (BIMB) (2006). *Annual Report 2006*. Kuala Lumpur: BIMB.

BCBS (2005). *Textbody of the Basel II Accord*. Basel: BCBS.

Čihák, M. and Hesse, H. (2008). *Islamic Banks and Financial Stability: An Empirical Analysis*, IMF Working Paper No. WP/08/16.

Daníelsson, J. (2008). 'Blame the models', *Journal of Financial Stability* 4(4): 321–8.

el-Hawary, Dahlia Anwar, Grais, Wafic and Iqbal, Zamir (2006). 'Regulating Islamic financial institutions, the nature of the regulated', in T. Khan and D. Muljawan (eds), *Islamic Financial Architecture: Risk Management and Financial Stability*. Jeddah: IRTI, pp. 51–94.

Gibson, C. (2009). *Financial Reporting and Analysis, Using Financial Accounting Information*. 11th edn, Mason, OH: South Western Cengage Learning.

De Graeve, F., Kick, T. and Koetler, M. (2008). 'Monetary policy and financial (in)stability: An intergrated micro/macro approach', *Journal of Financial Stability* 4(3): 205–31.

Greuning, H. V. and Iqbal, Z. (2008). *Risk Analysis for Islamic Banks*. Washington, DC: World Bank.

Greuning, H. V. and Iqbal, Z. (2007). 'Banking and risk environment', in S. Archer and

R. Karim (eds), *Islamic Finance: The* Regulatory Challenge. Singapore: John Wiley and Sons, pp. 11–39.

Haron, A. and Hock, J. (2007). 'Inherent risk: Credit and market risks', in S. Archer and R. Karim (eds), *Islamic Finance: The* Regulatory Challenge. Singapore: John Wiley and Sons, pp. 94–120.

Hoggarth, Glenn, Reis, Ricardo and Saporta, Victoria (2002). 'Cost of banking system instability, some empirical evidence', *Journal of Banking and Finance* 26(5): 825–55.

Holt, C. (2009). 'Herding behaviour in asset markets', *Journal of Financial Stability* 5(1): 35–56.

Hussin, A. (2005). 'The Islamic financial landscape in Malaysia', in A. Anwar and M. Haneef (eds) *Studies in Islamic Banking and Finance in the 21st Century, Theory and Practice.* Kuala Lumpur: IIUM Publication.

Kulathunga, A. and Grais, W. (2007). 'Capital structure and risk in Islamic financial institutions', in S. Archer and R. Karim (eds) *Islamic Finance: The Regulatory Challenge*, pp. 69–93.

Marston, D. and Sundararajan, V. (2006). 'Unique risks of Islamic banks: Implications for systematic stability', in T. Khan and D. Muljawan (eds), *Islamic Financial Architecture: Risk Management and Financial Stability.* Jeddah: IRTI, pp. 93–108.

Mavrotas, G. and Vinogradov, D. (2007). 'Financial sector structure and financial crisis burden' *JFS*: 295–323.

Nier, E. (2005). 'Bank stability and transparency', *Journal of Financial Stability* 1(3): 342–54.

Peter, G. van (2009). 'Asset prices and banking distress, A macro-economic approach', *Journal of Financial Stability* 5(3): 298–319.

Podpiera, J. and Weill, L. (2008). 'Bad luck or bad management? Emerging banking market experience', *Journal of Financial Stability* 4(2): 135–48.

Saunders, A. and Cornett, M. (2006). *Financial Institutions Management: A Risk Management Approach.* New York: McGraw-Hill.

Sundararajan, V. (2007). 'Risk characteristics of Islamic products: Implications for risk measurement', in S. Archer and R. Karim (eds) *Islamic Finance: The Regulatory Challenge.* Singapore: John Wiley and Sons, pp. 40–68.

Uhde, A. and Heimshoff, U. (2009). 'Consolidation in banking and financial stability in Europe: Empirical evidence', *Journal of Banking and Finance* 33(7): 1,299–311.

Usmani, Muhammand Taqi (2002). *An Introduction to Islamic Finance.* The Hague: Kluwer Law International.

Vogel, F. and Hayes, S. (1998). *Islamic Law and Finance, Religion, Risk and Return.*

Wagner, W. (2007). 'The liquidity of bank assets and banking stability', *Journal of Banking and Finance* 31(1): 129–39.

Wagner, W. and Marsh. J. (2006). 'Credit risk transfer and financial sector stability', *Journal of Financial Stability* 2(2): 173–93.

White, W. (2008). 'Past financial crisis, the current financial turmoil and the need for a new macro financial stability framework', *Journal of Financial Stability* 4(4): 307–12.

Appendix

Abbreviations

AB	Affin Bank Bhd
AFG	Alliance Finance Group Bhd
Bhd	Berhad
BIMB	Bank Islam Malaysia Bhd
BMMB	Bank Muamalat Malaysia Bhd
BNM	Bang Negara Malaysia
CCR	Core Capital Ratio
CRT	credit risk transfer
D/C	Deposits times Capital Ratio
ECTA	Equity Capital to Total Assets Ratio
HLB	Hong Leong Bank Bhd
HSBC	Hongkong and Shanghai Banking Corporation
IFSB	Islamic Financial Services Board
IMF	International Monetary Fund
JBF	Journal of Banking and Finance
JFS	Journal of Financial Stability
L/D	Loans to Deposits Ratio
NR	Northern Rock
ROA	Return on Assets Ratio
ROE	Return on Equity Ratio
RWCR	Risk Weighted Capital Ratio
SSC	*Sharīʿah* Supervisory Committee
Tier-I	Tier I Capital Ratio
ECB	European Central Bank

Table 4.1 Analysis of HSBC and NR

	HSBC (31.12.) $ millions					Northern Rock (31.12.) £ millions				
	HSBC 2004	HSBC 2005	HSBC 2006	HSBC 2007	HSBC 2008	NR 2004	NR 2005	NR 2006	NR 2007	NR 2008
1 EBIT	18,943	20,966	22,086	24,212	9,307	431.2	494.2	626.7	-167.6	-1,355.9
2 Net profit	14,258	15,873	16,871	20,455	6,498	306.2	349.9	443	-199	-1,399.7
3 Sh. equ.	85,522	92,432	108,352	128,160	93,591	1,541.9	1,575.6	2,174.8	1,663.5	-402.2
4 Deposits	693,072	739,419	896,834	1,228,321	1,245,411	21,543.6	25,209.4	29,003.8	12,307	25,347.8
5 Total loans	816,340	865,967	1,053,338	1,218,914	1,086,634	33,104.8	75,149.9	92,306.4	100,127.1	76,106.2
6 Total assets	1,279,974	1,501,970	1,860,758	2,354,266	2,527,465	42,790	82,708.5	101,010.6	109,321	10,4346
7 ECTA	3.22%	3.33%	5.97%	5.61%	4.54%	3.61%	2.48%	2.04%	1.82%	0.59%
8 D/C	16.98	15.48	8.15	8.99	11.16	14.51	15.00	14.46	10.76	29.85
9 L/D	115.50%	117.44%	117.30%	106.92%	93.20%	146.66%	231.55%	308.88%	465.82%	468.02%
10 Tier-1	8.90%	9.00%	9.40%	9.30%	8.30%	8.70%	7.70%	8.50%	7.70%	-4.00%
11 TCR	12.00%	12.80%	13.50%	13.60%	11.40%	14.00%	12.30%	17.50%	14.40%	10.80%
12 ROA	1.23%	1.14%	1.00%	0.97%	0.27%	0.77%	0.56%	0.48%	-0.19%	-1.23%
13 ROE	38.25%	34.31%	16.81%	17.30%	5.86%	21.25%	22.45%	23.62%	-10.37%	-207.67%

Table 4.2 Balance Sheet and Income Statement Excerpts

Bank Islam Malaysia Bhd (30.6.)

RM'000	BIMB 2004	BIMB 2005	BIMB 2006	BIMB 2007	BIMB 2008	BIMB 2009
EBIT	98,298	−479,778	−1,277,160	211,971	316,942	235,866
Net profit	75,262	−507,807	−1,296,789	207,617	389,600	161,876
Shareh. equ.	1,163,188	730,181	−277,840	1,019,109	1,319,269	1,531,182
Deposits	11,618,023	14,840,697	14,449,544	17,611,652	20,812,762	25,212,709
Total loans	7,640,474	9,168,596	8,501,362	8,422,014	9,061,318	9,661,864
Total assets	12,958,514	15,848,906	14,605,316	19,058,301	23,556,443	27,488,507

Bank Muamalat Malaysia Bhd

RM'000	BMMB 2004	BMMB 2005	BMMB 2006	BMMB 2007	BMMB 2008	BMMB 2009
EBIT	−26,819	41,251	103,409	64,238	44,068	142,061
Net profit	−26,302	32,328	72,520	48,138	31,951	98,834
Shareh. equ.	498,147	523,683	716,637	737,331	702,236	1,319,131
Deposits	7,459,031	9,606,333	12,278,841	12,400,882	12,698,395	14,937,217
Total loans	2,703,321	3,962,527	5,148,171	5,585,247	6,027,516	6,630,159
Total assets	8,0614,14	10,269,647	13,450,636	13,808,090	14,398,645	16,714,212

Hong Leong Bank (30.6.)

RM'000	HLB 2004	HLB 2005	HLB 2006	HLB 2007	HLB 2008	HLB 2009
EBIT	528,721	713,435	764,241	856,598	1,010,042	1,132,231
Net profit	381,960	513,439	549,920	619,449	741,861	904,625
Shareh. equ.	4,425,498	4,401,996	4,380,909	4,658,707	5,133,238	5,776,852
Deposits	39,253,777	41,982,652	47,072,382	61,833,017	68,920,523	73,955,933
Total loans	22,970,195	25,582,735	28,618,868	31,654,774	34,534,024	34,795,414
Total assets	49,060,405	57,709,713	60,596,250	71,423,739	77,461,205	79,494,542

Alliance Financial Group (31.3.)

RM'ooo	AFG 2004	AFG 2005	AFG 2006	AFG 2007	AFG 2008/ 09	AFG 2008
EBIT	299,679	18,437,227	150,812	502,050	303,312	408,938
Net profit	215,055	−201,424	107,363	380,095	228,888	301,500
Shareh. equ.	1,941,997	1,742,395	1,942,722	2,589,438	2,761,885	2,947,141
Deposits	17,679,198	1,134,284	19,586,770	22,805,884	26,766,223	25,917,997
Total loans	14,644,047	13,549,622	13,310,628	15,618,971	18,718,097	20,648,445
Total assets	23,645,878	23,581,197	26,399,289	27,674,926	31,854,432	31,663,615

Affin Bank (31.12)

RM'ooo	AB 2004	AB 2005	AB 2006	AB 2007	AB 2008	AB 2009
EBIT	174,641	229,352	272,314	322,003	454,628	425,147
Net profit	161,653	167,489	199,158	232,452	331,312	317,752
Shareh. equ.	15,487,14	20,918,20	22,732,71	2,511,000	2,709,538	2,967,018
Deposits	13,419,839	18,745,040	23,915,953	27,877,717	25,610,676	31,463,982
Total loans	10,708,147	16,436,195	16,986,653	16,848,690	19,516,255	21,989,304
Total assets	18,030,771	25,004,440	29,425,414	31,909,386	33,011,374	35,598,637

Table 4.3 Financial Ratios

BIMB	2004	2005	2006	2007	2008	2009
ECTA	8.53%	6.57%	1.49%	2.20%	5.49%	5.58%
D/C	10.55	13.97	64.75	43.25	16.43	16.15
L/D	60.51%	63.53%	60.33%	52.78%	45.50%	40.68%
CCR	10.60%	6.77%	−2.78%	9.74%	11.27%	12.25%
RWC	11.60%	9.06%	−2.84%	12.10%	13.15%	13.87%
ROA	0.56%	−3.53%	−8.52%	1.23%	1.83%	0.63%
ROE	6.61%	−53.64%	−573.37%	56.02%	33.32%	11.36%

BMMB	2004	2005	2006	2007	2008	2009
ECTA	5.54%	5.57%	5.23%	5.33%	5.10%	6.50%
D/C	16.81	16.70	17.64	16.97	17.44	13.67
L/D	33.86%	39.06%	41.63%	43.49%	46.27%	45.80%
CCR	13.40%	9.70%	10.70%	7.60%	8.80%	13.90%
RWC	14.60%	11.10%	15.80%	11.20%	12.90%	17.60%
ROA	−0.34%	0.35%	0.61%	0.35%	0.23%	0.64%
ROE	−6.18%	6.33%	11.69%	6.62%	4.44%	9.78%

HLB	2004	2005	2006	2007	2008	2009
ECTA	9.00%	8.27%	7.42%	6.85%	6.58%	6.96%
D/C	9.08	9.20	10.14	12.05	13.35	13.10
L/D	60.16%	59.77%	60.86%	55.34%	50.62%	48.52%
CCR	17.49%	15.85%	13.76%	13.34%	13.30%	15.89%
RWC	18.99%	17.38%	17.52%	16.79%	16.36%	16.47%
ROA	0.82%	0.96%	0.93%	0.94%	1.00%	1.15%
ROE	9.17%	11.63%	12.52%	13.71%	15.15%	16.58%

AFG	2004	2005	2006	2007	2008	2009
ECTA	7.88%	7.80%	7.37%	8.38%	8.99%	8.99%
D/C	9.59	5.11	5.62	9.35	9.26	9.23
L/D	82.25%	149.86%	129.63%	68.24%	69.27%	74.72%
CCR	9.91%	10.23%	10.89%	11.42%	10.41%	11.13%
RWC	14.54%	15.08%	16.62%	16.29%	14.76%	15.40%
ROA	0.92%	−0.85%	0.43%	1.41%	0.77%	0.95%
ROE	11.62%	−10.93%	5.83%	16.77%	8.55%	10.56%

AB	2004	2005	2006	2007	2008	2009
ECTA	7.51%	8.46%	8.02%	7.80%	8.04%	8.27%
D/C	10.35	8.84	9.77	10.83	10.25	10.05
L/D	70.46%	84.39%	78.35%	65.33%	67.99%	72.72%
CCR	9.37%	9.48%	10.04%	10.56%	10.06%	11.42%
RWC	14.55%	13.51%	13.55%	13.88%	13.08%	13.04%
ROA	0.83%	0.78%	0.73%	0.76%	1.02%	0.93%
ROE	10.99%	9.20%	9.13%	9.72%	12.69%	11.20%

5

ISLAMIC BANKS' FINANCING BEHAVIOUR: A PILOT STUDY

Mohd Afandi Abu Bakar,
Radiah Abdul Kader and Roza Hazli Zakaria

5.1 Introduction

It is irrefutably true that bank-lending volume is stronger in periods of strong economic growth and weaker in periods of weak economic growth. During strong economic growth, due to high consumption spending by households, investment demand will increase; the opposite is true during weak economic growth. The nerve-racking issue is that empirical studies exhibit a pro-cyclical behaviour of the conventional banks' lending to the business cycle (Gruss and Sgherri, 2009; Albertazzi and Gambacorta, 2009; Rochet, 2008; Bouvatier and Lepetit, 2008; Quagliariello, 2007; Bikker and Metzemakers, 2005 are among the latest empirical studies that provide evidence on the matter). The conventional bank-lending operation even has the intrinsic tendency to worsen economic fluctuations and to some extent may even exacerbate the swing.

The failure of conventional banks to play their role in stabilising the economy and with the continuous global economic disorder has sparked the interest on the Islamic financial system. The pertinent question is whether the Islamic bank financing has a tendency to weather the economic climate as anticipated by most of its proponents. A bank behaviour that is counter-cyclical to the economic fluctuations shows that the reserve and *LLP* policy must be positively related to bank financing supply movement, which is proven not to be the case for the conventional bank.

Muslim scholars proposed that the virtue of the Islamic financial system will bring stability to the economic environment. They alleged that Islamic banks with profit and risk sharing are able to weather the economic and financial crisis better. However, many of the views presented are theoretical in concepts and descriptive in nature, with little empirical evidence. It is important to provide empirical evidence regarding the statements made concerning the Islamic banks' behaviour and capability. It is part of the theoretical framework explaining the nature of Islamic banks and should be followed by in-depth empirical evidence and not merely by theoretical description.

The more worrying issue is that at present the Islamic banks' financing practices are mostly in the form of fixed-rate financing (60 per cent to 80 per cent of total financing delivered by the institutions). Currently the use of profit- and risk-sharing instruments has decreased by an average of 11 per cent since the mid-1990s (Khan and Bhatti, 2008). Given the present situation, will the banks' financing behave pro-cyclical to the business cycle? With the financing operations presently practised, the capability of Islamic bank to smooth the economic cycles is now questionable.

With this in mind, this particular study is a pilot attempt to examine the impact of aggregate economic activity fluctuations on the Islamic banks' financing activities. This objective provides the direction of association between *GDP* growths as the main macro-economics aggregate indicators to the Islamic bank financing growth. If the Islamic banks' financing activities are stable and resilient, then the degree of *GDP* growth needs to have a smalleffect on the Islamic bank financing growth. More importantly, the objective of the study is to evaluate the cyclicality behaviour of Islamic banks' financing and the cyclicality behaviour of fixed-rate financing. In order to make it behaving counter-cyclically, the reserve and loan loss provision (*LLP*) growth should respond positively to the financing growth. The reserves and *LLP* policy verify the capability of the bank to control the financing volume to smooth the business cycle event, which was evidently not the case for conventional banks.

The importance of reserves and *LLP* instruments for managing the business cycle can be found in the *Qur'ānic* principles:

> He said: 'For seven years you shall sow continuously, then what you reap leave 5 it on the ear, except a little whereof you eat (47). Then thereafter there shall come upon you seven hard years, in which you shall devour all that you have reserved for them, except a little you keep in store (48). Then there shall come after that a year in which the people shall have rain and in which they shall press (fruit and oil) (49).
>
> (*Qur'ān*, 12: 47–9)

Reserves and *LLP* should act as the control device on banks' financing activities. *Allah*'s instruction is that, during high economic growth, spending needs to be reduced and in the event of economic downturn spending needs to be raised in order to generate economic growth. The policy should able to control financing growth so that it is able to put pressure on the financing activity in the event of economic expansion. During economic contraction, reserves and *LLP* growth should be able to amplify the financing activities.

This topic is essential since empirical study of the Islamic banks' cyclical behaviour is so far insufficient. This study will provide a better viewpoint and will bridge the gap between theoretical and conceptual literature with empirical evidence on the potential of Islamic bank. With empirical evidence hopefully it will verify the superiority of the Islamic financial system. More important is to build confidence and readiness of the major non-majority Muslim countries to start providing *Sharīʿah* -compliant financial instrument and establishing Islamic financial institutions.

5.2 Review of Literature

Empirical study shows that the pro-cyclical behaviour of the conventional banks is associated with the management practices on provisioning and credit rating policy (Bouvatier and Lepetit 2008; Quagliariello 2007; Bikker and Metzemakers, 2005; Laeven and Majnoni, 2003 and de Lis et al., 2000) and reserves (Bliss and Kaufman, 2002). Profit-driven enthusiasm is another determinant that is contributing to the pro-cyclical behaviour (Albertazzi and Gambacorta, 2009 and Bikker and Hu, 2002). Some have also argued that the regulation reforms such as Basel I and Basel II (Burger and Udell, 1994; Hancock and Wilcox, 1998; and Wagster, 1999) and IAS 39 (Gruss and Sgherri, 2009 and Rochet, 2008) are likely amplifying banks' pro-cyclical behaviour.

Muslim scholars on the other hand argued that the roots underlying this undesirable behaviour are the exercise of unfavourable instruments and activities from the *Sharīʿah*. Usage of interest-based instruments is the most undesirable instrument. Furthermore, financial transactions practised such as speculative activities, ambiguous and uncertain transactions and financial risk transactions exacerbated the swing. They believed that with the existing of *Sharīʿah*-compliant instruments the Islamic banking institutions will be more resilient, stable and better able to stabilise the economic environment.

However, empirical studies by Bakar (2001) and Ismail and Sulaiman (2006) provide symptoms of the pro-cyclical behaviour. Bakar (2001) observed that Malaysia Islamic bank investment margin fluctuates more strongly than its rival during an upswing and downswing of interest rate; this is one of the leading indicators of the business cycle. Ismail and Sulaiman (2006) analysed the recovery rates and default rates for Malaysian Islamic banks. Their findings show that, when the economy is expanding, the default rate is low and that the opposite happens when the economy is contracting. Based on the above findings it is argued that there is a possibility that, through fixed-rate financing instruments, the Islamic banks' financing might behave pro-cyclical. Approximately 90 per cent of Malaysian Islamic banks financing is in the form of fixed-rate financing. However, their study does not look at the cyclicality behaviour of Islamic banking operations. Therefore it cannot be used to draw conclusions regarding the cyclicality behaviour. Moreover, their study cannot be generalised for the Islamic banks' behaviour as a whole as the study was restricted to Malaysian Islamic banking institutions.

Other than that, previous studies usually fall under three broad subjects comprising the areas of financial management efficiency (for example, Kassim *et al.*, 2009; Yusoff *et al.*, 2008; Ismail and Sulaiman, 2006; Sanusi and Ismail, 2005 and Rosly and Bakar, 2003). The second area of concern is the effect of interest rate movement on the Islamic bank operations (for example, Yap and Kader, 2008; and Bacha, 2004). The latest area of study looks at the strength and stability of the institutions (Karwowski, 2009; Čihák and Hesse, 2008). The earliest empirical study on the Islamic financial relationship with monetary economics was in the work of Darrat (1988, 2002). Taking Tunisia (1988) and Iran and Pakistan (2002) as a case study, he provides some empirical evidence on the issue of the feasibility of an Islamic interest-free financial system. The empirical results consistently indicate the relative efficiency of the interest-free monetary system. Other empirical studies look at the possible instruments that can be used by Islamic banking in managing the monetary economics and its stability with the abolishment of interest instruments under the Islamic environment (Elhiraika, 2004; Kiaee, 2007; and Kia and Darrat, 2007). Elhiraika (2004) analyses the modes of finance in Sudan before and after the adoption of Islamic finance in 1990. He also explains the determinants of monetary growth and its effect on major policy objectives including real output growth and inflation by using data from 1970 to 2001.

Literature on the conventional banks' cyclicality behaviour, by contrast, presents more evidence. At the end of the 1980s and during the early 1990s concerns about the pro-cyclical behaviour of bank-lending activities begin to appear. Empirical works by Bernanke and Blinder (1992) and Kashyap and Stein (1993, 1994) estimate the credit channel hypothesis and the relevance of a credit crunch. In the 1990s empirical evidence demonstrated that excessive pro-cyclical behaviour of banks worsens the cyclical behaviour (Bernanke and Lown, 1991; Bernanke and Blinder, 1992; Kashyap and Stein, 1993, 1994; and Asea and Blomberg, 1998). In the 2000s the analysis was more focused on bank pro-cyclical determinants (Gruss and Sgherri, 2009; Bouvatier and Lepetit, 2008; Rochet, 2008; Quagliariello 2007; Bikker and Metzemakers 2005; Laeven and Majnoni, 2003; Bliss and Kaufman, 2002; and Bikker and Hu, 2002 and de Lis et al., 2000).

Adrian and Hyun's (2008) work is based on US bank holding companies; it found that banks increase their leverage during asset price booms and reduce it during busts. Bouvatier and Lepetit (2008) worked with European banks' data and found that *LLP* made in order to cover expected future loan losses ampli-fyies credit fluctuations. An earlier study by Quagliariello (2007) on Italian banks shows that, during economic downturns, banks tend to tighten the credit supply. Bikker and Metzemakers' (2005) study shows that provisioning turns out to be substantially higher when *GDP* growth is lower, reflecting increased riskiness of the credit portfolio when the business cycle turns downwards; this also increases the risk of a credit crunch. Laeven and Majnoni's (2003) work empirically shows that many banks around the world delay provisioning for bad loans until it is too late, that is, when cyclical downturns have already set in.

From the literature survey it is evident that the idea of the Islamic banks' capability of smoothing the fluctuations in the economic activities is somehow a lack of empirical evidence. Therefore this particular study tries to fill up the gap. With bank financing activities concentrating more on the fixed-rate instruments, there is a possibility that Islamic banks may behave pro-cyclically. The study predicts that bank operation will behave pro-cyclically if the reserve and *LLP* failed to give a positive impact on the financing growth. The financial institutions need to obey Islamic instruction (*Qur'ān*: 12: 46–9) related to their management of reserve and *LLP*. Failing to do so would no doubt result in the Islamic banking operations behaving like their conventional counterpart.

5.3 Islamic Banks and Economic Stability

In Islam, the foundation of institutional development is based on the principles of *Sharī^c^ah* with the objective to realise socio-economic goals. All transactions that depend on chance and speculations are prohibited (*Qur'ān*, 2: 219; 5: 90). No matter what the forms are, the essence of disapproved business conduct comprises unjustified appropriation of others' wealth and rights (*Qur'ān*, 2: 188; 4:2 9). The major principles of Islamic finance therefore ban interest-based financial instruments. In the opinion of Islamic jurists, the collection and payment of interest has a resemblance to the characteristic of usury (*ribā*), and for this reason it is prohibited. *Allah* (swt) has declared nothing can be had without effort or labour (*Qur'ān*, 53: 39). Income received from interest-based instruments is seen as a return without any labour activities and as an unproductive effort. Therefore the interest-based instruments will bring unfairness and unjustness to parties involved in a financial transaction.

As an alternative the Islamic scholars approved the application of equity-based and trade-based (*al-bai*) financing. With equity-based financing the relationship between lender, intermediaries and borrower is transformed into a partnership through profit and risk sharing investment. As for financing on consumption spending, the trade-based financing by price mark-up and the hire purchase formula is used. *Sharī^c^ah* also prohibit all financial transaction involving speculative, ambiguous and uncertain activities and financial risk transactions (*Qur'ān*: 2: 219, 5:90). This makes Islamic bank more cautious, very selective and more efficient in investment selection and financing activities. The financing and financial transaction must also tie to a 'tangible and identifiable underlying asset'. With *Sharī^c^ah*-approved instruments therefore the banking operations are free from any exploitation and excess.

In the profit and risk sharing model the money is now transformed to a productive use and risk must be undertaken to justify a return. Furthermore, returns should not be fixed regardless of profits to avoid usury. Theoretically, with this instrument, the fund provider has more attention in the soundness of the investment for the reason that return is directly related to the project success. At the same time the bank is also bound to the concept of being *amanah* (trustworthy) to the depositors. Thus the bank will attract entrepreneurs by ensuring efficient management and the highest possible productivity and return of the projects.

During an economic upswing investment-earning shows a positive trend with the low rate of non-performing loans; this motivates the bank to increase its financing supply. Concurrently an important characteristic of the Islamic banking operations is to follow *Allah*'s (*swt*) command during the economic swing (*Qur'ān*: 12: 46–9). In the event of an economic upswing, banks should increase their reserve and *LLP* for the reasons of increasing in financing risk, as this will lessen speculative motivated financial transaction. Increase in reserve and *LLP* reduces the excess fund for financing activities. As opposed to this, conventional banks that extend untied credit and pricing are influenced more by speculative pressures than the economic fundamentals benefit.

Speculative trading, financial risk and uncertain activities are avoided and free from all sorts of exploitation and excess. This makes the Islamic banks' selections of projects and investment more cautious and selective. The transaction is also tied to a 'tangible and identifiable underlying asset'. Islamic financing is also within the moral value structure with ethical investments and consumption spending. Financing by Islamic banks that is tied to real asset and based on profit and risk sharing allows market forces to work in a better way to achieve economic efficiency. With that Islamic banks will allocate the resources more efficiently without any exploitation. Referring to this argument the Islamic bank investment will not grow as steeply as the interest-based bank in the event of an economic upswing. Even though the earning and non-performing loans show encouraging signs during an economic upswing, the Islamic bank will not easily be extending the financing or loosening the requirements.

During economic downturn, when fewer profitable investment projects exist, although normally conventional banks tighten their underwriting standards, Islamic banks will not overreact to these swings. Although higher investment risk exists, and with an increasing number of non-performing loans when the economy contracts, the provision of equity-based financing from Islamic banks will not fall significantly. During this period the bank will reduce the reserve and *LLP* to increase the excess funds for financing as instructed by the *Qur'ān* (12: 46–9) to spend during the contracting economy. The excess reserve on provisioning during high economic growth will be utilised in this period to finance productive projects. With the decrease in banks' reserve, and *LLP* during economic downturn with more excess funds for financing, the volume will be pushed upwards. Islamic banks also will not hold to much cash reserve in the event of low economic growth due to the *zakāh* (obligatory charity) responsibility on the amount of cash reserve. *Zakāh* instruments play the role of automatic investment motivator to the economic agents. Holding of cash reserves therefore will be at minimum safety level and the excess cash reserve needs to be invested with a return at least equal to the *zakāh* rate. If it is not invested the cash assets will be depleted due to *zakāh* obligation.

With profit and risk sharing financing instruments, the profits are shared between the two parties according to some pre-agreed ratio, but if there are losses the investor bears all the financial losses (*muḍārabah* agreement) or shared (*mushārakah* agreement) with the entrepreneur. The entrepreneur will not be reluctant to invest due to the sharing of risk with the fund providers. Therefore, the financing activities' emphasis lies on productivity compared to creditworthiness. With those special characteristics of profit and risk sharing financing instruments underpinning the Islamic bank it should be able to smooth the downswing in the economic activity.

However, the operations of Islamic banking currently have not adopted these ideas; in fact, they opted to use more fixed-rate financing instruments. *Murābaḥah* (mark-up) and *ijārah* (lease purchase) instruments are the most widely applied presently by Islamic banks for the practical and operational reasons. Nevertheless the Islamic banks' fixed-rate financing instruments are still complying with the *Sharīᶜah* requirements.

During an economic upswing Islamic banks will not easily be extending the financing or loosening the financing requirements. The increase in reserve and *LLP* as obeying to *Qur'ān* (12: 46–9) during this period reduces the banks' earning assets that will reduce the amount of fixed-rate financing. With this argument Islamic banks' financing supply will not increase as steeply as interest-based financing. During the period of economic expansion the chances of over-extension of trade-based financing are still balanced because not only is the paying capacity of clients stable but also the value of the collateralised assets is rising. In the event of an economic upswing the Islamic bank will still be cautious and selective when providing the trade-based financing. The Islamic bank will definitely avoid all the prohibited activities. With asset-backing financial transactions, ethical investments and consumption financing operations Islamic banks will allocate the resources efficiently without any exploitation. When the economy is hit with a slow growth, Islamic banks, due to the cyclicality behaviour, are still protected when they use trade-based financing. Since trade-based financing is agreed in advance of the transaction, it cannot be altered during the life of the contract. With fixed due dates or a schedule of dates banks cannot recall it for early payments either. Therefore the likelihood of a 'run on debtors' by the banks, in expectation of a coming recession, is low.

With the unique characteristics of the Islamic bank this will ensure that the institutions' financing activities will not overreact to the economic swings. At any time the Islamic banks are able to mellow down their cyclicality behaviour by adjusting their reserve and provisioning policy. Diagrammatically it is shown in Figure 5.1.

The pertinent issue now is that of whether banks practically tend to use reserve and *LLP* to smooth their operations. Do Islamic banks reserve more and provision more when financing activities and earnings increase? Banks should make enough reserve and provisions when the economy is growing with high *GDP* growth rate and high loan growth. Failure to do so, when economic conditions reverse, will mean that loan losses start to emerge and profitability decrease; this will force banks to increase their provisioning, thus amplifying the effects of the recession.

The potential of Islamic banks in minimising the effect of the business cycle thus depends on their reserve and *LLP* policy and the ratio between equity-based financing to the trade-based financing. The higher provision for equity-based

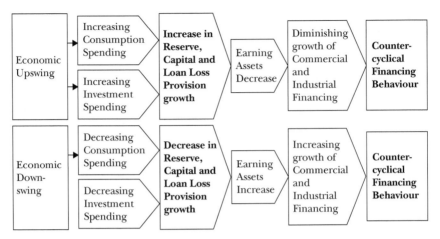

Figure 5.1 Islamic Bank Financing Counter-cyclical Framework

financing will ensure a more effective counter-cyclical behaviour of the banking sector.

5.4 Modelling

The fluctuations in business cycle result in changes in employment level, general price level and other macro-economic variables. The relevant variables indicating the event of bank cyclicality behaviour is as illustrated Figure 5.2:

In this study the model developed is a hybrid of the model developed by Laeven and Majnoni (2003) and Bikker and Metzemakers (2005). To estimate the Islamic banks' financing cyclicality behaviour this paper focuses on the growth rate of financing related to the growth of real *GDP*, bank reserve and *LLP* as the cyclicality indicator. To take into account the different characteristics of individual banks, the study used the ratio of banks' variable growth to the earning assets growth rate. This is to allow for the differences between banks' characteristics. The study uses growth value to avoid potential misspecification and endogeneity problems due to the differences in bank and country characteristics. Previous researchers used total assets growth rate as the denominator to control on banks' and country's characteristic differences (Laeven and Majnoni, 2003; Bikker and Metzemakers, 2005). In this particular study the rationale of using the earning assets as the denominator is that it is the item that actually generates income to the bank. The earning assets include all assets that generate explicit financing income or lease receipts. This is typically measured by subtracting all non-earning assets such as cash and short-term funds, statutory deposits, fixed assets and other assets from the total assets.

A counter-cyclical behaviour of bank financing during economic fluctuations is revealed by the slower growth of financing volume to the growth of real

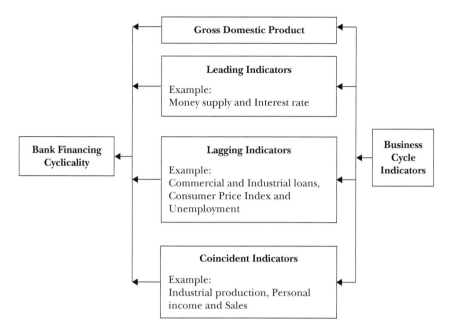

Figure 5.2 Bank Cyclicality Framework

GDP. The financing growth rate should diminish when the real *GDP* is growing and increase with slower economic growth. The slower growth of financing to *GDP* growth is caused by an increase in the reserve and *LLP*, the internal instrument for managing the financing volume. Therefore reserves and *LLP* growth must positively correlate to financing growth. In the event of economic upswing the reserve and *LLP* must also increase to safeguard the increase in financing. During economic downturn it should move the opposite way to boost up the financing volumes. Therefore the study hypothesises that Islamic banks' financing will behave counter-cyclically if the following conditions are met:

(i) Bank financing growth should be smaller compared to the real *GDP* growth.
(ii) Bank financing growth should positively correlate to the reserve growth.
(iii) Bank financing growth should positively correlate to the *LLP* growth.

In conducting the study, we employed the panel data method in analysing the bank financing behaviour. Annual data from 1998 to 2008 were gathered from twenty-four Islamic bank institutions from various countries including Malaysia, Bahrain, UAE, Turkey, Kuwait, Saudi Arabia, Pakistan and South Africa (Appendix 1). The data are obtained from bank's annual reports and various countries' central bank reports. This study employed various banks and data

from a range of countries in order to obtain a clear and comprehensive preliminary understanding of the Islamic banks' financing behaviour.

The specification model consists of variables categorised into two groups: the
macro-economic variables and bank's related variables. The function is specified
as follows:

Bank Financing = *f* {*Macro-economic variables and Institutional variables*}

The model estimates the Islamic banks' financing activities behaviour to the
fluctuation in real *GDP* as the macro-economic indicators. Bank reserves and
LLP are the institutional characteristics that indicate the financing cyclicality
behaviour.

The specific set of variables used in the study is as follows:
Dependent variables:

    (i) Total Financing growth to Earning Asset growth (*TF/EA*) ratio
   (ii) Fixed-Rate Financing growth to Earning Asset growth (*FR/EA*) ratio

Independent variables:

    (i) Macro-economic Indicators:
        (a) real Gross Domestic Product (*GDP*) growth
        (b) growth of money supply (*M3*)
   (ii) Banks' variables:
        (a) bank Reserves growth to Earning Asset growth ratio (*R/EA*)
        (b) bank capital growth to Earning Asset growth ratio (*K/EA*)
        (c) loan Loss Provision growth to Earning Asset growth ratio (*LP/EA*).

The financing figure used in the analysis is the net total financing and net
fixed-rate financing after deducting for the provision for bad and doubtful financing. The fixed-rate financing instruments is the sum of financing from *murābaḥah*,
ijārah, bai muajjal, istisnā and *bai bithaman ajil* financing instruments. The behaviour
of Islamic bank financing is given by the coefficient of correlation of the real
GDP growth to the ratio of total financing growth to earning assets growth (*TF/EA*)
and the ratio of fixed-rate financing growth to earning assets growth (*FR/EA*).
Bank reserves growth to earning assets growth ratio (*R/EA*) and ratio of *LLP*
growth to earning assets growth (*LP/EA*) play the role as regulator on the financing cyclicality behaviour.

To suit the present study purposes, the proposed empirical model is as
follows:

$$[F/EA]_{ijt} = \alpha_o + \beta_1 GDP_{ijt} + \beta_2 M3_{ijt} + \beta_3 [R/EA]_{ijt} + \beta_4 [LP/EA]_{ijt} +$$
$$\beta_5 [K/EA]_{ijt} + \varepsilon_{ijt}$$

$i = 1, \ldots, n$ (selected bank); $t = 1, \ldots, T$ (annual data); $j = 1, \ldots, n$ (selected
country);

where:

F_{ijt}/EA_{ijt} is total financing and fixed-rate financing growth to total assets growth ratio for bank i in country j at time t

GDP_{jt} is real Gross Domestic Product growth in country j at time t

$M3_{jt}$ is broad money supply M3 growth in country j at time t

R_{ijt}/EA_{ijt} is bank Reserve growth to total assets growth ratio for bank i in country j at time t

LP_{ijt}/EA_{ijt} is loan Loss Provision growth to total assets growth ratio for bank i in country j at time t

K_{ijt}/EA_{ijt} is bank capital growth to total assets growth ratio for bank i in country j at time t.

5.5 Findings

Table 5.1 reports the descriptive statistics of the variables employed in this study. From the mean, median, standard deviation, skewness, kurtosis and the Jarque-Bera value we can see that the sample data is not normally distributed. For all variables, the values of mean and median are not the same; the values of skewness are not equal to zero implying that data distributions are not symmetrical around mean. The values of kurtosis are not equal to three. The values of Jarque-Bera are significant with high probability value, which leads to the rejection of the null hypothesis of a normal distribution. Therefore, the Generalised Least Square (GLS) method is more appropriate and is expected to yield a much better result.

For the stationarity test of the sample data used in the analysis, the Levin, Lin and Chu (LLC) and Im, Pesaran and Shin (IPS) method was conducted for the panel unit root testing. LLC test is preferable because of its large potential power gains (Cosar, 2002). Given that the sample is relatively small, this study also considered the IPS panel data unit root test, since it has better small sample properties and has the additional advantage of simplicity (Cosar, 2002). Table 5.2 summarises the unit root test on each variable. The test shows that at level, $M3$ and LLP is non-stationary; therefore the study proceeds to test all the items for stationary at first difference. The result shows that both of the variables are stationary at first difference. Thus the analysis will be regressed at first difference.

5.5.1 Model Estimation

The models are estimated using both a fixed effects (FE) and random effects (RE) model with panel GLS. The estimation proceeds with panel GLS in the model for the reason that the model displays autocorrelation problems. The analysis also assigned the cross-section weight in the regression due to the presence of cross-section heteroskedasticity problems in the estimation.

The result for cyclicality behaviour of Islamic banks' total financing is given in Table 5.3. The Hausman test shows that the FE model explains the results better (Hausman $X^2 = 1.233$ and insignificant, $\rho = 0.9417$). Therefore the null

Table 5.1 Normality Test

Variables	Total Financing	Fixed Rate financing	GDP	M3	Reserve	Capital	LLP
Mean	0.956905	1.114117	5.425529	13.71587	−2.612786	−1.334341	2.698682
Median	0.953090	0.926694	5.788000	11.83526	0.967915	0.634123	0.799616
Maximum	49.38416	70.40527	17.32900	50.83661	334.4296	92.60785	425.0362
Minimum	−58.53142	−39.43389	−7.35900	1.613494	−437.0229	−536.5601	−395.711
Std. Dev.	7.814411	8.672229	2.916811	9.651401	54.45460	39.03878	56.65576
Skewness	−1.571268	1.650066	−0.89575	1.619302	−4.245084	−12.57880	−0.69846
Kurtosis	30.28181	27.44593	7.339536	5.598110	47.32196	173.4915	37.38809
Jarque–Bera	6473.315	5222.909	189.1859	147.9658	17480.12	254927.2	10166.89
Probability	0.000000	0.000000	0.000000	0.000000	0.000000	0.000000	0.000000
Sum	197.1225	229.5081	1117.659	2825.469	−538.2339	−274.8743	555.8050
Sum Square of Deviations	12518.33	15417.55	1744.096	19095.66	607887.2	312425.5	658024.5
Observations	206	206	206	206	206	206	206

Source: EViews software generated

Table 5.2 Unit Root Test

Method	Level				First Difference			
	LLC		IPS		LLC		IPS	
Variables	stat	Prob	stat	Prob	stat	Prob	stat	Prob
Total Financing	−10.9780	0.0000	−4.00631	0.000	−16.8915	0.000	−6.36168	0.000
Fixed Rate Financing	−13.6886	0.0000	−4.37591	0.000	−20.6295	0.000	−8.46047	0.000
GDP	−18.8176	0.0000	−9.25771	0.0000	−16.1141	0.0000	−10.9652	0.0000
M3	−5.78781	0.0000	−0.91271	0.1807	−33.5926	0.0000	−12.4451	0.0000
Reserve	−58.5980	0.0000	−24.7537	0.0000	−26.4095	0.0000	−12.7567	0.0000
Capital	−7.10103	0.0000	−3.07596	0.0010	−10.9047	0.0000	−5.73780	0.0000
LLP	3.02722	0.9988	4.12167	1.000	−2.75349	0.003	−3.65784	0.000

Source: EViews software generated

Table 5.3 Total Financing Cyclicality Analysis

Model	FIXED MODEL			RANDOM MODEL		
Variable	Coeff.	Std Error	t-stat	Coeff.	Std Error	t-stat
Constant	1.133913	0.156046	7.266523	1.443301	1.432969	1.007210
GDP	0.000153	0.022615	0.006783	−0.053770	0.220602	−0.243742
D(M3)	0.016263	0.010148	1.602631	0.056489	0.082193	0.687268
Reserve	0.024093*	0.009283	2.595345	0.032430**	0.014569	2.226003
Capital	0.019625**	0.008075	2.430483	0.009828	0.018556	0.529675
D(LLP)	0.009666*	0.003098	3.120230	0.022645*	0.007025	3.223228
R^2	0.511078			0.127030		
Adjusted R^2	0.421602			0.102230		
SEE	6.778451			7.548815		
F-test	5.711904*			5.122130*		
DW	2.200612			1.422136		

*Significant at 1%, **Significant at 5%

Correlated Random Effects - Hausman Test

Equation: Total Financing

Test cross-section random effects

Test Summary	Chi-Sq. Statistic	Chi-Sq. d.f.	Prob.
Cross-section random	1.232932	5	0.9417

Source: EViews software generated

hypothesis of the RE model can be rejected. From the coefficient of determination (R^2) we can see that 51.11 per cent variation in Islamic bank total financing behaviours can be explained by changes in the determinants with significant F-statistic at 1 per cent level of significance. The result provides evidence that Islamic banks' total financing does behave counter-cyclically to the business cycle.

The insignificance of real GDP growth in determining the Islamic banks' financing behaviour indicates that Islamic banks' financing decisions are not tied-up by the expansion and contraction of the economy shown by the growth in real *GDP*. These findings indicate that the Islamic financing behaviour is free of any speculative financing activities when there is fluctuation in the economic environment. This result shows that Islamic banks' financing activities are determined by other factors and not directly affected by changes in the real *GDP* growth.

More importantly, the operations of Islamic banks do follow the *Qur'ān*'s (12: 46–9) instruction concerning reserves and *LLP* management. The result demonstrates that the reserve, capital and *LLP* are positively correlated to the Islamic banks' financing activities. It shows that the buffer instruments manage the Islamic banks' financing cyclicality behaviour well, which is not the case for conventional banks (Laeven and Majnoni, 2003; Bikker and Metzemakers, 2005). All of the variables' results are significant at 5 per cent and 1 per cent level. The finding shows that a 1 per cent growth in reserve and capital is used to protect growth by 0.02 per cent of the financing activities. A 1 per cent growth of *LLP* is used to protect growth in financing activities by 0.01 per cent. More importantly, the growth of all the instruments is greater compared to the financing growth. This shows that the Islamic banks are more cautious as the economy grows and as the economy contracts, the reserve, capital and *LLP* fall faster compared to the financing to increase the amount of excess fund for financing activities. With the faster growth in bank reserve, capital and *LLP* during economic expansion the earning assets will reduce and this will reduce the excess funds for financing supply. During economic slowdown, a decrease in reserves, capital and *LLP* growth will increase the earnings assets of Islamic banks, and this will increase the excess funds available for financing by the Islamic bank. These excess funds need to be allocated for financing to avoid the depletion of its amount due to paying obligatory *zakāh*.

On the contrary, the insignificant relationship between money supply *M3* to the Islamic banks' financing needs some consideration by the Islamic bank practitioners. It indicates that the financing activities are not responding to changes in money supply *M3* as they should.

5.5.2 *Fixed-rate Financing Cyclicality Analysis*

In Table 5.4, the Hausman test result shows that the FE model explains the situation better. The value of the X^2 test statistic is 1.058 with $p = 0.9577$ and insignificant. The null hypothesis of the RE model is rejected. The study concludes that the FE model is the preferred specification for the data. The FE model shows that 61.25 per cent of the variation in fixed-rate financing can be explained from the changes in the independent variables ($R^2 = 0.6125$). The *F*-statistic is also significant at a 1 per cent level. Results for fixed-rate financing cyclicality shows that it does follow the normal institutional behaviour, that is, the lending growth is stronger during economic expansion and weakens when the economy is contracting. However, fixed-rate financing growth is slightly

Table 5.4 Fixed-rate Financing Cyclicality Analysis

Model / Variable	FIXED MODEL			RANDOM MODEL		
	Coeff.	Std Error	t-stat	Coeff.	Std Error	t-stat
Constant	1.015536	0.193510	5.247976	0.877718	1.494330	0.587365
GDP	0.078623**	0.032009	2.456273	0.108387	0.234064	0.463066
D(M3)	0.003436	0.012627	0.272152	−0.004908	0.087978	−0.055791
Reserve	0.055603*	0.011400	4.877506	0.051319*	0.015507	3.309424
Capital	0.009629	0.009861	0.976465	0.012688	0.019787	0.641226
D(LLP)	0.015010*	0.003776	3.975514	0.025364*	0.007533	3.367175
R^2	0.612530			0.180681		
Adjusted R^2	0.541621			0.157405		
SEE	7.899927			8.090381		
F-test	8.638198*			7.762524*		
DW	2.089156			2.108637		

*Significant at 1%, **Significant at 5%

Correlated Random Effects – Hausman Test

Equation: Fixed-rate Financing
Test cross-section random effects

Test Summary	Chi-Sq. Statistic	Chi-Sq. d.f.	Prob.
Cross-section random	1.058110	5	0.9577

Source: EViews software generated

slower compared to the growth in *GDP*. With growth in *GDP* by 1 per cent the Islamic bank fixed-rate financing grows by 0.08 per cent and it is significant at a 1 per cent level. This finding verifies the fear of some Islamic scholars regarding the possibility that the fixed-rate instruments will behave as their conventional counterparts.

On the other hand, the reserve and *LLP* growth is also positively correlated to the fixed-rate financing growth with the coefficient of correlation being 0.06 and 0.02 respectively and significant at the 1 per cent level. The result shows that a 1 per cent growth in reserve is used to manage and protect growth by 0.06 per cent of the financing growth. Then again a 1 per cent growth in *LLP* is used to protect 0.02 per cent of the fixed-rate financing growth. This result indicates that the argument by some scholars on the pro-cyclical behaviour of fixed-rate financing to the business cycle is groundless. The reserve and *LLP* policy manage to play their role to pressure down Islamic banks' fixed-rate financing cyclicality behaviour and also perform as the financing safety net. Thus the fixed-rate financing behaves counter-cyclically with the positive relationship to reserve and *LLP*. The reserve and *LLP* growth were also found to be larger compared to the growth of fixed-rate financing. This indicates that during business cycle expansion the reserve and *LLP* increase faster than the increase in financing. On the other hand, during a contracting economy both of the buffers instruments' growth decreases faster than the decrease in financing growth in order to increase the excess funds for financing. The insignificance of $M3$ growth in determining the Islamic banks' fixed-rate financing behaviour again indicates that Islamic banks' financing decisions are not influenced by the expansion and contraction of $M3$ growth. This result shows that Islamic banks' fixed-rate financing activities do not directly respond to changes in the $M3$ growth.

5.6 Conclusions

The increase in the instability of the economic environment for the past thirty years related to the instability in the conventional financial system has raised concerns among economists and regulators. For the Islamic scholars the Islamic financial system with its unique characteristics is the ultimate solution for achieving a stable economic environment. This particular study provides preliminary empirical evidence concerning the behaviour of Islamic banks' financing in relation to the aggregate economic activities' fluctuations. The original idea of the profit and risk sharing instrument is currently difficult to practice due to various practical and operational reasons. Therefore the financing is largely in the form of fixed-rate financing. The empirical results of this research present initial evidence for the resiliency and stability of the Islamic banks' financing operations to the expansions and contractions of the economic activities. The findings show that the financing activities of Islamic banks with a reserve and LLP policy that adhered to the $Qur'\bar{a}n$'s instruction (12: 46–9) manage to reduce the bank financing pro-cyclical behaviour. By avoiding speculative financial transactions and financial risk transactions, the Islamic banks are able to protect themselves from the economic fluctuation. The concern is that the large amount of fixed-rate financing instruments used by the Islamic banks may distort the capability of the system to stabilise the economy. Although the degree of association is low as opposed to the GDP growth and the buffers policy that is positively associated with it, the institutions need to be more careful so that over-financing of fixed-rate financing can be avoided.

Although the results of this research show an impressive economic behaviour of the Islamic banks, this study has its own limitations in the form of a small sample size and the fact that the study only analyses the short-run cyclical behaviour of the Islamic banks' financing activities. A larger sample size with a longer time span would be able to provide more concrete evidence and increased understanding of the Islamic banks' cyclical behaviour. Those limitations invite the need for further research.

Bibliography

Adrian, T. and Hyun, S. S. (2008). 'Liquidity, monetary policy, and financial cycles', *Current Issues in Economics and Finance* Jan/Feb 14(1): 1–17.

Albertazzi, U. and Gambacorta, L. (2009). 'Bank profitability and the business cycle', *Journal of Financial Stability* 5(4): 393–409.

Asea, P. K. and Blomberg, B. (1998). 'Lending cycles', *Journal of Econometrics* 83: 89–128.

Bacha, O. I. (2004). *Dual Banking Systems and Interest Rate Risk for Islamic Banks*, MPRA Paper No. 12763.

Bakar, A. (2001). *An Empirical Analysis of Islamic Banking Division Profitability Performance*, Research Paper for the Degree of Master in Economics, Kulliyyah of Economics and Management, International Islamic University Malaysia.

Bakar, A. (2006). *Profitability Performances of Islamic Banking: An Empirical Evaluation*. Universiti Teknologi MARA, IRDC, Shah Alam, Malaysia.

Baltagi, B. H. (2008). *Econometric Analysis of Panel Data*. 3rd edn. Chichester: John Wiley and Sons.

Berger, A. N. and Udell, G. F. (2003). *The Institutional Memory Hypothesis and The Procyclicality Of Bank Lending Behaviour*, BIS Working Papers, No. 125.

Bernanke, B. S. and Blinder, A. S. (1992). 'The federal funds rate and the channel monetary transmission', *The American Economic Review* 82(4): 901–21.

Bernanke, B. S. and Lown, C. (1991). 'The credit crunch', *Brookings Papers on Economics* 2: 205–48.

Bikker, J. A. and Hu, H. (2002). *Cyclical Patterns in Profits, Provisioning and Lending of Banks*, De Nederlandsche Bank Staff Reports, No. 86, Amsterdam.

Bikker, J. A. and Metzemakers, P. A. J. (2005). 'Bank provisioning behaviour and procyclicality', *Journal of International Financial Markets, Institutions and Money* 15: 141–57.

Bliss, R. R. and Kaufman, G. G. (2002). *Bank Procyclicality, Credit Crunches, and Asymmetric Monetary Policy Effects: A Unifying Model*, Federal Reserve Bank of Chicago, WP 2002-18.

Bouvatier, V. and Lepetit, L. (2008). 'Banks' procyclical behavior: Does provisioning matter?', *Journal of International Financial Markets, Institutions and Money* 18: 513–26.

Brambilla, C. and Piluso, G. (2007). *Are Banks Procyclical? Evidence from the Italian Case (*1890–1973)*. Quarderni del Dipartimento Di Economia Politica, Universita Degli Studi Di Siena.

Burger, Allen and Udell, Gregory (1994). *Lines of Credit and Relationship Lending in Small Firm Finance*. Financial Institutions Centre Working Paper No. 94-11, The Wharton School, University of Pennsylvania.

Chapra, M. U. (1985). *Towards a Just Monetary System: A Discussion of Money, Banking and Monetary Policy in the Light of Islamic Teaching*. Leicester: The Islamic Foundation.

Chapra, M. U. (1996). 'Monetary management in an Islamic economy', *Islamic Economic Studies* 4(1): 21.

Čihák, M. and Hesse, H. (2008). *Islamic Banks and Financial Stability: An Empirical Analysis*, IMF Working Paper WP/08/16.

Cosar, E. E. (2002). 'Price and income elasticities of Turkish export demand: A panel data application', *Turkish Central Bank Review* 2: 19–55.

Darrat, A. F. (1988). 'The Islamic interest-free banking system: Some empirical evidence', *Applied Economics* 20: 417–25.

Darrat, A. F. (2002). 'The relative efficiency of interest-free monetary system: Some empirical evidence', *Quarterly Review of Economics and Finance* 42: 747–64.

de Lis, Santiago Fernandez, Pages, Jorge Martinez and Saurina, Jesus (2000). 'Credit growth, problem loans and credit risk provisioning in Spain', *Documento de trabajo* N. 0018, Banco de Espana.

Elhiraika, A. D. (2004). *On The Design and Effects of Monetary Policy in an Islamic Framework:The Experience of Sudan*. Islamic Research and Training Institute, Islamic Development Bank, Research Paper, No. 64, Jeddah.

Gambacorta, L. and Mistrulli, P. E. (2004). 'Does bank capital affect lending behaviour', *Journal of Financial Intermediation* 13(4): 436–57.

Gertler, M. and Gilchrist, S. (1994). 'Monetary policy, business cycles, and the behavior of small manufacturing firms', *Quarterly Journal of Economics* (May): 309–40.

Green, W. H. (2008). *Econometric Analysis*. 6th edn. New York: Pearson Prentice Hall.

Gruss, B. and Sgherri, S. (2009). *The Volatility Costs of Procyclical Lending Standards: An* Assessment Using a DSGE Model, IMF Working Paper, WP/09/35.

Hancock, D. and Wilcox, J. A. (1998). 'The "credit crunch" and the availability of credit to small business,' *Journal of Banking and Finance* 22: 983–1,014.

Ismail, A. G. and Sulaiman, A. A. (2006). *Default and Recovery Rates on Islamic Banks Financing: Implications for New Capital Adequacy Standard*, Working Paper in Islamic Economics and Finance No. 0606, Islamic Economics and Finance Research Group, Universiti Kebangsaan Malaysia, Malaysia. Available at: http://ekonis-ukm.my/administrator/components/com_jresearch/files/publications/wpiefo606_default_n_recovery.pdf.

Karwowski, E. (2009). *Financial Stability: The Significance and Distinctiveness of Islamic Banking in Malaysia*, Working Paper No. 555, The Levy Economics Institute.

Kashyap, A. K. and Stein, J. C. (1993). *Monetary Policy and Bank Lending*, National Bureau of Economic Research Working Paper 4317, April.

Kashyap, A. K. and Stein, J. C. (1994). *The Impact of Monetary Policy on Bank Balance Sheets*, National Bureau of Economic Research Working Paper #4821, August.

Kashyap, A. K. and Stein, J. C. (2004). 'Cyclical implications of the Basel II Capital Standards', *Federal Reserve Bank of Chicago Economic Perspectives* 28: 18–31.

Kassim S.H. *et al.* (2009). 'Impact of monetary policy shocks on the conventional and Islamic bank in a dual banking system: Evidence from Malaysia', *Journal of Economic Cooperation And Development* 30(1): 41–58.

Khan, M. M. and Bhatti, M. I. (2008). 'Development in Islamic banking: A financial risk-allocation approach', *Journal of Risk Finance* 9(1): 40–51.

Khan, M. S. (1986). 'Islamic interest-free banking: A theoretical analysis', *International Monetary Fund Staff Papers* 33: 1–27.

Khan, M. S. and Mirakhor, A. (1989). *Islamic Banking: Experiences in the Islamic Republic of Iran and Pakistan*, International Monetary Fund Working Papers, WP/89/12.

Kiaee, H. (2007). *Monetary Policy in Islamic Economic Framework: Case of Islamic Republic of Iran*, Munich Personal RePEc Archive (MPRA), Paper No. 4837.

Kia, A. and Darrat, A. F. (2007). 'Modeling money demand under the profit-sharing banking scheme: Some evidence on policy invariance and long-run stability', *Global Finance Journal* 18: 104–23.

Laeven, L. and Majnoni, G. (2003). 'Loan loss provisioning and economic slowdowns: Too much, too late?', *Journal of Financial Intermediation* 12: 178–97.

Nan, K. C. and Hung, J. W. (2007). 'The procyclical leverage effect of collateral value on bank loans', *Economic Inquiry* 45(2): 395.

Quagliariello, M. (2007). 'Banks' riskiness over the business cycle: A panel analysis on Italian intermediaries', *Applied Financial Economics* 17: 119–38.

Quagliariello M. (2008). 'Does macroeconomy affect bank stability? A review of the empirical evidence', *Journal of Banking Regulation* 9(2): 102–15.

Rochet, J. C. (2008). 'Procyclicality of financial systems: Is there a need to modify current accounting and regulatory rules?' *Banque de France, Financial Stability Review* (Special issue – Valuation and financial stability), 12. October, pp. 95–9.

Rosly, S. A. and Abu Bakar, M. A. A. (2003). 'Performance of Islamic and mainstream banks in Malaysia', *International Journal of Social Economics* 30(11/12): 1,249.

Sanusi, N. A. and Ismail, A. G. (2005). *A Panel Data Analysis of the Determinants of Malaysian Islamic bank Returns: 1995–2004*, Working Paper in Islamic Economics and Finance No. 0508, Universiti Kebangsaan Malaysia, Malaysia.

Siddiqi M.N. (1981). *Rationale of Islamic Banking*. Jeddah, Saudi Arabia: International Centre for Research in Islamic Economics.

Verbeek M. (2004). *A Guide to Modern Econometrics*. 2nd edn. Chichester: John Wiley and Sons Ltd.

Wagster, J. D. (1999). 'The Basle Accord of 1988 and the international credit crunch of 1989–1992', *Journal of Financial Services Research* 15: 123–43.

Yap, K. L. and Kader, R. A. (2008). 'The impact of interest rate changes on the performance of Islamic and conventional banks', *Malaysian Journal of Economic Studies* 45(2): 113–34.

Yusof, R. *et.al.* (2008). *Monetary Policy Shocks and Islamic Banks' Deposits in a Dual Banking System: A Comparative Analysis between Malaysia and Bahrain*, Paper presented at 8th Global Conference on Business and Economics, 18–19 October 2008, Florence, Italy.

Appendix 1

Islamic Bank List

Table 5.5 Islamic Bank List

Islamic Bank Institution	Country	Year
1. Bank Islam Malaysia Berhad (BIMB)	Malaysia	1998–2008
2. Maybank Bhd	Malaysia	1998–2008
3. HongLeong Bank Bhd (HLB)	Malaysia	1998–2008
4. Public Bank Bhd (PB)	Malaysia	1998–2008
5. RHB Bhd (RHB)	Malaysia	2000–2008
6. Affin Bank Bhd (Affin)	Malaysia	2000–2008
7. AM Bank Bhd (AMB)	Malaysia	1998–2008
8. Alliance Bank Bhd	Malaysia	2000–2008
9. Hongkong and Shanghai Bank Malaysia Bhd (HSBC)	Malaysia	1998–2008
10. Citibank Malaysia Bhd	Malaysia	1998–2008
11. Standard Chartered Bank Malaysia Bhd (SCB)	Malaysia	1999–2008
12. Overseas Chinese Bank Malaysia Bhd (OCBC)	Malaysia	2000–2008
13. Bank Rakyat	Malaysia	1998–2008
14. Abu Dhabi	UAE	1998–2008
15 Development Islamic bank	UAE	2001–2008
16. Kuveyt	Turk	1999–2008
17. Baraka	Turk	2000–2008
18. Kuwait Finance House (KFH)	Kuwait	1998–2008
19. Al Jazira Bank	Saudi Arabia	1999–2008
20. Baraka	South Africa	2000–2008
21. Shamil Bank	Bahrain	2000–2008
22. Gulf Finance House	Bahrain	2002–2008
23. ABC Islamic bank (ABC)	Bahrain	2003–2008
24. Meezan	Pakistan	2002–2008

6

RISK MANAGEMENT PRACTICES OF ISLAMIC BANKS: INTERNATIONAL EVIDENCE

Romzie Rosman and Abdul Rahim Abdul Rahman

6.1 Introduction

The esteemed status that Islamic banking has achieved, as well as the evident proof of its practical and viable system is noteworthy. The increasing development of Islamic financial institutions worldwide demonstrates the desire for Muslims to use Islamic financial institutions that are interest-free and that adhere to the Islamic principles of *Sharīᶜah* legislated in the *Qur'ān* (Sundararajan and Errico, 2002). The Islamic financial industry is currently comprised of Islamic commercial and investment banks, *takāful* (mutual insurance) companies, leasing and *muḍārabah* companies, and other non-bank financial institutions (Sundararajan and Errico, 2002). Iqbal and Llewellyn (2002) emphasised that, by various means, international financial systems can benefit from diversified financial products and operations, such as those available in Islamic banks, which are characterised by distinct risk-sharing features for each type of contract.

However, significant concerns have been raised surrounding the practice of risk management in Islamic banks. This is a result of the precedence to safeguard the viability and sustained growth of Islamic financial institutions in order to improve their input to financial stability and economic development (Chapra and Khan, 2001). In addition, prudent risk management in Islamic banking has gained substantial attention as Islamic financial institutions work to combat the challenges of globalisation (Sundararajan and Errico, 2002).

Risk management in banking is not a new phenomenon (Schroeck, 2002), as dealing with risk has always been the essence of financial intermediation (Scholtens and van Wensveen, 2000). Banks as financial intermediaries are prone to both financial and non-financial risks (Khan and Ahmed, 2001). Financial risks consist of market risk and credit risk, whereas non-financial risks include, but are not limited to operational risk, regulatory risk and legal risk (Khan and Ahmed, 2001). The performance of institutions depends largely on how well they manage these different risks that arise from their operations (Sundararajan and Errico 2002; and Khan and Ahmed, 2001). The establishment of the IFSB's Guiding Principles on Risk Management in 2005 reflects the growing importance of prudent risk management in Islamic banking as risk management is paramount to maintaining the responsiveness that organisations need to gain success as stipulated by Furash (1996). Another advantage of good risk management, as argued by Nocco and Stulz (2006), is that an integrated, holistic, approach to risk management can create shareholder value. Thus it is expected that Islamic banks make it their priority to develop appropriate risk management systems to effectively manage their unique risks, which, accordingly, will improve their performance and provide the strength to withstand a financial crisis.

The objectives of this paper are twofold. First, to examine the nature of risk management practices in Islamic banks; and, second, to describe the extent of risk reporting, risk measurement approaches and risk mitigation techniques that are currently adopted by Islamic banks. The dynamic nature of global financial markets highlights the need for continuous research on risk management. It is anticipated that this empirical study will benefit academics and professionals in the Islamic financial industry who constantly have to deal with risk in their daily operations. Furthermore, it is expected that this paper will generate opportunities for further research in this area.

The paper will initially present a review of the existing literature on risk management issues in Islamic banks in Section Two. Section Three provides an explanation of the IFSB guiding principles on risk management for institutions (other than insurance institutions) offering only Islamic financial services (IIFSs). Subsequently, Section Four explains the research methodology used in this study. Section Five provides a discussion of the research findings, followed by the conclusion in Section Six.

6.2 Risk Management Issues in Islamic Banking

Risk management is more important in the financial sector than in other parts of the economy (Carey, 2001). Prudent risk management is crucial and is the foundation of successful banking practice (for example, Al-Tamimi, 2002; Al-Tamimi and Al-Mazrooei, 2007). Thus the survival and success of financial organisations depends on the efficiency in which they can manage risk, and thus, effective risk management is critical in providing better returns to shareholders (Akkizidis and Khandelwal, 2008). Risk management can be described as:

> the overall process that a financial institution follows to define a business strategy, to identify the risks to which it is exposed, to quantify those risks, and to understand and control the nature of risks it faces.
>
> (Cumming and Hirtle, 2001: 3)

Santomero (1997) established that implementing a risk management system includes four parts: (i) standards and reports, (ii) position limits or rules, (iii) investment guidelines or strategies, and (iv) incentive contracts and compensation. Similarly, Khan and Ahmed (2001: 30–2) asserted that the fundamentals of the risk management process comprise three main features:

(i) establishing an appropriate risk management environment and sound policies and procedures
(ii) maintaining an appropriate risk measurement, mitigating and monitoring process and
(iii) adequate internal controls.

There are unique risks in Islamic banks due to the nature of their operations, particularly the *Sharīʿah*-compliance requirements. Islam completely acknowledges risk that is caused by financial and commercial factors as external to the formation of the business transaction (Mohd Arrifin et al., 2009). As stated by IFSB (2005b), the essential feature of IIFSs' activities is the requirement to comply with *Sharīʿah* rules and principles, especially the prohibitions of generating profits without bearing risks. Hence, it is Islamic bank's fiduciary duty to apply *Sharīʿah*-compliant risk mitigation techniques in their operations. The processes of risk management and the specific risk management practices for each unique risk in Islamic banks are well documented. Several earlier studies have focused on risk management practice in Islamic banks (Khan and Ahmed, 2001; Iqbal and Mirakhor, 2007; Akkizidis and Khandelwal, 2007; Grais and Kulathunga, 2007; Haron and Hin Hock, 2007; Greuning and Iqbal, 2007; Sundararajan, 2007; Archer and Haron, 2007; Cox, 2007; and Mohd Ariffin et al., 2009).

Akkizidis and Khandelwal (2008) conducted a comprehensive study on risk management issues in Islamic financial contracts. They established that, typically, Islamic banks had a unique mix and a transformation of risk for each financial contract. Haron and Hin Hock (2007) discussed the inherent risks such as credit and market risk exposures that existed in Islamic banks. Credit risk is the potential that a counter-party fails to meet its obligations in accordance with agreed terms; market risk is the risk of losses in on- and off-balance sheet positions arising from movement in market price (IFSB, 2005a). The notion of displaced commercial risk is when banks may be under market pressure to pay a return that exceeds the rate that has been earned on assets financed by Investment Account Holders (IAHs), at what time the asset yield returns are lower in comparison to competitors' rates (IFSB, 2005a, 2005b). These certain risks are inherent in the operations of both Islamic and conventional banks.

Alternatively, Archer and Haron (2007) argued that Islamic banks are exposed to a number of operational risks that are different from those faced by conventional banks. Their study asserted that, in Islamic banks, operational risk is a very important consideration due to the intricacies of a number of their products as well as their relative novelty in the contemporary financial services market, combined with the fiduciary obligations of Islamic banks when they act as a *mudarib* (investment manager).

Risk management in Islamic banks incorporates risk measurement, risk management and risk control (mitigation) (Iqbal and Mirakhor, 2007). Extensive risk measurement and mitigation methods for various risks, derived from Islamic financing activities, and from profit-sharing investment accounts, are also explained by Sundararajan (2007). Risk measurement is the evaluation of the likelihood and extent of a risk; risk mitigation is a technique that reduces the extent of risk exposures. The application of modern approaches to risk measurement, predominantly for credit and overall banking risks, is important for Islamic banks (Sundararajan, 2007).

Cox (2007) examined the importance of liquidity in the Islamic financial marketplace and conducted an analysis on ideal liquidity management tools and the structural issues that have affected the formation of Islamic capital and inter-bank markets. Greuning and Iqbal (2007) presented the three modifications of theoretical balance sheets of an Islamic bank that have implications for the overall riskiness of the banking. Here, the roles of Islamic banks as *mudarib* that have fiduciary duties are important aspects of risk management in Islamic banks.

An empirical survey conducted among seventeen Islamic banks in ten different countries discovered that, overall, risk management procedures in Islamic financial institutions were satisfactory (Khan and Ahmed, 2001). However, measuring, mitigating and monitoring processes, along with internal controls, needed to be further improved. Mohd Ariffin et al. (2009) surveyed twenty-eight Islamic banks in fourteen different countries to investigate the perception of risk management practices in Islamic banking. The study found that Islamic banks were not fully applying the *Sharīʿah*-compliant risk mitigation techniques and employed more traditional methods such as maturity matching, gap analysis and credit ratings. The main explanation is that Islamic banks are still new and lack the sufficient resources and systems required to use more technically advanced techniques. In addition, the results show that Islamic banks are not fully using the *Sharīʿah*-compliant risk mitigation methods, which are different from the ones used by conventional banks. One reason for this is that these methods are still subject to several objections by *Fiqh* scholars which, according to them (for example, parallel *baiʾ salam*), may lead to speculation (Usmani, 2007).

This literature review provided some insight into the unique types of risks in Islamic banks and also gave some examples of their risk measurement approaches and risk mitigation techniques.

6.3 IFSB and Guiding Principles of Risk Management

Due to the rapid development of Islamic banks in the financial industry, there has been growing effort to develop effective and prudent standards to supervise Islamic banking operations. The establishment of the IFSB is a consolidation of these efforts. The IFSB, which is based in Kuala Lumpur, was officially inaugurated on 3 November 2002. Malaysia, as the host country of the IFSB, enacted a law known as the Islamic Financial Services Board Act 2002, to serve as an international standard-setting body for regulators for the soundness and stability of the Islamic financial services industry. The Islamic financial services industry is broadly defined to include banking, capital markets and insurance. The IFSB has promoted the development of a prudent and transparent Islamic financial industry, especially to Islamic banks, by introducing new and adapting existing international standards that are consistent with *Sharīᶜah* principles.

The IFSB issued a comprehensive document of standards entitled 'Guiding Principles of Risk Management for Institutions (other than Insurance Institutions) Offering Only Islamic Financial Services (IIFS)' in December 2005. The guidelines, apart from the general requirement, are in the form of fifteen principles on risk management, which are clustered into six categories of major risk areas: 1) credit risk, 2) equity investment risk, 3) market risk, 4) liquidity risk, 5) rate of return risk/displaced commercial risk, 6) and operational risk including *Sharīᶜah* non-compliance risk. The central characteristic of IIFSs' activities is the requirement to abide by the *Sharīᶜah* rules and principles, especially the prohibitions of generating revenues without bearing any risks. A brief summary of these standards are provided in Table 6.1.

The first principle under the general requirements on risk management is the need for the board of directors (BOD) and for senior management to govern the risk management process. This includes, for instance, the regular appraisal of the effectiveness of risk management activities and ensuring an effective management structure. The principles under the credit risk category apply to specific products in relation to receivables, leases and profit-sharing assets. The IFSB focused on default, downgrading and concentration risks relating to credit risk. In dealing with credit risk is the need to recognise the credit risk exposures that arise from different stages in financing and also to carry an appropriate and diligent evaluation of the financing products. The principles also recommend remedial actions in the case of financial distress with a counter-party. These proactive measures comprise frequent contact with the counter-party, the use of debt-scheduling, restructuring arrangements and the use of *Sharīᶜah*-compliant insurance (*takāful*).

The third category is equity investment risk and deals with risks inherent in equity instruments, which are held for investment purposes, in particular for *mushārakah*[1] and *muḍārabah*.[2] This category covers the setting of objectives and policies and procedures of investments that use profit-sharing instruments. The need to engage independent parties to carry out audits and valuations of the investments is also emphasised in relation to managing equity investment risk.

The fourth category is market risk; exposure to this risk may occur at certain times throughout the Islamic financing contracts. Market risks exist in the case of tradable, marketable or leasable assets and off-balance sheet, individual portfolios. There is a need for the establishment of a sound and comprehensive management process and information system that comprises a framework to assist in identifying market risks, as well as guidelines governing risk taking activities in different portfolios, and a solid information management system for controlling, monitoring and reporting market risk exposure and performance.

The fifth category is liquidity risk. The principles highlighted in this category cover the key elements for effective liquidity management within the scope of

Table 6.1 The IFSB Guiding Principles on Risk Management

Risk	Principle	Guidelines
General Requirement	Principle 1.0	IIFS shall have in place a comprehensive risk management and reporting process.
Credit Risk	Principle 2.1	IIFS shall have in place a strategy for financing, recognizing the potential credit exposures at various stages of the agreement.
	Principle 2.2	IIFS shall carry out due diligence review.
	Principle 2.3	IIFS shall have in place an appropriate methodology for measuring and reporting the credit risk exposures.
	Principle 2.4	IIFS shall have in place *sharīʿah*-compliant credit risk mitigating techniques.
Equity Investment Risk	Principle 3.1	IIFS shall have in place appropriate strategies, risk management, and reporting processes in respect to the risk characteristics of equity instruments.
	Principle 3.2	IIFS shall ensure that their valuation methodologies are appropriate and consistent.
	Principle 3.3	IIFS shall define and establish the exit strategies in respect of their equity investment activities.
Market Risk	Principle 4.1	IIFS shall have in place appropriate framework for market risk management.
Liquidity Risk	Principle 5.1	IIFS shall have in place a liquidity management framework.
	Principle 5.2	IIFS shall assume liquidity risk that commensurate with their ability to have sufficient recourse to *sharīʿah*-compliant funds.
Rate of Return Risk	Principle 6.1	IIFS shall establish a comprehensive risk management and reporting process to assess the potential impact of market factors affecting rate of return on assets.
	Principle 6.2	IIFS shall have in place an appropriate framework for managing displaced commercial risk.
Operational Risk1	Principle 7.1	IIFS shall have in place adequate systems and controls.
	Principle 7.2	IIFS shall have in place appropriate mechanisms to safeguard the interests of all fund providers.

Note: IIFS = Institutions (other than Insurance Institutions) offering only Islamic Financial Services.
Source: IFSB (2005b)

Islamic banks' exposure. The concern is on the two major types of fund providers: (i) current account holders and (ii) unrestricted IAHs, who require a degree of liquidity to be maintained by Islamic banks in order to meet their requirements for withdrawal. Hence, Islamic banks are advised to have a separate liquidity management framework for each category of current accounts and investment accounts. Likewise, Islamic banks should have in place a liquidity management policy that covers sound processes for measuring and monitoring liquidity; an adequate system for monitoring and reporting liquidity exposures on a periodic basis; adequate funding capacity; and access to liquidity through fixed assets realisation and sale and lease-back arrangement. They should also develop a liquidity crisis management system.

The sixth category is on the rate of return risk, which includes displaced commercial risk. The rate of return risk is a strategic management risk issue since the Islamic banks are responsible for managing their IAHs' expectations and liabilities to current account holders. Islamic banks need to be aware of the possible factors that give rise to rate of return risk. For example, an increase in benchmark rates may result in IAHs' having expectations of a higher rate of return. Additionally, there is the need to have appropriate systems for identifying and measuring the factors that give rise to rate of return risk. Islamic banks are encouraged to employ balance sheet techniques to minimise their exposure using certain strategies by taking into account the future profit ratios. For this, developing new *Sharīʿah*-compliant instruments will be instrumental as well. For the purpose of managing displaced commercial risk, Islamic banks should develop and maintain the appropriate level of profit equalisation reserve (PER).

Finally, the seventh category relates to operational risks, which consists of risks from futile or inadequate internal processes, people and systems alongside the *Sharīʿah* non-compliance requirements and the failure of fulfilling Islamic banks' fiduciary responsibilities. Islamic banks are recommended to anticipate the events that could affect their operations. A prudent and controlled environment for operational risk management and periodic reviews to detect and address operational efficiencies are required to be conducted. Furthermore, it is essential to have an independent audit and assessment conducted by internal and external auditors for evaluating a bank's internal control. For the purposes of *Sharīʿah*-compliance, the Islamic banks have to ensure that they comply at all times with *Sharīʿah* rules and principles including their contract documentations. It is also recommended to have the separate *Sharīʿah* department conduct a *Sharīʿah*-compliance evaluation at least annually.

6.4 Research Methodology

This study attempted to examine the degree to which Islamic banks, internationally, practice risk management and techniques in dealing with different types of risk by answering the following two key research questions:

(i) What is the nature of risk management practices in Islamic banks, internationally?

(ii) To what degree are risk reports, risk measurement methods and risk mitigation techniques currently being utilised by Islamic banks, internationally?

A questionnaire was developed for this study, primarily based on the IFSB guiding principles on risk management. The questions were designed to evaluate the risk management practices by assigning a score for each answer. A pilot study was conducted among academics in the *Kulliyyah* (Faculty) of Economics and Management Sciences at the International Islamic University of Malaysia (IIUM), practitioners from Islamic banks, and a representative from the IFSB, all of whom either specialised in or had adequate knowledge of the field of risk management in Islamic banking. This was done to ensure the reliability and the relevance of the questions.

As regards to the samples of the study, the target population chosen for this study were banks that were in existence from 2006 and that categorised themselves as Islamic banks in the BankScope database.[3] The initial sampling population selected were seventy-two Islamic banks from twenty-one countries. The questionnaire was sent to the CEOs who represented the banks. The final sampling population that returned the survey included thirty-two Islamic banks from sixteen different countries. Table 6.2 consists of a list of the Islamic banks that returned the questionnaire.

6.5 Data Analysis and Findings

In this study, in collecting the primary data through a questionnaire for Islamic bankers' perceptions in relation to risk management practices in their institutions, a 5 level Likert scale was used. The scale of 1 (strongly disagree) to 5 (strongly agree) is the most commonly used in research.[4] The higher that the response sits on the scale is indication that the respondent strongly agrees that such practices were adopted by their banks.

6.5.1. Categories of Risk Management Practices

Table 6.3 shows the ranking based on the overall mean score on each of the categories of risk management practice. It is found that the highest score is for operational risk management. This is followed by general requirements for risk management, market risk management, equity investment risk management, credit risk management, liquidity risk management, and finally rate of return/displaced commercial risk management. The following sections attempt to discuss the implications of these findings.

(i) Operational Risk Management

Khan and Ahmed (2001) deemed operational risk to be among the most critical risks perceived by Islamic bankers.[5] As a result, it is expected that Islamic banks

Table 6.2 List of Islamic banks

No.	Name of Bank	Country
1	Abu Dhabi Islamic Bank	UAE
2	Asian Finance Bank	Malaysia
3	A'Ayan Leasing and Investment	Kuwait
4	Al Rajhi Bank	Saudi Arabia
5	Al Salam Bank	Bahrain
6	Arab Finance House	Lebanon
7	Arab Islamic Bank	Palestine
8	Arcapita	Bahrain
9	Bank Al Bilad	Saudi Arabia
10	Bank Islam Brunei	Brunei
11	Bank Islam Malaysia	Malaysia
12	Bank Maskan	Iran
13	Bank Muamalat Malaysia	Malaysia
14	Bank Syari'ah Mandiri	Indonesia
15	Bank Tejarat	Iran
16	Bank Islami Pakistan	Pakistan
17	Bank Ettamouil Saudi Tounsi (BEST Bank)	Tunisia
18	CIMB Islamic Bank	Malaysia
19	EONCAP Islamic Bank	Malaysia
20	Emirates Global Islamic Bank	Pakistan
21	Industrial Development Bank	Sudan
22	Jordan Islamic Bank	Jordan
23	Khaleeji Commercial Bank	Bahrain
24	Kurdistan International Bank	Iraq
25	Kuwait Turkish Participation Bank	Turkey
26	Meezan Bank	Pakistan
27	RHB Islamic Bank	Malaysia
28	Standard Chartered Modaraba	Pakistan
29	Tadamon Islamic Bank	Sudan
30	Turkiye Finans Katilim Bankasi	Turkey
31	United Capital Bank	Sudan
32	Venture Capital Bank	Bahrain

Table 6.3 Categories of Risk Management Practices

Categories	Ranking	Mean
Operational risk[a] management	1	4.475
General requirement on risk management	2	4.446
Market risk management	3	4.025
Equity investment risk management	4	3.735
Credit risk management	5	3.709
Liquidity risk management	6	3.679
Rate of return risk/Displaced commercial risk management	7	3.665

[a] Operational risk includes *sharīʿah* non-compliance risk.

should make it their priority to manage operational risks. The management of operational risks is essential both due to the *Sharīʿah* non-compliance risks (risks related to potential non-compliance with *Sharīʿah* rules and principles in the bank's operation) and fiduciary risks associated with the Islamic bank's fiduciary responsibilities as *mudarib*, towards fund providers under the *muḍārabah* form of contract. Accordingly, the funds invested by the fund providers become a liability of the *mudarib* in an event of misconduct or negligence by the *mudarib*. These risks may result in the fund providers' withdrawal, loss of income or the voiding of contracts leading to a diminished reputation or the limitation of business opportunities (IFSB, 2005a). Hence, the high mean score for operational risk management, which includes the *Sharīʿah* non-compliance risk, illustrates the importance for Islamic banks to fulfil the *Sharīʿah* requirements at all times.

(ii) General Requirements for Risk Management

The high mean score in the general requirement category for risk management practices indicates that Islamic banks have in place a comprehensive risk management system and that they practice good governance by assigning suitable boards and senior management to oversee their operations. As argued by Khan and Ahmed (2001), Islamic banks need to create an appropriate risk management environment and sound policies and procedures as fundamentals of their risk management system. Here, the BOD is responsible for outlining the overall objectives, policies and strategies of risk management. Moreover, the risk management activities of Islamic banks require active supervision by the BOD and senior management (IFSB, 2005a). From the survey, it is found that the BOD must ensure adequate capital in order to meet capital requirements and to maintain an effective management structure. This may be due to the fact that sufficient capital is mandatory to protect the bank from insolvency. The IFSB (2005a) guiding principles for capital adequacy stipulate that Islamic banks need to meet the capital requirements based on their risk exposures, particularly credit risk, market risk and operational risk exposures.

(iii) Market Risk Management

Market risk management ranked third; this suggests that market risk is also a significant risk to control, as their risk exposures are to be included in the calculation of regulated capital under Basel II and IFSB standards. Moreover, the unique nature of market risk, due to the trading activities of real assets of Islamic banks, signifies the importance of managing this risk. In addition, market risk exposure needs to be managed because of the nature of Islamic banking operations, which are affected by the volatility of market price for assets or commodities.

(iv) Equity Investment Risk Management

Although Islamic banks have less exposure to equity investment risks, this risk is still an important consideration to Islamic banks due to the nature of profit-sharing of Islamic banks, and especially for banks that focus on equity types of financing like *muḍārabah* and *mushārakah*. Islamic banks were lacking in the practice of engaging independent parties to carry out audits and valuation of their investments. Islamic banks, therefore, need to frequently review and update their policies and procedures of profit-sharing investments.

(v)   Credit Risk Management

Credit risk remains the most common risk in Islamic banking activities, since a majority of Islamic banking activities are using *murābaḥah* [6] and *ijārah* [7] financing. The findings were that Islamic banks on average attained a low score in credit risk management and ranked fifth among other types of risk management practices. The majority of Islamic banks choose not to adopt some of the administrative remedial actions proposed by IFSB such as establishing a debt-collection agency or *Sharīʿah*-compliant insurance to manage problematic credits and defaulting counter-parties.

(vi) Liquidity Risk Management

The second lowest score was liquidity risk management. This indicates a serious concern for Islamic banks as this is a very significant risk due to the limited availability of *Sharīʿah*-compatible money market instruments and lender of last resort (LOLR) facilities (Sundararajan and Errico, 2002; Sundararajan, 2007). Moreover, Chapra and Khan (2000) argued that Islamic banks may face liquidity problems as Islamic banks are over-relying on current accounts for liquidity and restrictions on the sale of debts; furthermore, the market for short-term Islamic instruments is still not developed. Thus, adequate systems for measuring, monitoring and controlling liquidity risk are required in Islamic banks. The relatively low score may be attributed to the Islamic banks' limited access to liquidity either through fixed asset realisations of sale or through lease-back arrangements. If this risk exposure is not well-managed and mitigated, it can ultimately threaten the sustainability of Islamic banks.

(vii) Rate of Return Risk/Displaced Commercial Risk Management

The lowest score was the management of rate of return/displaced commercial risk. Rate of return risk is generally associated with overall balance sheet exposures where mismatches arise between assets and balances from fund providers (IFSB, 2005a). It stems from the uncertainty in the returns earned by Islamic banks on their assets (Iqbal and Mirakhor, 2007). Furthermore, displaced commercial risk arises as the consequence of rate of return risk (IFSB, 2005a). This indicates that Islamic banks may be under pressure to pay a return that exceeds the rate that has been earned on assets financed by IAHs when the return on assets is under-performing as compared to competitors' rates. It is found that the method of smoothing the return, for example, the use of PER on rate of return risk/displaced commercial risk management practice, is not widely favoured by Islamic banks. However, Greuning and Iqbal (2007) argued that maintaining reserves to smooth income distributed to IAHs over periods of time has become a common practice. In their view the objective of such a PER is to hedge against future low-income distributions by keeping a portion of the current profits to pay out to IAHs in the future. So, it is crucial for Islamic banks to manage this risk in order for them to attract and maintain investors, especially the IAHs, who are one of their main sources of funds.

6.5.2 Risk Reporting

This study provides a comparison using figures from the empirical study developed by Khan and Ahmed (2001), which included seventeen Islamic banks that represented the Islamic financial industry in 2001. This study identified that the majority of Islamic banks produced many types of risk reports in their operations. Table 6.4 provides a list of the various risk reports produced by Islamic banks. Currently, most Islamic banks produce all types of risk reports except for the Commodities and Equities Positions Risk Reports, as well as Country Risk reports. This demonstrates that Islamic banks are aware of all the reports that must be produced, which should illustrate the improvements in risk reporting. This may consequently lead to improved transparency and accountability.

Mohd Ariffin (2005) claimed that risk reporting and disclosure were perceived to be more important in Islamic banks than conventional banks due to the existence of profit-sharing IAHs in Islamic banks. The IFSB (2005b) also emphasised the requisite to report on each specific risk and to ensure the adequacy of relevant risk reporting to supervisory authorities. Most of the Islamic banks (96 per cent of the banks) produced reports for credit risk. This may be due to the fact that credit risk is the most common source of risk in Islamic banking.

Significantly, there has been a high percentage of improvement in risk reporting, particularly in operational risk and market risk reporting. The overall high score on the operational risk management practice has perhaps

Table 6.4 Types of Risk Reports Used by Islamic Banks

	2001[a] (n=17)	2010 (n=32)	Changes (+/−)
Capital at risk report	65%	74%	14%
Credit risk report	71%	96%	35%
Market risk report	30%	74%	147%
Rate of return risk report	N/A	71%	N/A
Interest rate risk report	24%	N/A	N/A
Liquidity risk report	77%	84%	9%
Foreign exchange risk report	41%	84%	105%
Commodities and equities position risk report	59%	45%	−24%
Operational risk report	18%	74%	311%
Shariᶜah non-compliance risk report	N/A	68%	N/A
Country risk report	35%	36%	3%

[a] These results are obtained from Khan and Ahmed (2001).

reinforced Islamic banks regularly disclosing information on their operational risk. Discrepancies in the operations of firms such as Barings and Allfirst have generally given rise to the most significant, catastrophic loss events, which have caused the collapse of a number of big firms (Jackson-Moore, 2007). Similarly, risk reporting of market risks has also improved significantly. This may be due to the requirement for capital adequacy, which utilises market risk, credit risk and operational risk exposures in capital adequacy calculation (IFSB, 2005b). Therefore, the major progress of operational and market risk reporting in Islamic banks signifies the priority given to risks that need to be measured for capital adequacy purposes.

6.5.3 Risk Measurement Approaches

Previous studies confirmed that Islamic banks were deficient in the use of advanced risk measurement approaches (Khan and Ahmed, 2001; Mohd Ariffin, Archer and Karim, 2009). Similarly, this study found that apart from the measurement of value at risk, the majority of Islamic banks were using less technical risk measurement approaches. Currently, most of the Islamic banks in this study use all of the existing risk measurement approaches except for duration analysis, simulation technique and risk adjusted rate of return (RAROC). Table 6.5 illustrates the risk measurement approaches currently used by Islamic banks. By estimating the percentage of Islamic banks that use 'more technically advanced risk measurement approaches', it is evident that, currently, there has only been a slight increase in the usage of these approaches by Islamic banks. For instance, in 2010, the percentage of usage was 50 per cent as compared to 38 per cent in 2003 and 47 per cent in 2001. As stated by Mohd Ariffin, Archer and Karim (2009), Islamic banks are still new and do not have sufficient resources and systems to use more technically advanced techniques.

6.5.4 Risk Mitigation Techniques

An analysis of the various risk mitigation techniques used in Islamic banks is displayed in Table 6.6 below. The comparison was made based on figures from the empirical study of Khan and Ahmed (2001). In the past, a high percentage of Islamic banks utilised risk mitigation techniques that were widely used by conventional banks, and a small percentage of Islamic banks were using *Sharīʿah*-compliant risk mitigation techniques. Likewise, this study also reported that, in 2010, the majority of Islamic banks remained using the same risk mitigation techniques that were generally used by conventional financial institutions.

Only a minority of Islamic banks use the *Sharīʿah*-compliant risk mitigation technique. Instead, Islamic banks have opted to use *hamish jiddiyah* (security deposit) as their risk mitigation technique. Since the introduction of *hamish jiddiyah* and *urboun* (earnest money), there has only been a slight improvement on

Table 6.5 Risk Measurement Approaches Used by Islamic Banks

	2001[a] (n=17)	2003[b] (n=28)	% Changes (+/−)	2003[c] (n=28)	2010 (n=32)	% Changes (+/−)
Credit ratings	76.5%	57%	−25%	57%	81%	42%
Gap analysis	29.4%	68%	131%	68%	71%	4%
Duration analysis	47.1%	43%	−9%	43%	48%	12%
Maturity matching analysis	58.8%	82%	39%	82%	81%	−1%
Earnings at risk	41.2%	43%	4%	43%	55%	28%
Value at risk	41.2%	71%	72%	71%	55%	−23%
Simulation technique	29.4%	18%	−39%	18%	42%	133%
Estimates of worst case scenarios/ stress testing	52.9%	43%	−19%	43%	71%	65%
Risk adjusted rate of return on capital (RAROC)	47.1%	14%	−70%	14%	29%	107%
Internal based rating system	64.7%	46%	−29%	46%	55%	20%
Less technically advanced risk measurement approaches [d] *(Average)*	*50.6%*	*58.6%*	*16%*	*58.6%*	*67%*	*14%*
More technically advanced risk measurement approaches [e] *(Average)*	*47.06%*	*38.4%*	*−18%*	*38.4%*	*50%*	*30%*

[a] These results are obtained from Khan and Ahmed (2001).
[b] These results are obtained from Mohd Ariffin *et al.* (2009), the study was conducted in 2003.
[c] These results are obtained from Mohd Ariffin *et al.* (2009), the study was conducted in 2003.
[d] Credit ratings, gap analysis, duration analysis, maturity matching analysis and earnings at risk are in the category of less technically advanced risk measurement approaches.
[e] Value at risk, simulation techniques, estimates of worst case scenarios/stress testing, RAROC and the internal-based rating system are in the category of more technically advanced risk measurement approaches.

average usage of the *Sharī‘ah*-compliant risk mitigation technique. The explanation for the absence in usage of the *Sharī‘ah*-compliant risk mitigation technique may be because the technique is subject to conflicting interpretations by different *Sharī‘ah* scholars. Another factor could be that *salam*[8] and *istisnā*[9] contracts are not widely used in Islamic banks (Mohd Ariffin et al., 2009).

6.6 Conclusion

This study identified the insufficiency of risk management practices in Islamic banks that may threaten their sustainability, especially during a financial crisis. This study discovered that the lack of effective risk management practices for both liquidity risks and rate of return risk/displaced commercial risk will be the

Table 6.6 Risk Mitigation Technique Used by Islamic banks

	2003[a] (n=27)	2010 (n=32)	% Changes (+/−)
On-balance sheet netting	22%	52%	136
Third-party enhancement	78%	48%	−38
Loan loss reserve	89%	77%	−13
Guarantees	93%	84%	−10
Collateral arrangement	93%	90%	−3
Islamic option	N/A	19%	N/A
Islamic swaps	N/A	32%	N/A
Islamic currency forwards	N/A	35%	N/A
Parallel *salam* contracts	11%	19%	73%
Parallel *istisnā'* contracts	15%	23%	53%
Hamish Jiddiyah (security deposit)	N/A	81%	N/A
Urboun (earnest money)	4%	32%	700%
Used by conventional financial institution[b] *(average)*	*75%*	*70%*	*−7%*
Sharīʿah-compliant risk mitigation technique[c] *(average)*	*10%*	*35%*	*250%*

[a] These results are obtained from Khan and Ahmed (2001).

[b] On-balance sheet netting, third-party enhancement, loan loss reserve, guarantees and collateral arrangement are under the category of risk mitigation technique that used by conventional financial institutions.

[c] Islamic option, Islamic swaps, Islamic currency forwards, Parallel *salam* contracts, Parallel *istisnā* contracts, *hamish jiddiyah* and *urboun* are under the category of *sharīʿah*-compliant risk mitigation technique.

primary concern for Islamic banks and regulatory agencies. A liquidity crisis can affect Islamic banks when there is a lack of access to liquidity, and the threat of displaced commercial risk (where a massive withdrawal by IAHs occurs when Islamic banks do not offer attractive rates of return) can cause liquidity problems.

The management of rate of return risk/displaced commercial risk management was also found to be generally deficient in Islamic banks. The method of smoothing the return (for example, the use of PER) is not widely adopted by Islamic banks. If Islamic banks cannot offer competitive rates, customers would be inclined to switch to the other banks that would give higher returns. Customers that desire higher returns can simply switch their savings or investments to conventional banks that provide higher returns. Hence, displaced commercial risk, if not well mitigated, can lead to a significant withdrawal from depositors, which may result in serious liquidity problems. If IAHs are not paid good returns on their investments or if they receive low returns compared to the market return of similar instruments, and are made to bear the risk of loss, they may withdraw their funds. As a result, this risk may lead to a liquidity crisis for the bank that could have effects similar to those of a conventional bank run (Archer and Karim, 2007).

Islamic banks, internationally, have substantially improved in risk reporting, especially in the areas of operational risk, market risk and credit risk. This could be due to the significant development, as identified by Greuning and Iqbal (2007), that Islamic banks internationally have made considerable efforts over the years to improve the level of transparency and the quality of information disclosure in the market. Greater transparency will improve economic decisions and foster accountability, internal discipline and better governance. Simultaneously, improved transparency and accountability will improve the quality of decision-making in policy-oriented institutions.

Generally, there has been the tendency for Islamic banks to use less technically advanced risk measurement approaches. Hence, to ensure the viability of Islamic financial institutions and their sustainability in facing a financial crisis, more enhanced risk measurement approaches are encouraged, for a greater ability to identify the complex risks such as liquidity risks and rate of return risks. As argued by Sundararajan (2007), the application of modern and advanced approaches to risk measurement is important to properly recognise the unique mix of risks in Islamic finance contracts.

Islamic banks have typically been complacent with their risk mitigation approaches and have remained practicing risk mitigation techniques that are widely used by conventional banks. Some of the risk mitigation techniques that Islamic banks were satisfied to use included collateral arrangement, guarantees and loan loss reserve. These findings highlight the necessity to develop unique *Sharīᶜah*-compliant risk mitigation techniques. As stipulated by Grais and Kulathunga (2007), adequate resources need to be devoted to risk identification and measurement in addition to sound risk management techniques, in order to increase the capacity to develop innovative risk mitigation and hedging instruments that are suitable to Islamic financial institutions.

Notes

1. A *mushārakah* is a contract between the IIFS and a customer to contribute capital to an enterprise, whether existing or new, or to ownership of a real estate or moveable asset, either on a temporary or permanent basis. Profits generated by that enterprise or real estate/asset are shared in accordance with the terms of a *mushārakah* agreement while losses are shared in proportion to each partner's share of capital. *Source*: IFSB (2005b).
2. A contract between two parties, capital owner(s) or financiers (called *rab al maal*) and an investment manager (called *mudarib*). Profit is distributed between the two parties in accordance with the ratio upon which they agree at the time of the contract. Financial loss is borne only by the financier(s). The entrepreneur's loss lies in not getting any reward for his or her services. Source: IFSB (2005b).
3. BankScope is a financial analysis tool, combining information on 11,000 world banks with a financial analysis software program. This database allows the user to search a combination of numerous criteria including: bank name, SWIFT number, specialisation, financial data, ratings, geographic location and financial affiliations (BankScope, 2001).
4. The original Likert scales by Renkis Likert (1930) used five points of scale. In addition,

for comparison purposes, Khan and Ahmed (2001) examined the severity of risk exposures also using five points of scales.

5. However, Mohd Ariffin *et al.* (2009) found that both operational risk and *sharīᶜah*
   non-compliance risk are among the least importance risks perceived by Islamic bankers
   compared to other types of risks.

6. A *murābaḥah* contract refers to a sale contract whereby the IIFS sell to a customer at an
   agreed profit margin plus cost (selling price), a specified kind of asset that is already in
   their possession. *Source*: IFSB (2005b).

7. An *ijārah* contract refers to an agreement made by the IIFS to lease to a customer
   an asset specified by the customer for an agreed period against specified instalments
   of lease rental. An *ijārah* contract commences with a promise to lease that is binding
   on the part of the potential lessee prior to entering the *ijārah* contract. *Source*: IFSB
   (2005b).

8. A parallel *salam* contract refers to a second *salam* contract with a third party acquiring,
   from the IIFS, a specified kind of commodity, which corresponds to that of the commodity specified in the first *salam* contract. *Source*: IFSB (2005b).

9. A parallel *istisnā* is a second *istisnā* contract where a third party will be manufacturing
   for the IIFS a specified kind of asset, which corresponds to the specification of the first
   istisnā contract. *Source*: IFSB (2005b).

Bibliography

Akkizidis, I. and Khandelwal, S. K. (2008). *Financial Risk Management for Islamic Banking and
Finance.* Basingstoke: Palgrave Macmillan.

Al-Tamimi, H. (2002). 'Risk management practices: An empirical analysis of the UAE
commercial banks', *Finance India* 16(3): 1,045–57.

Al-Tamimi, H. and Al-Mazrooei, M. (2007). 'Banks' risk management: A
comparison study of UAE national and foreign banks', *The Journal of Risk Finance* 8(4):
394–409.

Archer, S. and Haron, A. (2007). 'Operational risk exposures of Islamic banks', in
S. Archer and R. A. A. Karim (eds), *Islamic Finance: The Regulatory Challenge.* Singapore:
John Wiley and Sons (Asia) Pte Ltd, pp. 121–31.

Archer, S. and Karim, R. A. A. (2007). 'Measuring risk for capital adequacy: The issue
of profit-sharing investment accounts', in S. Archer and R. A. A. Karim (eds) *Islamic
Finance: The Regulatory Challenge.* Singapore: John Wiley and Sons (Asia) Pte Ltd,
pp. 223–36.

Carey A. (2001). 'Effective risk management in financial institutions: the Turnbull
Approach', *Balance Sheet* 9(3): 24–7.

Chapra, M. U. and Khan, T. (2000). *Regulation and Supervision of Islamic Bank,* Occasional
Paper No. 3, Islamic Development Bank, Jeddah.

Cox S. (2007). 'The role of capital markets in ensuring Islamic financial liquidity', in
S. Archer and R. A. A. Karim (eds), *Islamic Finance: The Regulatory Challenge.* Singapore:
John Wiley and Sons (Asia) Pte Ltd, pp. 271–81.

Cumming, C. and Hirtle, Beverly J. (2001). 'The challenges of risk management in diversified financial companies', *Economic Policy Review* 7: 1–17.

Furash E. (1996). 'Getting over the hump in camel', *The Journal of Lending and Risk
Management* 78: 7–11.

Grais, W. and Kulathunga, A. (2007). 'Capital structure and risk in Islamic financial
services', in S. Archer and R. A. A. Karim (eds), *Islamic Finance: The Regulatory Challenge.*
Singapore: John Wiley and Sons (Asia) Pte Ltd, pp. 69–93.

Greuning, H. V. and Iqbal, Z. (2007). 'Banking and risk environment', in S. Archer and

R. A. A. Karim (eds), *Islamic Finance: The Regulatory Challenge*. Singapore: John Wiley and Sons (Asia) Pte Ltd, pp. 11–39.

Haron, A. and Hin Hock, J. L. (2007). 'Inherent risk: Credit and market risks', in S. Archer and R. A. A. Karim (eds), *Islamic Finance: The Regulatory Challenge*. Singapore: John Wiley and Sons (Asia) Pte Ltd, pp. 94–120.

Hull, J. C. (2005). *Options, Futures and Other Derivatives*, 6th edn. Upper Saddle River, NJ: Prentice Hall College Div.

IFSB (2005a). *Capital Adequacy Standard for Institutions (Other than Insurance Institutions) Offering only Islamic Financial Services*, Islamic Financial Services Board, Kuala Lumpur, Malaysia.

IFSB (2005b). *Guiding Principles of Risk Management for Institutions (Other than Insurance Institutions) Offering only Islamic Financial Services*, Islamic Financial Services Board, Kuala Lumpur, Malaysia.

Iqbal, M. and Llewellyn, D. T. (2002). *Islamic Banking and Finance: New Perspectives on Profit Sharing and Risk'*, Cheltenham: Edward Elgar.

Iqbal Z. and Mirakhor, A. (2007). *An Introduction to Islamic Finance: Theory and Practice*. Singapore: John Wiley and Sons (Asia) Pte Ltd.

Jackson-Moore, E. (2007). 'Measuring operational risk', in S. Archer and R. A. A. Karim (eds), *Islamic Finance: The Regulatory Challenge*. Singapore: John Wiley and Sons (Asia) Pte Ltd, pp. 237–46.

Khan, T. and Ahmed, H. (2001). *'Risk Management: An Analysis of Issues in Islamic Financial Industry'*, IRTI/IDB Occasional Paper, No. 5.

Kunhibava, Sherin (2010). *Derivatives in Islamic Finance*. Research Paper No: 7/2010, International Shari'ah Research Academy for Islamic Finance (ISRA), Kuala Lumpur, Malaysia.

Mitchell R. (2010). *Rebuilding Trust: Next Steps for Risk Management in Financial Services*, Economist Intelligence Unit Limited report. Available at: http://graphics.eiu.com/upload/eb/SAS_2010_Rebuilding_trust_WEB.pdf, last accessed 6 February 2010.

Mohd Ariffin, Noraini (2005). *Enhancing Transparency and Risk Reporting in Islamic Banks*. Unpublished PhD Thesis, School of Management, University of Surrey.

Mohd Ariffin, N., Archer, S. and Karim R. A. A. (2009). 'Risk in Islamic banks: Evidence from empirical research', *Journal of Banking Regulation* 10(2): 153–63.

Nocco, B. W. and Stulz, R. (2006). *Enterprise Risk Management: Theory and Practice*, Ohio State University Working Paper.

Santomero, A. M. (1997). 'Commercial bank risk management: An analysis of the process', *Journal of Financial Research*, 12(2–3): 83–115.

Schroeck, G. (2002). *Risk Management and Value Creation in Financial Institutions*. Hoboken, NJ: John Wiley and Sons.

Scholtens, B. and van Wensveen, D. (2000). 'A critique on the theory of financial intermediation', *Journal of Banking and Finance*, 24(8): 1,243–51.

Sundararajan, V. and Errico, L. (2002). *Islamic Financial Institutions and Products in the Global Financial System: Key Issues in Risk Management and Challenges Ahead'*, IMF Working Paper, International Monetary Fund.

Sundararajan V. (2007). 'Risk characteristics of Islamic products: Implications for risk measurement and supervision', in S. Archer and R. A. A. Karim (eds), *Islamic Finance: The Regulatory Challenge*. Singapore: John Wiley and Sons (Asia) Pte Ltd, pp. 40–68.

Usmani, Muhammand Taqi (2002). *An Introduction to Islamic Finance*. The Hague: Kluwer Law International.

7

LIQUIDITY RISK MANAGEMENT AND FINANCIAL PERFORMANCE OF ISLAMIC BANKS: EMPIRICAL EVIDENCE

Noraini Mohd Ariffin and Salina Hj. Kassim

7.1 Introduction

Managing liquidity is one of the top priorities of a financial institution's assets and liabilities management. In the context of banking, liquidity, or the ability to fund increases in assets and meet obligations as they come due, is critical for the ongoing viability of the banking institution. Since there is a close association between liquidity and the solvency of banks, sound liquidity management reduces the probability of banks becoming insolvent, thus reducing the possibilities of bankruptcies and bank runs. Ultimately, prudent liquidity management as part of the overall risk management of the banking institutions ensures a healthy and stable banking sector.

Liquidity management is just as important to the Islamic banks as it is to the conventional banks. However, compared to the conventional counterpart, liquidity management for the Islamic banks is unique and even more challenging due to the fact that most of the existing instruments used for liquidity management are interest-based and therefore not *Sharīʿah*-compatible. In addition, the rationality of bank customers in the conventional sense, in which profit motives prevail in any economic transaction, could result in liquidity withdrawal from the Islamic banks when return in the conventional counterpart is higher (Kassim, Majid and Yusof, 2009). The Islamic banks may also experience a severe liquidity mismatch when the market interest rate changes due to the changing economic environment. For example, in a high interest rate environment, the Islamic banks experience severe liquidity mismatch when assets (financing) tend to be more attractive relative to the conventional banks' loans while Islamic banks' deposit is relatively less attractive compared to the conventional banks' deposits.

In managing liquidity, the Islamic banks' dealings are restricted in the Islamic inter-bank market due to the requirement to avoid interest-bearing instruments. Traditionally, many Islamic banks rely heavily on commodity *murābaḥah* (markup basis) based on *tawarruq* for short-term investment and liquidity management. As an increasing number of *Sharīʿah* scholars are against the adoption of this arrangement, since it is considered as a grey area, several new *Sharīʿah*-compatible instruments have been introduced for liquidity management. Among others, several applications of the *sukuk* structure have been adopted in which the Islamic bank would buy or sell the *sukuk* (depending on its liquidity position) and, in return, pay or earn profit on the *sukuk*. Several other instruments to fulfil the Islamic banks' liquidity needs involve the applications of other contracts including *muḍārabah*, *ijārah* and parallel *salam* (Ayub, 2007).

At the moment, the IFSB's principles of risk management outline general guidelines pertaining to the liquidity management framework of the Islamic banks. In particular, the IFSB emphasises that the Islamic banks shall assume liquidity risk commensurate with their ability to have sufficient recourse to mitigate risk in respect of the restricted or unrestricted current accounts. Since the current account holders and unrestricted account holders require a degree of liquidity to be maintained by Islamic banks in order to meet their requirements for withdrawal, the IFSB principle suggests the Islamic banks to have a separate liquidity management framework for each category of current accounts and investment accounts. In addition, the Islamic banks are required to recourse to *Sharīʿah*-compliant funds in their liquidity management. The Islamic banks should have in place liquidity management policies that cover a sound process for measuring and monitoring liquidity, adequate systems for monitoring and reporting liquidity exposures on a periodic basis, and adequate funding capacity; they should also have access to liquidity through fixed assets realisation and through sale and lease-back arrangement, and they should develop liquidity crisis management (IFSB, 2005).

Due to the importance of liquidity risk management to the growth and survival of the Islamic banking institutions, this study attempts to analyse this topic from a new perspective. In particular, this study focuses on the management and disclosure of liquidity risks by the Islamic banks and relates these to the Islamic banks' performance. To the best of our knowledge, studies focusing on the relationship between liquidity risk management and performance in the case of the Islamic banks have been very limited when compared to the case of the conventional banks; this is mainly due to the recent nature of the Islamic banking industry. In this regard, this study contributes towards enriching the literature on the risk management of the Islamic banks by providing deeper understanding on issues relating to liquidity risk management by the Islamic banks. In particular, the study aims to answer the following research questions:

(i) What is the extent of liquidity risk in the Islamic banks in Malaysia?
(ii) Does the current crisis have a significant effect on the liquidity risk among the Islamic banks?
(iii) What is the extent of liquidity risk management disclosure in the annual report?
(iv) Is there any link between liquidity risk and the financial performance of Islamic banks?

The rest of the study is organised as follows: the next section discusses the existing literature on liquidity risk and its management as well as the link between risk management practices and banks' profitability. The following section presents the research methodology, focusing on the nature and sources of data, while the discussions on the findings of the study are presented in the subsequent section. Lastly, the final section summarises the conclusions.

7.2 Literature Review

7.2.1 Liquidity Risk and its Management

Liquidity risk arises from maturity mismatches where liabilities have a shorter tenor than assets. A sudden rise in the borrowers' demands above the expected level can lead to shortages of cash or liquid marketable assets (Oldfield and Santamero, 1997). Liquidity crisis in a banking institution could lead to insolvency and bank runs. Consequently, minimising the liquidity risk is one of the most important aspects of banks' asset and liability management. In essence, the objective of liquidity risk management is to mitigate the effect of the maturity mismatch on the banks' balance sheet. This requires the understanding of how cash flows are moving within an organisation, identifying the existence and location of cash flow strains by measuring emerging liquidity pressures and taking corrective actions to prevent these pressures from growing (Taylor, 2001).

As banking institutions, Islamic banks also have to meet their liquidity needs and obligations to ensure the smooth running of their business, as is the case with their conventional counterparts. However, the unique nature of Islamic banks with their objective of avoiding *ribā* (interest) in any form requires additional issues to be addressed in order to meet their liquidity needs in a *Sharīʿah*-compliant manner. Many have argued that liquidity risk is a major risk facing the Islamic banks (see, for example, Ray, 1995). Apart from the financing nature of the Islamic banks, which rely on long-term equity contracts such as *muḍārabah* and *mushārakah*, another reason for the potential liquidity problem in Islamic banks is due to the limited number of financial instruments that are accepted by *Sharīʿah* scholars. As a result, Islamic banks do not have the same funding options that are available to conventional banks in the inter-bank market. The absence of an adequate money market or a secondary capital market for Islamic financial instruments complicates the problem of mismatched maturities. Liquidity problems have also been purported to be the major impediment to the growth of Islamic banking (Vogel and Hayes, 1998).

Essentially, the liquidity risk in the Islamic banks arises from the lack of sufficient *Sharīʿah*-based liquid instruments. From the *Sharīʿah* perspective, additional issues arise in transforming the financial modes into negotiable financial instruments due to the maxim that once a debt has been created it cannot be transferred to other parties except at par value. On the other hand, depositor funds are either callable on demand or require very short withdrawal notice periods. Thus, the possibility of the Islamic bank to experience liquidity shortage is rather high in the event of a sudden rise in the borrowers' withdrawal of deposits.

In addition, the Islamic banks are prohibited by the *Sharīʿah* from borrowing at short notice by discounting debt obligation receivables (for example, through a central bank discount window). There is also no *Sharīʿah*-compliant lender of the last resort facility offered by many central banks. This means that Islamic banks are particularly exposed to liquidity risk because they tie up their investment account holders' funds in illiquid long-term assets, such as *ijārah* assets, or *muḍārabah/mushārakah* profit-sharing arrangements. However, Al-Sadah (1999) found that several Islamic banks in Bahrain take into consideration the level of liquidity on each type of account (investment, savings and current accounts) in order to meet investors' withdrawals. The level of liquidity is influenced by the liquidity requirements imposed by the regulatory agencies on the Islamic banks. Each Islamic bank uses different liquidity systems in order to achieve the same aim; there is some portion in the accounts that acts as a liquidity cushion for satisfying unexpected withdrawals. This enables the Islamic banks to meet the unexpected liquidity demands by current and investment account holders and prevents the possibility of a run on the bank.

Unlike the conventional banks, the Islamic banks' liquidity management is strictly limited in the Islamic inter-bank market. The Islamic inter-bank money market in Malaysia was introduced in January 1994 as a short-term intermediary to provide a ready source of short-term investment outlets based on *Sharīʿah* principles. This market is considered to be the first Islamic money market in the world. Inter-bank trading in Islamic financial instruments such as Islamic banker's acceptances, Islamic inter-bank investments where a bank with surplus funds can make an investment with another bank in deficit on the basis of *muḍārabah* (profit-sharing arrangements) and inter-bank cheque clearing systems are the key activities of this market. Here, the Islamic banks would be able to match their funding requirements effectively and efficiently.

Similarly, in Bahrain, the Bahrain Monetary Agency facilitated the setting up of the Liquidity Management Centre in 2002 to sell *Sharīʿah*-compliant securities that Islamic banks can hold as liquid asset. The short-term securities (that is, three-month) known as *sukuk al-salam* are issued monthly, are to be held until maturity and are non-tradable. In addition, *ijārah sukuk*, which are tradable but are exposed to rate of return risk,[1] are issued for longer periods (that is, from four to six years). It should be noted *sukuk salam* securities are bills, whereas *ijārah* securities are bonds. The main objective of issuing *ijārah* securities is to address the requirements and needs of Islamic financial institutions and investors for attractive investment opportunities.

In the case of Malaysia, Bank Negara Malaysia introduced the Liquidity Framework in 1998 to replace the liquid asset ratio requirement. This framework, which is based on international best practices for liquidity management, focuses on an efficient matching of the assets and liabilities profile that will enable banks to be better positioned in times of liquidity shocks and will allow for better utilisation of funds, as well as removing price distortion on liquid assets resulting from the captive demand created under the previous framework.

The Basel Committee on Banking Supervision (BCBS), in its 2000 paper 'Sound Practices for Managing Liquidity in Banking Organisation', sets out several principles that highlight the key elements for effectively managing liquidity. One of the principles relating to disclosure is that a bank must have adequate information systems for measuring, monitoring, controlling and reporting liquidity risk. Reports should be provided on a timely basis to the bank's board of directors, senior management and other appropriate personnel. The other important principle is that each bank should have in place a mechanism for ensuring that there is an adequate level of disclosure of information about the bank in order to manage public perception of the organisation and its soundness.

With regard to the accounting standard that deals with liquidity risk, the Financial Accounting Standard No. 1, 'General Presentation and Disclosure in the Financial Statements of Islamic banks and Financial Institutions' (FAS 1), issued by AAOIFI, is applicable to the financial statements published by Islamic banks to meet the common information needs of the main users of such statements. This standard is applicable to all Islamic banks regardless of their legal form, countries of incorporation or size.

FAS 1 demands that disclosure be made of any amount an Islamic bank is obligated to deposit with others as compensating balances. Islamic banks should also disclose the distribution of unrestricted investment accounts and their equivalent and other accounts (assets), by type, in accordance with their respective periods to maturity or expected periods to cash conversion (for assets). This can disclose liquidity requirements during the next period and liquidity requirements during the following periods.

7.2.2 Banks' Risk Management and Financial Performance

Studies on the relationship between risk management and the financial performance of banks have been mostly conceptual in nature, often drawing the theoretical link between good risk management practices and improved bank performance. Schroeck (2002) and Nocco and Stulz (2006) stress the importance of good risks management practices to maximise firms' value. Several studies draw the link between good risk management practices with improved financial performances. In particular, these studies propose that prudent risk management practices reduce the volatility in banks' financial performance, namely operating income, earnings, firm's market value, share return and return on equity (Smith, 1995). In addition, Schroeck (2002) proposes that ensuring best practices through prudent risk management results in increased earnings.

There are limited studies providing empirical evidence as to the link between risk management practices and bank financial performance. The study by Drzik (2005) shows that bank investment in risk management during the 1990s helped reduce earnings and loss volatility during the 2001 recession. In the same vein, the study by Pagach and Warr (2009) examines factors that influence the firms' level of enterprise risk management and finds that the more leveraged the firms are, the more volatile are their earnings.

Angbazo (1997) offers another dimension of analysing the relationship between risk management and financial performance by testing the influence of risk factors in determining banks' profitability. In particular, the study finds that default risk is a determinant of banks' net interest margin (NIM), and the NIM of super-regional banks and regional banks are sensitive to interest rate risk as well as default risk. The study by Saunders and Schumacher (2000) provides further support for the importance of controlling risks to financial performance. By investigating the determinants of NIM for 614 banks of six European countries and the US from 1988 to 1995, the study finds that interest rate volatility has a positive significant impact on the banks' profitability.

Hakim and Neamie (2001) examine the relationship between credit risk and performance of Egypt and Lebanon banks in the 1990s. The findings show that the credit variable is positively related to profitability, and the liquidity variable is insignificant across all banks and has no impact on profitability.

7.3 Research Method

The financial performance measures used in this study include the rate of return on assets (*ROA*) and the rate of return on equity (*ROE*). *ROA* is the most comprehensive accounting measure of a bank's overall performance. Since it is defined as net income over total assets, it shows the profit earned per dollar of assets. It is an indicator of a bank's efficiency and a measure of the bank's ability to earn rent from its total operations. The *ROE*, on the other hand, reflects how efficiently a bank management is using shareholders' investment. It tells the bank's shareholders how much the institution is earning on the book value of their investment (Goudreau, 1992). In fact, *ROE* is the most important measurement of banking returns because it is influenced by how well the bank performs in all other return categories; it also indicates whether a bank can compete for private sources in the economy. *ROE* is defined as net income divided by average equity.

This study aims to assess the liquidity risk in selected Islamic banks in Malaysia from 2006 to 2008 to establish the link between the extent of liquidity risks and bank performance. In addition, the study attempts to examine the liquidity management disclosure in these Islamic banks. The study uses secondary data using the annual reports as the main source of reference. Following Angbazo (1997), the proxy of liquid assets to liabilities is used to measure liquidity risk. As the proportion of funds invested in cash or cash equivalents increases, a bank's liquidity risk declines. This measurement is consistent with that proposed by Bank Negara Malaysia (BNM).

The study focuses on the top six Islamic banks in Malaysia, which are Bank Islam Malaysia Berhad (BIMB), Bank Muamalat Malaysia Berhad (BMMB), CIMB Islamic bank (CIMB), Affin Islamic bank (AFFIN), RHB Islamic bank

(RHB) and EON Capital Islamic bank (EONCAP). The period 2006 to 2008 was selected because the study also attempts to analyse the effect of the recent financial crisis on the liquidity risk. In particular, the year 2006 is before the crisis while the years 2007 and 2008 are the years of the crisis.

7.4 Results and Discussions

7.4.1 Extent of Liquidity Risk

Table 7.1 provides the liquidity risk of the banks included in the sample for the period of analysis, 2006 to 2008. In order to determine the liquidity risk of the selected Islamic banks, as mentioned in Section 2, the total liquid assets over liabilities are used as a proxy.

On average, the results suggest that the liquidity risks faced by the selected Islamic banks have remained relatively stable at about 0.3 over the three-year period. However, based on the individual bank data, the results show that the liquidity risk for BIMB continued to rise from 0.19 in 2006 to 0.27 in 2007 and to 0.55 in 2008. Similarly, the liquidity risk for EONCAP was also on a rising trend from 0.096 in 2006 to 0.18 in 2007 and to 0.27 in 2008. By contrast, the liquidity risk for CIMB declined over the three-year period, while that of AFFIN showed mix results, and BMMB and RHB were relatively stable during the same period. Based on this trend analysis, we find that the crisis has no definite effect on the extent of liquidity risk in the Islamic banks.

Second, the extent of the liquidity risk of the individual Islamic banks is compared with the industry average. The results show that RHB and EONCAP consistently reported a lower liquidity risk as compared to the industry average liquidity risk. BIMB has lower liquidity risk as compared to average risk for 2006 and 2007, and CIMB for only 2008. Table 7.1 also indicates that BIMB and EONCAP banks had a significant increase in liquidity risk from 2006 to 2008. On average, EONCAP Islamic bank exhibits the highest liquidity risk (0.55), followed by AFFIN (0.52) and then CIMB (0.43).

Table 7.1 Liquidity Risks of Selected Islamic Banks in Malaysia

	2006	2007	2008	Average
BIMB	0.19	0.27	0.55	0.34
BMMB	0.39	0.34	0.37	0.37
CIMB	0.69	0.48	0.13	0.43
AFFIN	0.58	0.58	0.41	0.52
RHB	0.18	0.25	0.16	0.20
EONCAP	0.096	0.18	0.27	0.55
Average	0.35	0.35	0.32	0.31

Note: Liquidity risk is calculated based on the proxy of liquid assets to liabilities. Liquid assets used in the calculations are only cash and short-term funds, and liabilities used are total liabilities in the banks.

Table 7.2 Liquidity Risk Disclosure in Islamic banks, 2008

	BIMB	BMMB	CIMB	AFFIN	RHB	EONCAP
Definition of liquidity risk	Yes	Yes	Yes	Yes	Yes	Yes
Frequency of meeting	Not available	Not available	Once	Not available	Twice	Not available
Monitoring frequency	Not available	Not available	Daily	Monthly	Not available	Not available
Risk Management	Liquidity Framework	Liquidity Framework	Liquidity Framework	Liquidity Framework	Liquidity Framework	Liquidity Framework
Risk Measurement	Not available	Stress testing	Stress testing	Not available	Stress testing	Not available
Responsibility	Not available	Not available	Asset Liability Management and Group Treasury	Bank Risk Management Committee	Asset Liability Committee (ALCO)	Not available

Note: Not available means that the information on the items is not disclosed in the annual reports of the Islamic banks.

7.4.2 Liquidity Risk Management Disclosure in Islamic Banks

All Islamic banks in the study disclose the definition of risk in the annual reports. Table 7.2 provides a summary of the items disclosed in the Islamic banks' annual report for the year 2008. With regard to the liquidity risk management disclosure, all the selected Islamic banks disclose that the banks use the Liquidity Framework approved by Bank Negara Malaysia to manage liquidity. The banks' liquidity framework is subject to stress tests and the results are constantly reviewed. The liquidity framework ascertains the liquidity condition based on the contractual and behavioural cash flow of assets, liabilities and off-balance sheet commitments, taking into consideration the realisable cash value of the eligible liquefiable assets.

The risk measurement used by Islamic banks is stress tests but only three banks in the study disclose the information (BMMB, CIMB and RHB).

The liquidity risk management in Islamic banks is the responsibility of a Risk Management Committee in these banks, where this committee provides oversight and management of all risks including liquidity risk. There is a continuous review of business activities and processes to identify significant risk areas and to implement control procedures to operate within established corporate policies and limits. The banks' risk management strategy seeks to ensure that risks undertaken are well managed within the boundaries of its risk appetite. However, only three banks disclose this information (CIMB, AFFIN and RHB). The majority of the Islamic banks in the study also did not provide disclosure on the frequency of the meetings for the liquidity risk management and also the monitoring frequency.

However, there is no disclosure in these annual reports with respect to quantitative information on the management of the liquidity risk, for example, the techniques used to manage the liquidity risks, which is crucial to the market participants.

7.4.3 Liquidity Risk and Banks' Financial Performance

Table 7.3 shows the profitability ratios on the selected Islamic banks. In this study, the financial performance is assessed based on return on assets (ROA) and return on equity (ROE).

On average, the descriptive statistics show that ROA is higher for the year 2007 than it is for 2008 and 2006. Also, for the year 2008, BIMB has the highest ROA among all the Islamic banks being considered at 1.83 and followed by RHB at 0.97. The remaining banks in the sample have lower ROA as compared to the average ROA. For the year 2007, RHB has the highest ROA, followed by BIMB (1.34) and then CIMB (0.94).

Meanwhile, the ROE gives a different perspective compared to ROA. In particular, for the year 2008, based on the ROE, BIMB has the highest ROE at 32.90. BIMB's ROE was also high compared to the industry average at 12.43 in 2008 and 19.47 in 2007. The remaining banks in the sample have a lower ROE as compared to the average ROE for both 2007 and 2008. In 2006, due to the exceptionally high ROE in 2006 at 508.2 for BIMB, it is difficult to make a comparison with the average ROE. Regardless, there is a general decline in the ROE of the

Table 7.3 Financial Performance for the Period 2006 to 2008

	2006	2007	2008	Average
Return On Assets (*ROA*)				
BIMB	−8.63	1.34	1.83	−1.82
BMMB	0.61	0.35	0.23	0.40
CIMB	0.22	0.94	0.53	0.56
AFFIN	0.94	0.77	0.45	0.72
RHB	1.10	1.43	0.97	1.17
EONCAP	0.25	0.54	0.25	0.35
Average	**−0.92**	**0.90**	**0.71**	**0.23**
Return On Equity (*ROE*)				
BIMB	508.23	56.52	32.90	199.27
BMMB	11.69	6.62	4.45	7.59
CIMB	1.92	11.42	11.48	8.27
AFFIN	18.61	18.23	11.24	16.02
RHB	14.20	17.01	10.85	14.02
EONCAP	3.07	7.01	3.67	4.58
Average	**93**	**19.47**	**12.43**	**41.63**

Source: BankScope Database

Islamic banks from 2006 to 2008. Relating this to the global financial crisis, the crisis seems to have an adverse effect on the Islamic bank's financial performance as being shown by the declining *ROE* over the three-year period.

From the descriptive statistics, it is quite difficult to ascertain the link between the liquidity risk and financial performance. A more reliable statistical investigation using statistical or data-processing software is needed to link the Islamic banks' liquidity risk and financial performance. Despite this, several interesting observations can be made in the context of the individual Islamic bank. Relating this to financial performance, the findings show that BIMB has the highest *ROA* and *ROE* for 2008, yet it has the highest liquidity risk. This is consistent with the financial theory where it claims that risk and return have a linear relationship, that is, low risk is associated with low return and consequently high risk brings high return. In the case of outliers such as BIMB, the mathematical explanation could be the reason behind the relationship between the liquidity risk and financial performance. Second, the descriptive statistics show that RHB is among the top Islamic banks in terms of financial performance (ranked first in terms of *ROA* and ranked third in terms of *ROE*). Third, it shows that AFFIN essentially exhibited a positive relationship between liquidity risk and financial performance. This is reflected by its high liquid assets to liabilities and second rank in terms of *ROA* and second rank in terms of *ROE*.

7.5 Conclusion and Recommendations

Based on a sample consisting of the top six Islamic banks in Malaysia, this study attempts to relate the liquidity risk with the banks' financial performance. The study finds that the financial crisis has no definite effect on the extent of liquidity risk in the Islamic banks as the trend in liquidity risks in the Islamic banks over the three-year period has been inconsistent throughout the banks. Second, assessing the performance of the Islamic bank through the *ROE* suggests that there is a general decline in the *ROE* of the Islamic banks from 2006 to 2008, indicating that the crisis has an adverse effect on the Islamic banks' profitability. Third, relating liquidity risk to bank's financial performance, the findings show that the relationship between liquidity risk and financial performance is as predicted by the conventional financial theory of 'high risk–high return' as shown by BIMB, which has the highest *ROA* and *ROE* for 2008 and yet has the highest liquidity risk.

In addition, the findings show that the level of liquidity risk reporting is still at a minimum. The disclosure of firms' risk-management positions and strategies is crucial to improve corporate transparency for market participants and to enhance corporate governance.

Based on the findings in this study, it is important for the standard setters and the bank regulators to work together to improve the risk disclosures, including liquidity risk. The prudential standard issued by the Islamic Financial Services Board (IFSB) in December 2005 entitled *Guiding Principles on Risk Management* is similar to the BCBS's guidelines on sound practices and principles pertaining to market, credit and operational risk management of banks but caters for the specificities of Islamic banks, provides Islamic banks with the fifteen guidelines for risk management, including liquidity risk. However, these guidelines do not look specifically into risk disclosure.

It is hoped also that by having adequate disclosure in the annual reports, particularly information on risks, future banking crises could be avoided. This is because research has shown that one of the causes of the Asian banking crises was the lack of transparency in the annual reports. However, not all information should be made available to the public because some of the information such as the nature and the amount of investments of the restricted investment account holders should be made available to restricted investment account holders.

Notes

1. *Sukuk salam* securities are bills, whereas *ijārah* securities are bonds.

Bibliography

Abdul Rahman, Y. (1999). 'Islamic instruments for managing liquidity', *International Journal of Islamic Financial Services*, 1(1). Available at: www.islamic-finance.net/journal.html, last accessed 1 July 2006.

Accounting and Auditing Organisation for Islamic Financial Institutions (2001). *Accounting, Auditing and Governance Standards for Islamic Financial Institutions*. Bahrain: AAOIFI.

Al-Omar, F. and Abdel-Haq, M. (1996). *Islamic Banking: Theory, Practice and Challenges*. Karachi, Pakistan: Oxford University Press.

Al-Omar, Fouad and Iqbal, M. (2000). 'Some strategic suggestions for Islamic banking in the 21st century', *Review of Islamic Economics* 9: 37–56.

Al-Sadah, A. K. I. (1999). *Regulation of Financial Reporting by Islamic Banks*, unpublished M Phil Thesis, Guildford, UK: University of Surrey.

Angbazo, L. (1997). 'Commercial bank net interest margins, default risk, interest-rate risk, and off-balance sheet banking', *Journal of Banking and Finance* 21: 55–87.

Ayub, M. (2007). *Understanding Islamic Finance*, Singapore: John Wiley and Sons, Ltd.

Bank Negara Malaysia – Liquidity Framework. Bank Negara website. Available at: www.bnm. gov.my/guidelines/01_banking/04_prudential_stds/02_liquidity.pdf, last accessed 8 February 2010.

Basel Committee on Banking Supervision (2000). *Sound Practices for Managing Liquidity in Banking Organisations*. Basel: Basel Committee on Banking Supervision.

Drzik, J. (2005). 'New directions in risk management', *Journal of Financial Econometrics* 3(1): 26–36.

Goudreau, R. (1992). 'Commercial banks profitability rises as interest margins and securities sales increase', *Economic Review, Federal Reserve Bank of Atlanta* 77: 33–52.

Hakim, S. and Neamie, S. (2001). *Performance and Credit Risk in Banking Performance: A comparative study of Egypt and Lebanon*, ERF Working Paper Series, WP 0137.

How, J. C. Y., Karim, M. A. and Verhoeven, P. (2005). 'Islamic financing and bank risks: The case in Malaysia', *Thunderbird International Business Review* 47(1): 75–94.

IFSB (2005). *'Guiding Principles of Risk Management for Institutions (Other than Insurance Institutions) Offering only Islamic Financial Services'*, Islamic Financial Services Board.

Kassim S. H., Abdul Majid, M. S. and Mohd Yusof, R. (2009). 'Impact of monetary policy shocks on the conventional and Islamic banks in a dual banking system: Evidence from Malaysia', *Journal of Economic Cooperation and Development* 30(1): 41–58.

Khan T. and Ahmed, H. (2001). *Risk Management: An analysis of issues in Islamic financial industry*, Occasional Paper No. 5, Islamic Research and Training Institute (IRTI), Islamic Development Bank, Jeddah.

Nocco, B. W. and Stulz, R. M. (2006). 'Enterprise risk management: Theory and practice', *Journal of Applied Corporate Finance* 18(4): 8–20.

Oldfield, G. and Santomero, A. (1997). 'Risk management in financial institutions', *Sloan Management Review*, Fall: 33–46.

Pagach, D. and Warr, R. (2009). *Corporate Reputational Risk and Enterprise Risk Management: An Analysis from the Perspectives of Various Stakeholders*. Hoboken, NJ: John Wiley and Sons.

Ray, N. (1995). *Arab Islamic Banking and the Renewal of Islamic Law*. London: Graham and Troutman.

Saunders, A. and Schumacher, L. (2000). 'The determinants of bank interest rate margins: An international study', *Journal of International Money and Finance* 19: 813–32.

Schroeck, G. (2002). *Risk Management and Value Creation in Financial Institutions*. Hoboken, NJ: John Wiley and Sons.

Smith, W. (1995). 'Corporate risk management: Theory and practice', *The Journal of Derivatives* 2(4): 21–30.

Taylor, J. B. (2001). 'The role of the exchange rate in monetary-policy rules', *American Economic Review, Papers and Proceedings* 91(2): 263–67.

Vogel, F. and Hayes, S. (1998). *Islamic Law and Finance: Religion, Risk and Return*. The Hague: Kluwer Law Intl.

8

RISK MANAGEMENT AND ISLAMIC FORWARD CONTRACTS

Sherin Binti Kunhibava

8.1 Introduction

This chapter explores risk management and the current use of Islamic forward contracts in Islamic banks around the world. While Islamic banking facilities and Islamic capital market instruments such as *sukuk ijārah*, *sukuk mushārakah* and *sukuk muḍārabah* are well documented, widely understood and known, Islamic derivatives, on the other hand, are not. The possible reason for this is that there are a number of objections towards derivatives in *Sharīʿah* that make conventional derivatives,[1] such as forwards, futures and options impermissible (Obaidullah, 1998; Kamali, 2002). However, due to the need for risk management tools (Bacha, 1999), 'Islamic' derivatives have been created and are now being used in the Islamic financial industry. These derivative-like products use *Sharīʿah*-approved contracts and instruments, such as *inter alia*, *waʾd*, *musawamah*, *murābaḥah*, *muqassah* and commodity *murābaḥah*. The structure of the Islamic derivatives uses a combination of the above-mentioned contracts. How exactly these Islamic derivatives work and how they are used is not well known or understood. Increasing the transparency of these products would open up the market to better governance and comprehension. This chapter focuses on Islamic forward-like contracts as used in Islamic banks.

8.2 Background

Collection of primary data for this research included two focus group discussions with treasury personnel of a total of eleven Islamic banks in Malaysia. This was followed with interviews and sharing knowledge sessions with seven Islamic banks' treasury departments, within and outside Malaysia. The interviewing and sharing knowledge session with the Islamic banks enabled data to be gathered on the nascent usage of Islamic derivatives in Islamic banks. The last stage of data collection involved interviewing *Sharīʿah* advisors of Islamic banks and other scholars conversant in *Sharīʿah* on the *Sharīʿah* issues and parameters of Islamic derivatives.

Not all Islamic banks use the same Islamic derivative instruments. Thus, this study does not intend to explain the universal practice of Islamic forward contracts as used in Islamic banks in Islamic finance today. Another point that needs clarification is that this chapter does not assess whether Islamic forward contracts as used today are *Sharīʿah*-compliant or otherwise; this has already been deliberated by the *Sharīʿah* advisory panel of each of the Islamic banks. Rather, this study seeks to lift the mist that engulfs the practice of Islamic derivatives. The focus of this research is on Islamic forward-like contracts. This chapter is divided in the following manner: First, risk in Islamic finance is explained. Next, forward contracts as used in conventional finance are defined, and the problems with conventional forwards from *Sharīʿah*'s perspective are explained briefly. Thereafter, Islamic forward contracts are explained. Lastly, *bai-al sarf* in Islamic finance and the way forward are explored.

8.3 Risk in Islamic Finance

'Risk' is the possibility that the outcome of an event could result in an adverse result. More specifically, in finance, 'risk refers to the probable loss of income and asset value' (Ismail, 2010: 227). There are a number of risks in finance, the common ones being market risk, credit risk, liquidity risk, operational risk, equity investment risk and displacement commercial risk. Each category of risk involves the possibility of suffering adverse effects in that category. Thus market risk is the risk of losses arising from adverse movements in market prices. Market risk includes foreign exchange risk (unanticipated movements in exchange rates), profit rate risks (changes in the net profit income as a result of changes in profits and shifts in composition of assets and liabilities) and equity risk (changes in the prices of equities on equity positions) (Ismail, 2010).

In Islamic banking and finance two well-known Islamic legal maxims (*Qawaid Fiqiah*) explain the status of risk and return in Islamic financial transactions; these are *al-kharaj bin daman* and *al-ghunm bi al-ghurm*. These legal maxims come from the following *ḥadīth*:

> Narrated by Aisha (may *Allah* be pleased with her): *Allah*'s Messenger (*pbuh*) said, 'Any profit goes to the one who bears responsibility.'[2]

> Narrated by Amr bin Shu'aib on his father's authority from his grandfather (may *Allah* be pleased with his): *Allah*'s messenger (*pbuh*) said, 'The condition of a loan combined with a sale is not lawful, nor two conditions relating to one transaction, *nor the profit arising from something which is not in one's charge*, nor selling what is not in your possession.'[3]

> (Emphasis added)

These legal maxims indicate that without risk or liability there cannot be profit, or 'return should be proportional to the risk assumed' (Dar, 2007), and any gain that has not accompanied some liabilities is *ḥarām* (Kamali, 2001). Thus risk is part and parcel of a financial transaction in Islam; for example, in a sales contract the profit of a sale is an outcome of the risks a trader takes. The trader takes risks in relation to the price of the commodity, the condition of the commodity, the transport of the commodity, or any natural calamity that may befall his or her goods. If there are any adverse events that take place in relation to the transport, condition of the commodity, or even natural calamity, then the trader will lose money. Thus the seller bears the risk that makes it legitimate to gain when there is a profit (Rosly, 2005). In other words, there has to be risk involved so that the profit can be enjoyed.

Does this now mean that risk management is not allowed in Islam? This is answered in the negative because of two important principles in *Sharīʿah*: the *maqasid al-Sharīʿah* (general objectives of *Sharīʿah*) on protection of property or material wealth (*al-mal*), and the prohibition of *gharar*.

Protection of property is one of the essentials (*daruriyyat*) that are necessary to human life. Thus steps taken to protect the property or wealth from losses as in risk management would be within the *maqasid al-Sharīʿah*. Further, according to one of the secondary sources of *Sharīʿah* – *maslahah*, any consideration that secures a benefit or prevents harm and is in harmony with the *maqasid al-Sharīʿah* is *maslahah*. *Maslahah* means benefit or interest of the public (Kamali, 1991) and thus any action for the benefit of the public and that is within the *maqasid al-Sharīʿah* should be furthered. It can be inferred thus that risk management is within the *maqasid al-Sharīʿah* as it protects the property from losses and harm and is for the benefit of the public.

Gharar is more difficult to define (Vogel and Hayes, 1998: 64), as it is more general and encompasses a number of other elements such as *maysir* and *jahalah*. *Gharar* has been defined as 'danger' (Al-Zuhayli, 2003: 82), 'risk' (El-Gamal, 2001: 2) and also a transaction equivalent to 'a zero-sum game with uncertain payoffs' (Al-Suwailem, 1999; 2000: 1). Al-Zuhayli's definition of a *gharar* sale, it is opined, is a more clear-cut definition: It is the sale of probable items whose existence or characteristics are not certain due to the risky nature that makes it similar to gambling (Al-Zuhayli, 2003: 83). Thus it is opined that *gharar* is a type of risk and relates to lack of certainty regarding the knowledge of the parties on all aspects of a sales contract and lack of certainty on the existence of the items of sale (Vogel and Hayes, 1998). In Islamic transactions the existence of *gharar* is prohibited. In other words, steps have to be taken to ensure that there is no *gharar* in a sale contract. This means ensuring certainty in the knowledge of the parties and the existence of the items for sale. From this we can induce that steps taken to minimise risky transactions are encouraged and required in Islamic financial transactions.

Having discussed the concept of risk in Islamic finance this paper goes on next to explain forward contracts and the concepts of 'speculation' and 'hedging'.

8.4 Forward Contracts Defined and *Sharīʿah's* Position Explained

Hull (2006: 3–4) defines a forward contract as an 'agreement to buy or sell an asset at a certain future time for a certain price'. Thus in the forward contract ownership obligations are transferred on the spot, but delivery obligations are at some future date; in other words, forward contracts are settled at maturity at the forward price agreed upon initially (Kolb and Overdahl, 2010). This means that the forward price may be different from the price at maturity (market value), and either party to the transaction will make a gain or suffer a loss.

A forward contract is traded over-the-counter and is usually between two financial institutions or between a financial institution and its client (Gupta, 2006). Due to the fact that forward contracts are bilateral and between two parties and there is no delivery or payment involved at the start of the contract, the risk of default is real. If the underlying asset price rises, the contract buyer gains on the contract, and will be exposed to the credit risk that the seller will default on forward contract delivery obligations, when the underlying asset can be sold for more at the spot market. This is because there has been no delivery at the initial stage of the agreement. Likewise, if the underlying asset can be bought at a lower price than the forward price, the contract seller is exposed to the credit risk that the buyer will default on the forward contract payment obligations (Kolb and Overdahl, 2010).

It is for these reasons that in *Sharīʿah* conventional forwards have been found to be impermissible.

Mahmassani (1983), for example, has stated that, since in a forward contract both counter-values are non-existent at the time of the contract (that is, neither the money, nor goods), it is therefore not a genuine sale but merely a sale or exchange of promises. A sale can only be valid in *Sharīʿah* if either the price or the delivery is postponed (for example, in a *salam* or *istisnā* arrangement) but not both. This view has also been taken by the OIC Fiqh Academy (OIC Fiqh Academy, 2000, Resolution no. 63/1/97). The non-existence of both counter-values of the contract, in the case of forwards, amounts to unwarranted risk-taking and *gharar* that is filled with uncertainties over the prospects of fulfilment.[4]

Gharar in the performance of the forward contract leads to the next objection of *Sharīʿah* scholars towards conventional forwards. Conventional forwards are likened to gambling (*maysir* and *qimar*) because of the highly risky and uncertain outcome (Al-Suwailem, 2006; Kahf, 2002; Khan, 2000). Further derivatives such as forward contracts are often used to speculate, that is, not to protect the value of the underlying assets, but to gain from the increase of value of the underlying asset (Elgari, 2009).

Speculation itself is not considered to be 'unIslamic' (Khan, 1988). This is because speculation exists in all forms of businesses, such as *muḍārabah* and *mushārakah* (Kamali, 1999). The concern is when speculation turns out to be a zero-sum nature of a game that resembles *maisir* and *gharar* (Obaidullah, 2002). What this means is that when speculation is used to create wealth, as in *muḍārabah* and *mushārakah*, it would be acceptable, but when speculation is used for wealth transfer only,[5] that is, from one party to another, as in cases of gambling and loaning money based on *ribā*, then this would amount to speculation that is a zero-sum game, as in gambling (Diwany, 2003).

Some argue that the advantage of the speculators' presence in the market enhances liquidity, which enables hedgers to pass their risk on to the speculators (Kamali, 1999; Smolarski, Schapek and Mohammad, 2006). Others argue that the benefits to the hedgers seem to be very few compared to the advantages gathered by speculators (Khan, 1997; Obaidullah, 1998).

Here an explanation of speculation and hedging in relation to derivatives has to be made. Hedging is defined as a 'transaction that offsets an exposure to fluctuations in financial prices of some other contract or business risk' (Gupta, 2006: 99) or 'to hedge is a position in a hedging instrument put on to reduce the risk resulting from the exposure to a risk factor' (Stulz, 2003: 56). Hedging thus means reducing one's exposure to risk. In the case of derivatives, hedging in financial risks such as currency risk is often managed with derivatives, such as forwards.

Speculators are defined in the Commodity Futures Trading Commission (CFTC) Glossary quoted in Kolb and Overdahl (2010: 44) as 'an individual who does not hedge, but who trades with the objective of achieving profits through the successful anticipation of price movements'. Speculation is thus the opposite of hedging because hedgers want to avoid exposure to risks or adverse movements in the price of an underlying, whereas speculators want to take a position in the market, hoping that the prices will go up or down.

Speculators are often referred to as investors (Kolb and Overdahl, 2010). Investment has been defined (investorwords.com, 2010) as 'the purchase of a financial product or other item of value with an expectation of favourable future returns. In general terms, investment means the use money in the hope of making more money.' Comparing the definitions of 'speculator' and 'investment', one may conclude that they are one and the same. However, there are different types of speculators. For example, there is the speculator who does market research and studies the trend of the market closely before making an investment. Or there may be a situation whereby the speculator just enters the market and recklessly makes a decision to bet on the rise of a certain stock with no prior research done; this would be excessive riskiness and may amount to gambling or betting. Is there a difference between speculation and gambling in this situation? The author posed this question to certain Sharīʿah scholars and the answer was that, yes, there is a difference. In speculation the speculator takes up existing risks in the market whereas in gambling a gambler himself or herself creates risks.[6]

In Sharīʿah gambling is strictly prohibited (Qur'ān, 2: 219), and as stated above speculation is not prohibited unless it amounts to a zero-sum game, which is akin to gambling. However, hedging and avoiding risk is in line with Sharīʿah and is encouraged (Qur'ān, 12: 47–9; and the tradition of the Prophet (pbuh) in Sunan al-Tirmidhi (4/668); Imam al-Bayhaqi, Syu'bul Iman (2/80); Sahih Ibnu Hibban (2/510)[7]). The following ḥadīth is one often quoted to illustrate the fact that in Sharīʿah risk management is necessary.

A companion of the Prophet (pbuh), Anas bin Mālik (may Allah be pleased with him), narrated that a man asked the Prophet: 'O Messenger of Allah, should I tie [my camel] and place my trust [in *Allah*], or should I leave it untied and trust [in *Allah*]?' The Prophet answered: 'Tie it and trust [in *Allah*].'

(Collected by al-Tirmidhi and al-Bayhaqi)

The sources from the *Qur'ān* and *ḥadīth* show that, as long as it is done through *Sharīʿah*, acceptable means risk avoidance and hedging should be pursued. As stated by Elgari:

There is nothing in *sharīʿah* that dictates on the believer to be reckless enough as to ignore risks around them. It is not contrary to basic Islamic belief, to reckon that God is the supreme power and eventually it is His will that will always prevail. Yet, His will remains supreme because even avoiding risk is happening within His glorious will.

(Elgari, 2009: 2)

Islamic forward-like contracts are used in Islamic banks' treasury departments to hedge against currency risk. This is exactly why Islamic derivatives have been approved in Islamic finance to hedge against currency risk.

For example, let us look at two scenarios:

Company *X* will be receiving USD10m, the price of crude oil exported by Company *X*, in six months. On the start date with a current spot rate of 3.2400, that will be equivalent to RM32.4m. However, after six months the rate is 3.2000. Company *X* exchanges its USD10m and receives RM32.00m and has a loss of RM400,000.

If, on the other hand, Company *X* enters into a forward contract and locks in the exchange rate at 3.2400 then they will be receiving RM32.4m and will suffer no loss.

Naturally, the exchange rate could move in an opposite direction to, for example, 3.2600, which would result in a loss to Company *X* if it had hedged its position at the exchange rate of 3.2400. However, by hedging its position, Company *X* can safely plan for its future costs and claims. Without hedging, Company *X* would be at the mercy of the prevailing exchange rate and this could cause tremendous uncertainty, especially if a lot of its business is in exporting and dealing with foreign currency.

How do *Sharīʿah* advisers ensure that the bank uses the instruments for hedging purposes only? As explained by *Sharīʿah* advisers of banks, the criteria used is the business requirement of a particular customer. For example, only businesses with trade commitments are allowed FX-related derivatives, which include the Islamic forward contract. The treasury personnel interviewed in the course of this research have also indicated that they make sure that there is an actual need for the client to enter into Islamic derivatives, that is, that it is for hedging purposes, before they carry out the transaction.

The following sections turn to the structures of Islamic fowards used in Islamic banks.

8.5 Islamic Forward Contracts Used in Islamic banks: Structures

In this section certain Islamic forward contracts are used as case studies to explain current Islamic forward contracts used in Islamic banks.

8.5.1 FX Forward Product -i

This is a contractual obligation by two parties to pay, on a forward value date, the price of a commodity purchased on the transaction date in order to facilitate the exchange of currencies between the two parties.

For example, let us say that a customer wants to buy USD/MYR on a forward date of 2 June 2010. On the transaction date, the customer approaches the bank expressing the need to enter into a Forward-i. The bank will quote the forward USD/MYR rate based on the Forward-i structure of Commodity *bai muajjal*. If both parties agree, the transaction will be done through the Forward-i structure. On the forward value date, the customer will pay MYR while the bank will pay USD at the rate as agreed on the transaction date. The process is explained in Figure 8.1.

The customer wants to buy USD 1 million against MYR for a forward value at USD/MYR of 3.50.

(i) The customer appoints the Islamic bank as agent to buy commodity X from broker B for RM3.50 million on deferred payment. Payment will be made on the forward value date. Delivery of commodity X is on a spot basis.

(ii) The customer then sells the commodity X to the Islamic bank for USD 1 million on deferred payment. Payment will be made on the forward date. Delivery of commodity X is on spot basis.

(iii) The Islamic bank sells commodity X to broker A for RM3.5 million on deferred payment. Payment will be made on the forward value date. Delivery of commodity X is on a spot basis.

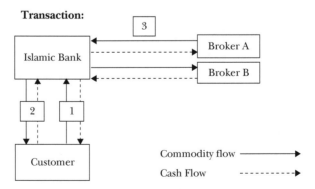

Figure 8.1 FX Forward Product –i

The above structure uses a commodity as an underlying and thus does not affect the rules of *sarf*. The next two structures on the other hand are currency exchanges without any commodities underlying.

8.5.2 FX Forward Wa'd-i Product

A FX forward *wa'd*-i product is a unilateral contract involving two parties, where the first party promises with the later party to buy/sell currency for settlement on a forward value date at the rate and amount agreed today. The party who makes the promise is obliged to honour the contract; however, the other party is not obliged to do the same. The process is decpicted in Figure 8.2.

(i) The customer promises on 24 June 2010 to buy USD 10 million from an Islamic bank on 24 July 2010 at exchange rate 3.2700. The customer is bound by the unilateral promise.

(ii) On 24 July 2010, the bank will pay USD 10 million and receives MYR 32.7 million from the customer.

The currency exchange is complete and the customer receives USD 10 million at the exchange rate 3.27000 regardless of the market rate.

Transaction:

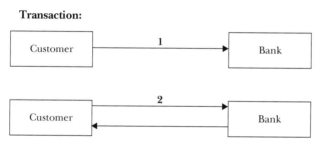

Figure 8.2 FX Forward *Wa'd*-i Product

8.5.3 Islamic FX Outright (Based on Unilateral wa'ds)

The Islamic FX Outright is used to manage currency risks and allows customers to exchange one currency into a second currency at a future date at a pre-agreed rate. The transaction process is depicted in Figure 8.3.

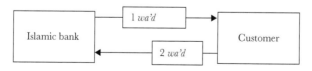

Figure 8.3 Islamic FX Outright (Based on Unilateral *wa'ds*)

Transaction:

  (i) The Islamic bank will undertake (*wa'd*) to the customer to exchange currency 1 against currency 2 at a pre-agreed rate at a future date. Through a second and independent *wa'd*, the customer will undertake to the Islamic bank to exchange currency 2 against currency 1 at a pre-agreed rate at a future date.

  (ii) On the future date, the investor and the bank agree to execute one *wa'd* and to give up the other one.

  (iii) On the maturity date, one promise will be given up, and the other one will be executed in order to exchange the two currencies.

In the above two structures the dominant Islamic instrument used is the *wa'd*, unilateral promise. The issue arises as to the rules of *sarf*, which is addressed next.

8.6 *Bai Al-Sarf* (Currency Exchange)

Islamic forward contracts, as discussed above, involve the exchange of money of different type or *genus*. When currency exchange is involved the rules of *sarf* apply:

> Ubida b. al-Simit (*Allah* be pleased with him) reported *Allah*'s Messenger (*pbuh*) as saying: gold is to be paid for by gold, silver by silver, wheat by wheat, barley by barley, dates by dates, and salt by salt, like for like and equal for equal, payment being made hand to hand. If these classes differ, then sell as you wish if payment is made hand to hand.
>
> (*Sahih Muslim*, Book 10, The Book of Transactions, *ḥadīth* 3853)[8]

> Narrated by Abdullah ibn Umar: I used to sell camels at al-Baqi for dinars and take dirhams for them, and sell for dirhams and take dinars for them. I would take these for these and give these for these. I went to the Apostle of *Allah* (*pbuh*) who was in the house of Hafsah. I said: Apostle of *Allah*, take it easy, I shall ask you (a question): I sell camels at al-Baqi'. I sell (them) for dinars and take dirhams and I sell for dirhams and take dinars. I take these for these, and give these for these. The Apostle of *Allah* (*pbuh*) then said: There is no harm in taking them at the current rate so long as you do not separate leaving something to be settled.
>
> (*Sunan Abu Dawud*, Book 22, Commercial Transactions, No. 3348)[9]

Trading of currencies is thus required to be done hand-to-hand in equal quantities in the same *genus*, or with different amounts in different *genera*. There are four general conditions for a currency exchange contract: first, the mutual receipt prior to the parting of the contracting parties, second the equality of quantities if monies of the same *genus* are traded, third the inapplicability of options and fourth there should not be deferment (Al-Zuhayli, 2003).

How does this ruling apply in Islamic forwards? To start with, let us discuss the second and third conditions. The second condition would not apply in the exchange of two different currencies because they are of different *genera* and therefore can be exchanged for different quantities. As for the third condition as to options, there are no options in these Islamic forward contracts, thus this condition is not violated.

The first and fourth condition (that there must be mutual receipt of the currency before the parting of the two contracting and that there must be no deferment), are two requirements that work hand-in-hand, since deferment prevents immediate receipt. Thus in currency exchange one of the important rules of exchange is that there must not be any deferment. Is this satisfied in an Islamic forward contract?

Is the *wa'd* made at the beginning of the Islamic forward transaction considered to be part of the *sarf?* If it is considered to be part of the currency exchange then there would seem to be deferment as one of the parties is promising to exchange one currency with another at a later date. However, a *wa'd* is a promise and may not be part of the *sarf.* In other words, the currency exchange takes placeonly at the forward date and that would be the date when the conditions for *sarf* apply.

Further, according to Accounting and Auditing Organization for Islamic Financial Institutions (AAOIFI) *Sharī'ah* Standard 1: Trading in currencies, 2/9:

> Bilateral Promises in Currency Trading: A bilateral promise is prohibited in currency trading when it is binding upon both parties, even when it is done to treat the risk of decline in a currency's value. As for a unilateral promise from one party, that is permissible, even if it is binding.

The AAOIFI Standard allows a unilateral promise or *wa'd* to be given in a currency exchange. Here distinctions have to be drawn between *al-wa'd*, a unilateral promise by one party, *al-wa'dan*, which are two independent unilateral promises given by two parties to each other but dependent on two different conditions, and *al-muwa'adah* where two bilateral promises are made by two parties which are dependent on each other. The first two promises are permissible; however, the last, bilateral, promise would seem to be prohibited in currency trading. In the Islamic forward structures that are discussed in this paper there were only unilateral promises and no bilateral promises discussed.

In summation, the rules of *sarf* may not be violated in the case of Islamic forward contracts.

8.7 The Way Forward

More transparency and clarity is required regarding the usage of Islamic derivatives. It is easy to criticise the structures; however, reality proves that currency risks are real and can cost businesses a lot of losses. If Islamic derivatives are not created and are dismissed as being nothing more than duplication of conventional counterparts, how can businesses compete in the real world and hedge against losses? However, at the same time it is hard to deny the uneasiness in usage in the Islamic financial industry. This was gathered when the author was collecting data for this research.

There is an avenue for further research in risk shifting or risk sharing. The solution for hedging at the moment is through Islamic derivatives; however, research has to be done in the field for the underlying cause and the need of Islamic derivatives. By introducing Islamic derivatives the symptoms of the problems are being treated – fluctuations in currency exchange. If the industry really wants to deal with the problem more research and resources must go into researching solutions to treat the source and not the symptoms. Once the source is treated the symptoms will automatically be eliminated and the need for suspect instruments will be done away with.

Currently, there is a definite need for hedging instruments; the risks are real and can affect businesses adversely. If Islamic banking and finance cannot provide for the needs of the industry then the industry will seek conventional financing solutions. The lesser evils should always be pursued and thus Islamic banking and finance has to provide solutions for hedging. For a start Islamic forward contracts are being used to hedge against currency risk.

Notes

1. A derivative is defined as 'a financial instrument whose value depends on the value of other, more basic variables' (Hull, 2005: 1). For definitions of futures and options see Kunhibava (2010) available at www.isra.my/publications/research-paper.html.
2. Reported by Al-Khamsa. Bukhari and Abu Dawud graded it *Daif* (weak). Al-Tirmidhi, Ibn Khuzaima, Ibn Al-Jarud, Ibn Hibban, Al-Hakim and Ibn Al-Qattan graded it *Sahih* (authentic). No. 685, 'The Book of Business Transactions', compiled by Ibn Hajar al-Asqalani (2002) in Bulugh Al-Maram, *Attainment of the Objective According to the Evidence of Ordinances*.
3. Reported by Al-Khamsa. Al-Tirmidhi, Ibn Khuzaima, and Al-Hakim graded it *Sahih* (authentic). No. 667, 'The Book of Business Transactions', compiled by Ibn Hajar al-Asqalani (2002) in Bulugh Al-Maram, *Attainment of the Objective According to the Evidence of Ordinances*.
4. See Kunhibava (2010) available at www.isra.my/publications/research-paper.html, for full set of arguments and counter-arguments on this issue.
5. In Islam, wealth creation is important rather than wealth transfer because wealth decays and new wealth must be created in order to replace the old wealth (Diwany, 2003). If only wealth transfer was to take place the stock of wealth would not be enough and would eventually be held by a few fortunate human beings. Wealth creation is therefore necessary for the equal distribution of wealth and more fundamentally for the survival of humankind (Diwany, 2003).
6. This answer was from *Sharīᶜah* scholars of an international bank. Question was asked in March 2010.
7. For further discussion on hedging in *Sharīᶜah* see Dusuki (2009).
8. Translated by Abdul Hamid Siddiqui ('Sahih Muslim').
9. Translated by Ahmad Hasan, see 'Sunan Abu Dawud'.

References

Al-Asqalani, Al-Hafiz Ibn Hajar (2002). *Bulugh Al-Maram Attainment of the Objective According to Evidence of the Ordinances*. Riyadh: Darussalam.

Al-Suwailem, S. (1999) 'Towards an objective measure of *gharar* in exchange', *Islamic Economic Studies* 7: 61–102.

Al-Suwailem, S. (2002) 'Decision-making under uncertainty: An Islamic perspective', in M. Iqbal and D. Llewellyn (eds), *Islamic Banking and Finance*. Cheltenham: Edward Elgar, pp. 15–30.

Al-Suwailem, Sami (2006). *Hedging in Islamic Finance*, Occasional Paper No. 10, Jeddah: Islamic Research and Training Institute.

Al-Tirmidhi (1975). *Sunan al-Tirmdhi*. Mesir: Maktabah Mustafaal-Babi al-Halabi.

Al-Zuhayli, Wahbah (2003). *Financial Transactions in Islamic Jurisprudence*. Vol. 1. Trans. M. A. El-Gamal. Damascus: Dar al-Fikr.

Bacha, Obiyathulla Ismath (1999). 'Derivative instruments and Islamic finance: Some thoughts for a reconsideration', *International Journal of Islamic Financial Services* 1(1) (April–June).

Dar, Humayon (2007). *Sharīᶜah Issues with Islamic Hedge Funds*. Available at: http://islamicfinanceandbanking.blogspot.com/2007/01/shariah-issues-with-islamic-hedge.html, last accessed 18 January 2010.

Diwany, Tarek El (2003). *The Problem with Interest*. 2nd edn. London: Kreatoc Ltd.

Dusuki, Asyraf Wajdi (2009). '*Sharīᶜah* parameters on the Islamic foreign exchange swap as a hedging mechanism in Islamic finance', *ISRA International Journal of Islamic Finance*, 1(1): 77–99.

El-Gamal, M. (2001). *An Economic Explication of the Prohibition of Gharar in Classical Islamic Jurisprudence*. Paper prepared for the 4th International Conference on Islamic Economics to be held in Loughborough University, UK, 13–15 August 2000. Available at: http://www.ruf.rice.edu/~elgamal, last accessed 1 October 2010.

Elgari, Mohammed Ali (2009). *The Islamic Perspective on Derivatives*, Paper presented at The Frontiers of Innovation in Islamic Finance, Second Oxford Islamic Finance Roundtable, organised by Oxford Centre for Islamic Studies and Securities Commission, Malaysia.

Gupta, S. L. (2006). *Financial Derivatives Theory, Concepts and Problems*. New Delhi: Prentice-Hall of India.

Hull, J. C. (2005). *Options, Futures and Other Derivatives*. 6th edn. Upper Saddle River, NJ: Prentice Hall.

Hull, John C. (2006). *Options, Futures and Other Derivatives*. 7th edn. Upper Saddle River, NJ: Pearson Education Inc.

Investorwords.com (2010). *Investment*. Available at: www.investorwords.com/2599/investment.html, last accessed 30 March 2010.

Ismail, Abdul Ghafar (2010). *Money, Islamic Banks and the Real Economy*. Singapore: Cengage Learning Asia Pte Ltd.

Kahf, M. (2002). *Islam's Stance on Commodities or Futures Market*, 6 September. Available at: www.islamonline.net/servlet/Satellite?cid=1119503544954&pagename=IslamOnline_English-Ask_Scholar52FFatwaE%2FPrintFatwaE, last accessed 11 October 2006.

Kamali, M. H. (1991). *Principles of Islamic Jurisprudence*. Cambridge: Islamic Text Society of Cambridge.

Kamali, M. H. (1999). 'Prospects for an Islamic derivative market in Malaysia', *Thunderbird International Business Review* 4(5): 523–40.

Kamali, Mohammad Hashim (2002). *Islamic Commercial Law: An Analysis of Futures and Options*. Cambridge: Islamic Texts Society.

Khan, Akram (1988). 'Commodity exchange and stock exchange in Islamic economy', *The American Journal of Islamic Social Sciences* 5(1): 91–114.

Khan, M. Fahim (1997). 'Islamic futures markets as a means for mobilizing resources for development', in A. Ausaf and T. Khan (eds), *Islamic Financial Instruments for Public Sector Resource Mobilization*. Jeddah: IRTI, pp. 133–63.

Khan, M. Fahim (2000). *Islamic Futures and their Markets: With Special Reference to their Role in Developing Rural Financial Market*, Research Paper No. 32, Jeddah: Islamic Research and Training Institute.

Kolb, Robert W. and Overdahl, James A. (eds) (2010). *Financial Derivatives Pricing and Risk Management*. Hobohen, NJ: John Wiley and Sons.

Kunhibava, Sherin (2010). *Derivatives in Islamic Finance*. Kuala Lumpur: ISRA.

Mahmassani, Subhi (1983). *al Mawjibat wa al-uqud fi al Fiqh al-Islami*. Beirut: Dar al Ilm al Malayin.

Obaidullah, M. (1998). 'Financial engineering with Islamic options', *Islamic Economic Studies* 6(1): 73–103.

Obaidullah M. (2002). 'Islamic risk management: Towards greater ethics and efficiency', *International Journal of Islamic Financial Services* 3: 1–18.

OIC Fiqh Academy (2000). *Resolution and Recommendations of the Council of the Islamic Fiqh Academy (1985–2000)*. Available at: www.islamibankbd.com/page/oicres.htm#10(10/2), last accessed 2 January 2007.

Rosly, S. A. (2005). *Critical Issues on Islamic Banking and Financial Markets*. Kuala Lumpur: Dinamas.

Sahih Muslim. Available at: www.searchtruth.com/hadith_books.php, last accessed 12 April 2010.

Smolarski, Jan, Schapek, Michael and Tahir, Mohammad Iqbal (2006). 'Permissibility and use of options for hedging purposes in Islamic finance', *Thunderbird International Business Review* 48(3): 425–43.

Stulz, Rene M. (2003). *Risk Management and Derivatives*. Ohio: Thompson Southwestern.

Sunan Abu Dawud. Available at: www.searchtruth.com/book_display.php?book=22&translator=3&start=10&number=3335, last accessed 12 April 2010.

Vogel, Frank E., and Hayes, III, Samuel L. (1998). *Islamic Law & Finance: Religion, Risk and Return*. The Hague: Kluwer Law International.

9

ENHANCING GOVERNANCE, ACCOUNTABILITY AND TRANSPARENCY IN ISLAMIC FINANCIAL INSTITUTIONS: AN EXAMINATION INTO *SHARĪ'AH* INTERNAL CONTROL AUDIT

Zurina Shafii and Supiah Salleh

9.1 Introduction

Malaysia has been embracing the practice of Islamic banking and finance for twenty-five years since its first establishment of Bank Islam Malaysia Berhad (BIMB) and Takaful Malaysia in 1984 and 1985 respectively. Since then, the investors have been relying on self-reporting regarding *Sharī'ah*-compliance by the *Sharī'ah* Committee (SC) of the relevant institutions. This is the requirement of Bank Negara Malaysia's (BNM) guidelines of GPS-1 on the role and responsibilities of *Sharī'ah* Supervisory Boards of Islamic financial institutions. The practice is similar to other Islamic Financial Institutions (IFIs) in the world, that is, reporting in IFIs is done at the internal level and only as related to the *Sharī'ah*-compliance matters and not to the internal control and financial statement audit.

There is an increasing need of external auditors' corroboration or audit on (a) the *Sharī'ah*-compliance of the IFIs, (b) internal control procedures and (c) the financial statements. This is for the following reasons:

(i) In the capital market, the *Sharī'ah* Advisory Council (SAC) of the Securities Commission Malaysia twice yearly announces to the public the *Sharī'ah*-compliant securities listed in Bursa Malaysia, including shares, warrants and other securities. The responsibility rests with the SAC team to audit the companies to ensure their *Sharī'ah*-compliant status. To enhance efficiency, the *Sharī'ah*-compliant companies could be given the responsibilities to report on their *Sharī'ah*-compliancy with the help of *Sharī'ah* external auditors.

(ii) In the banking sector, BNM requires the IFIs to comply with the *Sharī'ah* with its announcing the GPS-1 that states the roles and responsibilities of SAC at the BNM level and SC at the IFIs level. The reporting is done at the internal level with SC reports in the annual reports ensuring that IFIs comply with the *Sharī'ah*. The value of the report could be enhanced by making the IFIs have their audit performed by external *Sharī'ah* auditors.

External *Sharīʿah* audit in this paper is defined by the audit of (a) the *Sharīʿah*-compliance of the IFIs, (b) internal control procedures and (c) the financial statements of IFIs conducted by the *Sharīʿah* auditors appointed by the shareholders of the IFIs.

In the study we will highlight the need for an external *Sharīʿah* audit in order to address the specific risk of operational risk. We will distinguish the practice of *Sharīʿah*-compliance audits in comparison to the proposed practice of *Sharīʿah* external audits. We are proposing for the IFIs to engage in external *Sharīʿah* audits that have the characteristics of (a) to (c) above. Specifically, we are proposing one of the *Sharīʿah* internal control elements, that is, the use of *Sharīʿah* internal control lists/questionnaires. We adapt the *Sharīʿah* internal control list/questionnaire to the two banks, that is, BIMB and BIB. This *Sharīʿah* internal control list/questionnaire can be adopted by the external *Sharīʿah* auditors to audit the IFIs.

9.2 Framework for *Sharīʿah* Audit Process

In developing an overall audit plan, auditors have four types of tests that they can use to determine whether the financial statements are fairly stated. It can be divided into two major areas. The first part is to satisfy the demand of test of control. During normal audit practice a test of control is conducted during an interim audit whereby it is performed before the company's financial year ends. A test of control is done to check the internal control system of a company as well as whether the operational systems of the company comply with laws and regulations. The second part is to satisfy the substantive test requirement. A substantive test is conducted at the end of each accounting period, which is also known as final audit stage. At this stage the auditor will audit the financial statements of a company based on the samples taken.

This research identifies the audit test as a framework for the *Sharīʿah* audit process. The overall *Sharīʿah* audit process can be illustrated based on Figure 9.1.

In this study, we address issues related to the first part of the audit test, that is, the test of control. A test of control is performed to determine the appropriate-

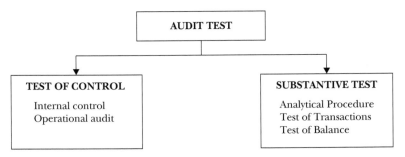

Figure 9.1 *Sharīʿah* Audit Test

ness of the design and operating effectiveness of specific internal controls. We have developed a *Sharīʿah* internal control checklist in order to assess the internal control system of two selected Islamic banks. The internal control checklist will be discussed thoroughly in the next section in this chapter.

9.3 Risk Management in Islamic Financial Institutions

The *Guiding Principles of Risk Management for Institutions (other than Insurance Institutions)* published by the Islamic Financial Services Board (IFSB) categorises risks in IFIs into six categories: credit risk, investment risk, market risk, liquidity risk, rate of return risk and, finally, operational risk. This chapter will focus on the management of operational risk in IFIs by way of carrying out proper *Sharīʿah*-compliance audits of the IFIs. The *Guiding Principles of Risk Management for Institutions (other than Insurance Institutions) offering only Islamic Financial Institutions (IIFS)* presents fifteen principles covering the general principles and specific risks mentioned above according to the IFSB, which are, as follows:

General Principle
Principle 1: Islamic Financial Institutions should have a comprehensive risk management and reporting process in place. The process should consider appropriate steps to comply with *Sharīʿah* rules and principles and to ensure the adequacy of relevant risk reporting to the supervisory authority.

Credit Risk
Principle 2: IFIs should have a strategy for financing. The instruments used must be in compliance with the *Sharīʿah*, whereby it recognises the potential credit exposures that may arise at different stages of the various financing agreements.

Principle 3: IFIs shall carry out a due diligence review in respect of counterparties prior to deciding on the choice of an appropriate Islamic financing instrument.

Principle 4: IFIs should have appropriate methodologies for measuring and reporting the credit risk exposures arising under each Islamic financing instrument.

Principle 5: IFIs should have in place *Sharīʿah*-compliant credit risk mitigating techniques appropriate for each Islamic financing instrument.

Investment Risk
Principle 6: IFIs should have appropriate strategies in place for risk management and reporting processes in respect of the risk characteristics of equity investments, including *mudārabah* and *mushārakah* investments.

Principle 7: IFIs must ensure that their valuation methodologies are appropriate and consistent, and they should conduct the assessment on the potential effects of their methods on profit calculations and allocations. The methods shall be mutually agreed between the IFI and the *mudarib* and/or *mushārakah* partners.

Principle 8: IFIs should, in respect of their equity investment activities, including extension and redemption conditions for *mudārabah* and *mushārakah* investments, define and establish exit strategies that must be subject to the approval of the institution's *Sharīʿah* board.

Market Risk
Principle 9: In respect of all assets held, IFIs should have in place an appropriate framework for market risk management (including reporting) and also for those that do not have a ready market and/or are exposed to high price volatility.

Liquidity Risk
Principle 10: IFIs should have in place a liquidity management framework (including reporting) taking into account separately and on an overall basis their liquidity exposures in respect of each category of current accounts, unrestricted and restricted investment accounts.

Principle 11: IFIs should assume liquidity risk commensurate with their ability to have sufficient recourse to *Sharīʿah*-compliant funds to mitigate such risk.

Rate of Return Risk
Principle 12: A comprehensive risk management and reporting process should be established by IFIs in order to assess the potential effects of market factors affecting rates of return on assets in comparison with the expected rates of return for investment account holders (IAHs).

Principle 13: IFIs must ensure that an appropriate framework for managing displaced commercial risk is in place, where applicable.

Operational Risk
Principle 14: IFIs should have in place adequate systems and controls, including *Sharīʿah* board or advisor, to ensure compliance with *Sharīʿah* rules and principles.

Principle 15: IFIs should have in place appropriate mechanisms to safeguard the interests of all fund providers.

After identifying the IFSB defined principles for the relevant risk areas, the following section discusses the operational risk in relation to *Sharīʿah* audit practice.

9.4 Addressing Operational Risk via *Sharīᶜah* Audit Practice

In developed economies, auditing is deemed significant because the process of wealth creation and political stability depends heavily on confidence in processes of accountability and on how well the expected roles are being fulfilled (Sikka *et al.*, 1998). As such, the courts, regulatory agencies and various stakeholder groups have played their parts in demanding that the profession move in an expeditious fashion to meet its responsibilities as perceived by the public (see Humphrey et al., 1992).

Grais and Pellegrini (2006) focused on the limitations in relying on the *Sharīᶜah* compliance assurance to the internal party (that is, the *Sharīᶜah* Committee). They also proposed in their study an effective framework to monitor and assess *Sharīᶜah* compliance. These findings are similar to those of the study conducted by Mansor (2007) that discovered that even though the auditors are responsible for auditing the financial statement and providing reasonable assurance that the financial statement is free from material misstatement, the external auditors did not assess or audit whether the transaction made by a *Sharīᶜah*-listed company is free from unlawful transactions, which are outlined by the *Qur'ān* and *Sunnah*. Mansor (2007) also proposed in his study that there should be a proper framework for the external auditors to check the IFIs.

In Malaysia's setting, a study by Shahul and Mulyany (2007) explores the perception of accounting academics, audit practitioners and Sharīᶜah scholars of the practice of Sharīᶜah audit for IFIs. The study highlights the importance of developing a proper governance of the *Sharīᶜah*-compliance issues.

The increased complexity of transactions in the unpredictable economy also increases the requirement of producing *Sharīᶜah* audits of the financial reporting. Even though there is discussion about the importance of corporate governance, the practical impact is still small when it comes to ensuring the quality of *Sharīᶜah* auditing in financial reporting (Adawiah, 2007).

According to Adawiah (2007), there are seven parts of *Sharīᶜah*-compliance governance that need to be fulfilled. These can be illustrated through Figure 9.2.

However, the current processes of *Sharīᶜah* audit in Malaysia are looking at only three aspects, which are inception and conceptualisation of an Islamic product, structuring the rules and principles according to the *Sharīᶜah*, and legal documentation procedures. The other four parts are still being developed in Malaysia. For the audit review stage, the process is still not yet formalised at the regulatory level. Even though some banks may impose it at an internal department level such as their internal audit department, there is no independent party being appointed to audit the financial report of the Islamic Financial Institutions.

The latest study, which is more comprehensive in identifying the issues and challenges of the *Sharīᶜah* audit, was conducted by Abdul Rahim (2008). He argued that the *Sharīᶜah* audit is needed to complement the current governance

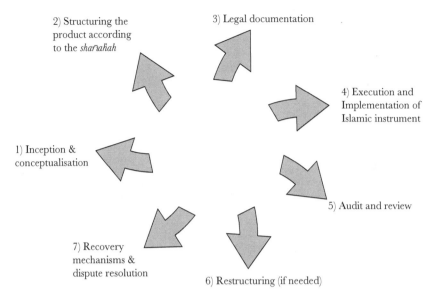

2) Structuring the product according to the *sharīaīah*

3) Legal documentation

4) Execution and Implementation of Islamic instrument

1) Inception & conceptualisation

5) Audit and review

7) Recovery mechanisms & dispute resolution

6) Restructuring (if needed)

Figure 9.2 *Sharīʿah*-Compliance Governance

mechanism of the Islamic financial services industry. Abdul Rahim (2008) also discussed in his paper some challenges that are considered as pre-requisites to effectively undertake a *Sharīʿah* audit.

The success of any kind of audit depends on the strength of human resources. The critical success factor is having expertise to do the *Sharīʿah* audit and having credible people setting the work plan and reviewing the results. Although *Sharīʿah* audits have not been made mandatory, hopefully such legislation will be passed since there is a gap between issued *fatwās* and the respective implementations. Even though there is no legislation requiring an external *Sharīʿah* audit, we expect the demand to grow and get more attention from the central banks, securities commissions and other Islamic Financial Institutions.

9.5 Governance, Accountability and Transparency measures in IFIs

9.5.1 Audit of Operations – Sharīʿah-Compliance

Accountability and transparency are major items in ensuring good governance. While governance itself is not uniquely defined in its various uses, as we shall discuss shortly, most definitions of the term implicitly or explicitly embrace the principles of accountability and transparency. Many examples can be cited in support of this position. A typical example of this is provided by Paul Wolfowitz, former president of the World Bank, who in a 2006 speech in Jakarta stated:

In the last half-century, we have developed a better understanding of what helps governments function effectively and achieve economic progress. In the development community, we have a phrase for it. We call it good governance. It is essentially the combination of transparent and accountable institutions, strong skills and competence, and a fundamental willingness to do the right thing.

According to the Governance Standard for Islamic Financial Institutions No. 6 (GSIFI) of AAOIFI, governance practices play a vital role in ensuring that businesses are run in a prudent and sound manner. A loss of confidence in financial institutions has the potential to create severe economic dysfunction, adversely affecting the general community in which they operate. A strong governance structure is expected to lead to an enhanced *Sharīʿah*-compliance structure.

IFIs are required to operate in a *Sharīʿah*-compliant manner. This is discharged through a report signed by the *Sharīʿah* advisor of the financial institutions that the company is operating under the *Sharīʿah* requirements. The *Sharīʿah* audit framework is the frame of reference to be used by the *Sharīʿah* auditors to audit the financial statements of Islamic financial institutions before they can decide that the operation of the business is performed in a manner that does not contradict the *Sharīʿah*. At present, the practice in the banking and *takāful* industry is that the *Sharīʿah* advisor depends on the work of internal auditors or on a voluntary appointment of external *Sharīʿah* auditors to audit the financial statements and determine that these documents reflect the compliancy of their operations with the *Sharīʿah*. In developing the Islamic capital market, several Islamic principles, such as the prohibition of *ribā*, *gharar* and *maysir*, dealing in sinful activities, must be integrated into the structure. In addition, every contract has to be performed lawfully, following the acceptable contract objectives. These requirements can be used as the guiding principles that have to be observed by the *Sharīʿah* committee.

As a *Sharīʿah* audit is the process to attest that all *Sharīʿah* concerns are being taken care of, the framework for the *Sharīʿah* audit can begin with the examination on the GPS-1 of BNM Guidelines on the Governance of the *Sharīʿah* Committee for the Islamic Financial Institutions. The guidelines state the roles of the *Sharīʿah* Committee towards the Islamic financial institution to which they are attached, which took effect on the 1 April 2005, and it has the broad objectives to become 'an effective *Sharīʿah* framework [which] would serve to ensure uniformity and harmonization of *Sharīʿah* interpretations that will strengthen the regulatory framework and governance practices for the Islamic financial industry'.

The *Sharīʿah* compliance audit framework should inform the *Sharīʿah* committee as to how they can discharge their professional duties to the board of directors, which has to make sure that the company operates under the *Sharīʿah* guidelines.

The guidelines by the BNM aim at achieving the following:

(i) to set out the rules, regulations and procedures in the establishment of a *Sharīʿah* Committee

(ii) to define the role, scope of duties and responsibilities of a *Sharīʿah* Committee
(iii) to define the relationship and working arrangement between a *Sharīʿah* Committee and the SAC of BNM.

Part E of the guidelinestates the duties and responsibilities of the *Sharīʿah* Committee and the Islamic financial institutions. The main duties and responsibilities of the *Sharīʿah* Committee are as follows:

(i) To advise the board on *Sharīʿah* matters in its business operation.
(ii) To endorse a S*harīʿah*-compliance manual. A document outlines that the request for advice is made to the *Sharīʿah* committee, outlines the conduct of the *Sharīʿah* committee's meeting as well as the manner of compliance with any *Sharīʿah* decision.
(iii) To endorse and validate relevant documentations, including the proposal form, contract, agreement or other legal documentation used in executing the transactions. Other documentations are product manuals, marketing advertisements, sales illustrations and brochures.
(iv) To assist related parties on *Sharīʿah* matters for advice upon request.
(v) To advise on matters to be referred to the SAC.
(vi) To provide written *Sharīʿah* opinion.
(vii) To assist the SAC on reference for advice.

The GPS-1 guidelines can be a starting point for us to establish a *Sharīʿah* compliance framework where it can enlighten the *Sharīʿah* Committee on how to discharge their duties and responsibilities stated above. In (a), the *Sharīʿah* Committee's duties to advise the board on *Sharīʿah* matters in its business operations encompass a large area of responsibilities. This document proposes that the *Sharīʿah*-compliance audit be carried out for all the products offered by the Islamic financial institutions, following the audit programs established by the IFIs and endorsed by the *Sharīʿah* Committee. This shall form part of the *Sharīʿah* Committee's disposal of duties under item (a).

The document can act as a theoretical framework of the *Sharīʿah*-compliance audit as the guidelines stated that the scope of documentation audit falls under the responsibility of the SC. The S*harīʿah*-compliance audit framework may begin by establishing an audit program to audit these documents (proposal form, contract, agreement or other legal documentation used in executing the transactions, product manuals, marketing advertisements, sales illustrations and brochures) for each of the products stated as *Sharīʿah*-compliant. The *Sharīʿah*-compliance of the operations based on these documentations, in turn, can be attested against the various sources ranging from regulations, *Sharīʿah* guidelines, accounting and auditing standards (AAOFIO).

Sources of attestation for *Sharīʿah* compliance audit for Islamic banks consist of the following, among others:

(i) Islamic banking Act 1983 (ACT 276)
(ii) Companies Act 1965

(iii) all guidelines and circulars issued by BNM regards to Islamic banking, that is, Financial Reporting – Guidelines on Financial Reporting for Licensed Islamic Banks

(iv) resolutions of *Sharīʿah* Advisory Council of Bank Negara Malaysia

(v) guidelines and circular by the *Sharīʿah* Advisory Council of the securities commission

(vi) *Sharīʿah* standards issued by AAOIFI

(vii) guiding principles issued by the Islamic Financial Services Board (IFSB)

(viii) internally developed standards (subject to *Sharīʿah* Committee approval), that is, a company's *Sharīʿah* manual

(ix) resolution and minutes of meetings of a company's *Sharīʿah* Committee

(x) additional reference (The OIC Fiqh Academy, the Islamic Research Institute of the al-Azhar University, Practise of internal auditing standard).

9.5.2 *Internal Control*

The internal control system is one of the areas that will be audited during the external audit process. However, in IFIs, the internal control system is being audited only from the point of conventional aspect. The elements of *Sharīʿah* are not included in the internal control framework. Since the *Sharīʿah* audit practices in IFIs at current covers the aspect of compliance only, the authors suggest that the internal control system of IFIs should be included when conducting *Sharīʿah* external audits.

9.5.2.1 *Defining and Describing Internal Control*

The role of internal control is to manage risk rather than to eliminate it. Internal control is one of the principal means by which risk is managed. Other devices used to manage risk include the transfer of risk to third parties, sharing risks, contingency planning and the withdrawal from unacceptably risky activities.

A system of internal control consists of policies and procedures designed to provide management with reasonable assurance that the company achieves its objectives and goals (Arens et al., 2008). A sound internal control system reflects the organisation being well managed by the company. An organisation that fails to impose a good internal control system may be facing a higher risk as compared to an organisation that has better control of its working environment. The higher the risk that the company faces the more likely it is to jeopardise the company's objectives. Generally, an organisation has three broad objectives in designing an effective internal control system, which can be outlined as follows:

(i) The reliability of financial reporting

Since the preparation financial reporting lies in the hand of the management, the management must ensure that the internal control system of the company is in good shape due to the expectations of external parties such as investors, creditors, financial institutions and other users. The management need to ensure that the financial reporting is not misleading. A good internal control system can ensure that the reporting is prepared in a truthful and fair way.

(ii) Efficiency and effectiveness of the operations

The management also holds responsibility for managing the resources efficiently and effectively in order to prevent the company from facing huge losses. Imposing a sound internal control system will minimise the risk of fraud and error among the workers in the organisation. Besides that it will also lead to better communication between the management and employees of the company.

(iii) Compliance with laws and regulations

All public companies are required to issue a report on the internal control system regarding the system's effectiveness. This report forms part of the annual report of each company.

The management thus designs a system of internal control to accomplish all three objectives mentioned above. The auditor's focus in both the audit of financial statements and the audit of internal controls is on those aspects related to the reliability of financial reporting plus those related to operations and to compliance with laws and regulations that could materially affect financial reporting.

According to *Internal Control: Guidance for Directors on the Combined Code* (the Turnbull Guidance), paragraph 17, the board's deliberations should include consideration of the following factors when determining a company's policies with regard to internal control and thereby assessing what constitutes a sound system of internal control in the particular circumstances of the company:

(i) the nature and extent of the risks facing the company
(ii) the extent and categories of risk that it regards as acceptable for the company to bear
(iii) the likelihood of the risks concerned materialising
(iv) the company's ability to reduce the incidence and effects on on the business of risks that do materialise; and the costs of operating particular controls relative to the benefit thereby obtained in managing the related risks.

In order to ensure the effectiveness of an internal control system, the operation and monitoring of the system of internal control should be undertaken by individuals who collectively possess the necessary skills, technical knowledge, objectivity and understanding of the company and the industries and markets in which it operates.

9.5.2.2 Components of Internal Control

A company's system of internal control commonly comprises five main components: control environment; identification and evaluation of risks and control

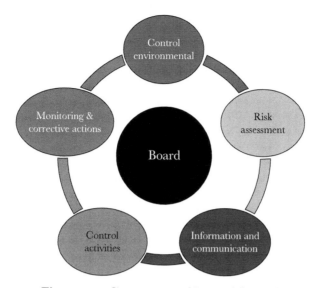

Figure 9.3 Components of Internal Control

Source: Adapted from The KPMG Review (1999: 22)

objectives; information and communication; control procedures; and monitoring and corrective action. The components of internal control can be seen as illustrated using the process in Figure 9.3.

Control environment

The control environment sets the tone of an organisation, influencing the control-consciousness of its people. It is the foundation for all other components of internal control, providing discipline and structure. Control environment factors include the integrity, ethical values and competence of the entity's people; management's philosophy and operating style; the way the management assigns authority and responsibility, organises and develops its people; and the attention and direction provided by the board of directors.

Identification and evaluation of risks and control objectives (risk assessment)

Every entity faces a variety of risks from external and internal sources that must be assessed. A precondition to risk assessment is the establishment of objectives, linked at different levels and internally consistent. Risk assessment is the identification and analysis of relevant risks to achievement of objectives, forming a basis for determining how the risks should be managed. Because economic, industry, regulatory and operating conditions will continue to change, mechanisms are needed to identify and deal with the special risks associated with change.

(a) Control activity

Control activities are the policies and procedures that help ensure that management directives are carried out. They help ensure that necessary actions are taken to address risks to achieve the entity's objectives. Control activities occur throughout the organisation, at all levels and in all functions. They include a range of activities as diverse as approvals, authorisations, verifications, reconciliations, reviews of operating performance, security of assets and segregation of duties.

(b) Information and communication

Pertinent information must be identified, captured and communicated in a form and timeframe that enables people to carry out their responsibilities. Information systems produce reports containing operational, financial and compliance-related information, which make it possible to run and control the business. They deal not only with internally generated data but also with information about external events, activities and conditions necessary to informed business decision-making and external reporting. Effective communication must also occur in a broader sense, flowing down, across and up the organisation channels. All personnel must receive a clear message from top management that control responsibilities must be taken seriously. They must understand their own role in the internal control system as well as how individual activities relate to the work of others. They must have a means of communicating significant information upstream. There also needs to be effective communication with external parties, such as customers, suppliers, regulators and shareholders.

(c) Monitoring

Internal control systems need to be monitored by a process that assesses the quality of the system's performance over time. This is accomplished through ongoing monitoring activities, separate evaluations, or a combination of the two. Ongoing monitoring occurs in the course of operations. It includes regular management and supervisory activities, and other actions personnel take in performing their duties. The scope and frequency of separate evaluations will depend primarily on an assessment of risks and the effectiveness of ongoing monitoring procedures. Internal control deficiencies should be reported upstream, with serious matters reported to top management and the board.

In order to ensure the effectiveness of the internal control system, all five common components of internal control and the nature and context of control should fit together. KPMG recommend that companies adopt or adapt a framework that can articulate how all the components fit together. Companies should then challenge themselves as to whether the standard is met. By using KPMG's Risk Management Diagnostic an organisation is able to challenge whether all the necessary components of a system of internal control exist. Furthermore, the existence of all components enables risk management to be embedded into the organisation. The framework is illustrated in Figure 9.4.

Furthermore, in order to understand the internal control system of an

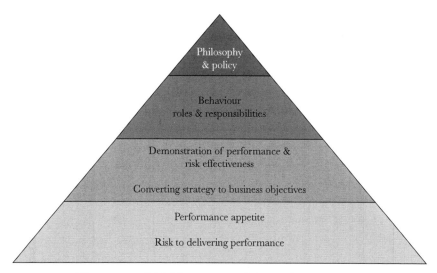

Figure 9.4 Risk Management Diagnostic Framework

Source: Adapted from The KPMG Review (1999: 25)

organisation, a few methods can be used such as the issuance of internal control questionnaires to employees, interviews to obtain client feedback, development of flowcharts of the system, and observation.

9.5.3 Sharīᶜah *Internal Control*

At current, the industry only focuses on the existing internal control system. With the emergence of Islamic Financial Institutions, there should be guidelines for measuring the *Sharīᶜah* internal control system. The definition for *Sharīᶜah* internal control also should be clearly outlined. Islamic Financial Institutions should include *Sharīᶜah* elements in designing their internal control system. This is because of the nature of the institutions that require the Islamic elements to be inculcated in the organisations.

A system of internal control of Islamic Financial Institutions consists of policies and procedures designed to provide the management with reasonable assurance that the company achieves its objectives and goals in line with the *Qur'ān* and *as-Sunnah*. The elements of *Sharīᶜah* should be inculcated in each of the components in the internal control system. According to the *Qur'ān* (4: 29):

> O ye who believe! Eat not up your property among yourselves in vanities: but let there be amongst you traffic and trade by mutual good-will: nor kill (or destroy) yourselves: for verily *Allah* hath been to you Most Merciful.

Overall, the *Sharīᶜah* internal control system can best be described by a combination of *Sharīᶜah*-compliance (as according to AAOIFI and BNM GPS1) and five major components of the internal control system. For example, in the control environment component, in order to ensure a higher level of integrity among the employees, the management of IFIs should explain to the employees the importance of the five pillars of Islam and the needs to fulfil these requirements. Employees with a high level of integrity will reduce the risk of fraud and error in the organisations. Only qualified, experienced and committed staff are recruited and retained as well as continuously trained and developed. SC involvement in the recruitment will encourage staff with the right aptitude and attitude. Thus, the organisation can rely on their employees to perform other important tasks and the other internal control components can be satisfied.

9.5.4 *Performing* Sharīʿah *Internal Control Audit in IFIs*

(i) Sharīʿah *ICQ*

Internal Control Questionnaires (ICQs) are a set of questionnaires that form one of the tools used to measure the effectiveness of the internal control system of an organisation. The set of questionnaires consists of a series of yes or no questions about the organisation's structure. Any no answers will help direct attention to areas and activities where there is a risk of human error and fraudulent activity. ICQs have been widely used by internal and external auditors during times of conducting audits. *Sharīʿah* ICQs are a set of questionnaires that have been proposed in this research as a tool to measure the effectiveness of the internal control system in Islamic Financial Institutions. By using this type of questionnaire, the management or auditors will be able to detect areas that need special attention and thorough investigation.

(ii) Sharīʿah *Internal Control Checklist*

Sharīʿah internal control checklist is a type of informational aid used to assist in performing audit work. It will reduce failure in detecting the risk by compensating for potential limits of human memory and attention. It helps to ensure consistency and completeness in carrying out a task. It is a list of schedules that lays out tasks to be done according to the area required. Since this research is using annual reports as main data, *Sharīʿah* control checklists are the most suitable tools to measure the effectiveness of internal control reporting in the annual report of IFIs.

(iii) *Interviews*

Interviews are often conducted to gather basic data or background knowledge on specific information needed. Interviews can be structured according to the following criteria:

(a) direction of the information flow: Information is given to or requested from the interviewee
(b) interview structure: one-to-one session or in groups
(c) form of communication: verbal or written.

Through interviews, any deficiency or loopholes in the internal control system can be detected, and corrective and preventive action can thus be implemented.

9.6 Proposed *Sharīʿah* Internal Control Checklist

This research focuses on two banks: Bank Islam Malaysia Berhad (BIMB) and Bahrain Islamic Bank (BIB). The selection of these two banks is based on the argument that they are established in two different countries where the Islamic banking and finance has been immensely developed. Other researchers such as Shahul and Mulyany (2007) also used BIMB and BIB in measuring the Islamicity index in their research. The use of an internal control system among these two banks will be measured using the *Sharīʿah* internal control checklist on the annual report of each bank. Any disclosure of information in the annual report is considered good and it reflects the transparency between the bank and the shareholders. One point will thus be awarded accordingly.

Sharīʿah ICQs are a set of questionnaires that have been proposed in this research as a tool to measure the effectiveness of internal control systems in Islamic Financial Institutions. All the items chosen are prepared according to GPS1 Bank Negara Malaysia Berhad, Guidelines on the Governance of *Sharīʿah* Committee for the Islamic Financial Institutions and Governance Standard for Islamic Financial Institutions (GSIFI) of Accounting, Auditing and Governance Standards for Islamic Financial Institutions (AAOIFI, 2008), which regulate the governance of the *Sharīʿah* Committee of an Islamic financial institution. However, *Sharīʿah* ICQs can only be used when a formal *Sharīʿah* audit is performed in IFIs. The data in this paper is obtained from the financial statements of IFIs and not through *Sharīʿah* audits, thus only the *Sharīʿah* internal control checklist can be produced.

This *Sharīʿah* internal control checklist can be segregated into two major parts, namely the *Sharīʿah*-compliance indicator and five main components of the internal control system indicator. For each piece of information disclosed, the symbol 'yes' will be given and subsequently will be awarded 1 point. However, if the item is not disclosed in the annual report, the symbol 'no' will be assigned and 0 points will subsequently be awarded. At the end of the marking process, the total information available will be divided by the total information that should be reported. Each indicator, that is, the *Sharīʿah*-compliance indicator and the five main components of the internal control system indicator will be assigned weights and each respective weight should reflect their level of importance.

In the research conducted by Shahul and Mulyany (2007) there are three major indicators being highlighted in order to calculate the Islamicity index for an Islamic bank, namely the *Sharīʿah*-compliance indicator, the corporate governance indicator and the social responsibility indicator. Since this paper focuses on enhancing governance, accountability and transparency in Islamic Financial Institutions, we chose to follow the guidelines according to GPS1 Bank Negara Malaysia Berhad, Guidelines on the Governance of *Sharīʿah* Committee for the

Islamic Financial Institutions and Governance Standard for Islamic Financial Institutions (GSIFI) of Accounting, Auditing and Governance Standards for Islamic Financial Institutions (AAOIFI, 2008).

Accordingly, Table 9.1 shows the internal checklist items as part of examining corporate governance.

Based on the internal control checklist above, the result can be summarised in Table 9.2.

Both of the banks are being measured using the AAOIFI standards and the BNM GPS1 in terms of *Sharīʿah* compliance and five major components of the existing internal control system. Due to the combination of two major elements (*Sharīʿah* compliance + five major components of internal control) it should be best described as a *Sharīʿah* Internal Control Framework.

Based on the score above, in terms of disclosure in the annual report for the year 2009, BIMB scored at 97.6 per cent as compared to BIB, which is only 69.8 per cent. This may be due to the fact that there are certain elements required in the standard that are not being reported in the annual report of BIB. However, this does not mean that BIB fails to comply with the standard. BIB may comply at the organisation level but is not reported in the annual report. For example, during appointment of the SC, the role, scope of duties and responsibilities of a SC should be clearly defined in the organisation. BIB did not mention it clearly in the annual report. The disqualification of the SC also is not being mentioned at all by BIB. BIB may assume that the role, scope and responsibilities of the SC as well as disqualification of the SC are general knowledge that should be known to the external parties. However, by disclosing such information, the users of annual reports will understand more and have a clearer picture of the SC's responsibilities.

During the analysis of the internal control checklist, there are some requirements that are not available in the BIB's annual report, for example the qualifications of BIB's SC. It is not being mentioned in the annual report. However, the information can be gathered by accessing BIB's website. It is suggested that the qualifications of the SC should be reported in the annual report so that the external users that have access to the annual report will not question the qualifications of the SC. This will encourage the IFIs to be more transparent in terms of appointment, qualifications, disqualification and duties and responsibilities of the SC.

In terms of the SC report of BIMB, the yearly *Sharīʿah* issues and the results are clearly stated in the annual report but are not discussed thoroughly. However, for BIB they still comply with the AAOIFI standard but there is no *Sharīʿah* issue being shared and discussed with the public for that particular year. If the *Sharīʿah* issues are being discussed and highlighted in the annual report, it will increase the level of transparency to the shareholders. The shareholders will at least appreciate the information given through the annual report.

In the AAOIFI standards, there is a requirement for IFIs to establish an Audit & Governance Committee (AGC). After reviewing both of the annual

Table 9.1 The Internal Checklist

No.	Question	BIMB	BIB
	PART A : *Sharīʿah*-Compliance		
	Appointment of *Sharīʿah* Committee		
1	The role, scope of duties and responsibilities of a *Sharīʿah* Committee clearly defined in the organization.	Yes	No
2	The appointment and reappointment of a *Sharīʿah* Committee member have obtained prior written approval from each country. (The appointment shall be valid for a renewable term of two years.)	Yes	Yes
	Qualification of *Sharīʿah* Committee		
3	A member of a *Sharīʿah* Committee shall be an individual. A company, institution or body shall not constitute a *Sharīʿah* Committee for the purpose of these Guidelines.	Yes	Yes
4	The *Sharīʿah* Committee in the organization have the qualification or possess necessary knowledge, expertise or experience in the following areas: (a) Islamic jurisprudence (*Usul al-Fiqh*); or	Yes	Yes
	(b) Islamic transaction/commercial law (*Fiqh al-Mu'amalat*). (c) Accounting background	No	No
5	The composition of the *Sharīʿah* Committee shall consist a minimum of three (3) members.	Yes	Yes
6	In addition to the *Sharīʿah* Committee, this organization hires at least one person with knowledge in *sharīʿah*, who serves as the secretariat to the *Sharīʿah* Committee.	Yes	No
	Disqualification of *Sharīʿah* Committee		
7	The SC should not act in a manner which may cast doubt on his fitness to hold the position of a *Sharīʿah* Committee member.	Yes	No
8	The SC attends at least 75% of meeting on average.	Yes	No
9	The SC is not bankrupt, or a petition under bankruptcy laws is filed against them.	Yes	No
10	The SC is not guilty for any serious criminal offence or any other offence punishable with imprisonment of one year or more.	Yes	No
11	The SC is not subject to any order of detention, supervision, restricted residence or banishment.	Yes	No
	Duties and responsibilities of the *Sharīʿah* Committee.		
12	The SC advise the Board on *sharīʿah* matters in order to ensure that the business operations of the organization comply with *sharīʿah* principles at all times	Yes	Yes
13	SC endorse *Sharīʿah* Compliance Manuals	Yes	No
14	The *Sharīʿah* Committee endorses the following relevant document: i) the terms and conditions contained in the proposal form, contract, agreement or other legal documentation used in executing the transactions; and	Yes	Yes

Table 9.1 (continued)

No.	Question	BIMB	BIB
	PART A : *Sharīʿah*-Compliance		
	Duties and responsibilities of the *Sharīʿah* Committee.		
	ii) the product manual, marketing advertisements, sales illustrations and brochures used to describe the product.	Yes	Yes
15	The SC assists related parties on *sharīʿah* matters for advice upon request. (Legal officer, auditor and etc.)	Yes	Yes
16	The *Sharīʿah* Committee prepares written *sharīʿah* opinions (*Sharīʿah* Committee Report) in the annual report on matters pertaining *sharīʿah* issues.	Yes	Yes
17	The *Sharīʿah* Committee explains the *sharīʿah* issues involved and the recommendations for a decision in the *Sharīʿah* Committee report. Does it offer support from relevant *sharīʿah* jurisprudential literature from the established sources?	Yes	No
	Policies and Procedures		
18	The organization refers all *sharīʿah* issues to the *Sharīʿah* Committee.	Yes	Yes
19	The organization adopts the *Sharīʿah* Committee's advice.	Yes	Yes
20	The organization ensures that the product documents are validated.	Yes	Yes
21	The organization has a *Sharīʿah* Compliance Manual.	Yes	No
22	The *Sharīʿah* Committee is given access to relevant records, transactions, manuals or other relevant information, as required by them to perform their duties.	Yes	Yes
23	The organization remunerates the members of the *Sharīʿah* Committee accordingly.	Yes	Yes
24	The *Sharīʿah* Committee reports functionally to the Board of Directors of the organization.	Yes	Yes
	Audit & Governance Committee (AGC) for IFIs (known internationally as the Audit Committee)		
25	The AGC are from independent non-executive members of the board of directors.	Yes	No
26	The AGC is knowledgeable in *sharīʿah* rules and principles (at least one)	No	No
	Total Part A Score	25/27 **92.5%**	14/27 **51.8%**
	PART B : 5 Major Components of Internal Control		
	Control Environment		
27	Integrity, ethical values and competence of the entity's people;	Yes	Yes
28	Management's philosophy and operating style;	Yes	Yes
29	The way management assigns authority and responsibility, and organizes and develops its people;	Yes	Yes
30	The attention and direction provided by the Board of Directors	Yes	Yes

Table 9.1 (continued)

No.	Question	BIMB	BIB
	PART B : 5 Major Components of Internal Control Identification and evaluation of risks and control objectives (Risk Assessment)		
31	Identification and analysis of relevant risks to achievement of objectives	Yes	Yes
32	Designing strategies for managing risks	Yes	Yes
33	Implementing and integrating risk management	Yes	Yes
34	Measuring, monitoring, and reporting the risk area	Yes	Yes
	Control Activity		
35	Proper authorizations, verifications, and reconciliations of transactions and activities.	Yes	Yes
36	Reviews of operating performance.	Yes	Yes
37	Segregation of Duties	Yes	Yes
38	Physical control over assets and records	Yes	Yes
	Information and Communication processes		
39	Internal and External events being highlighted	Yes	Yes
40	Effective communication with external parties, such as customers, suppliers, regulators, and shareholders.	Yes	Yes
	Monitoring		
41	Ongoing monitoring activities	Yes	Yes
42	Separate evaluations from independent party in the organizations (internal audit)	Yes	Yes
	Part B Score	16/16	16/16
		100%	**100%**
	Total Score	42/43	30/43
	Overall Score	**97.6%**	**69.8%**

Table 9.2 The Results for the Internal Checklists

	BIMB	BIB
Part A : *Sharīʿah*-Compliance	92.5%	51.8%
Part B : 5 major components of ICS	100%	100%
TOTAL SCORE	**97.6%**	**69.8%**

reports, it is found that, in BIB, the members of the AGC are not chosen from non-independent, non-executive members of the board of directors. It is also being mentioned in the standard that the AGC of IFIs should be knowledge-able in *Sharīʿah* rules. However, both of the banks BIMB and BIB fail to comply with the standard. Their AGC are mostly from an accounting and business background.

Overall, in terms of *Sharīʿah* compliance, BIMB scored at 92.5 per cent, whereas BIB reached 51.8 per cent. This does not imply that BIB is not *Sharīʿah*-compliant. BIB may impose the framework at the organisation level, but is not disclosing it in the annual report. BIMB manages to score above 90 per cent due to their full disclosure in the annual report. It is proposed, in order to increase the level of awareness of the shareholders, that IFIs should increase the level of information disclosed in the annual report. This will uphold the governance, transparency and integrity of the Islamic Financial Institutions.

For Part B of the internal control checklist, both of the banks manage to score 100 per cent; in other words, full disclosure is reached in terms of the five major components of internal control system. The author assumes that the five major components of the internal control system are commonly practised by the conventional system. Therefore the framework of conventional internal control systems is already established in the existing industry, which leads to full compliance by the IFIs. However, as mentioned before, each of the five major components of the internal control system should include the *Sharīʿah* aspect as well.

9.7 Conclusion

External *Sharīʿah* audits will provide external corroboration to the IFIs' compliance with the *Sharīʿah*; they will emphasise that the IFIs have good internal control mechanisms as well as true and fair financial statements. For external *Sharīʿah* audits to be performed, proper mechanisms should be developed. This paper provides some propositions in the form of a *Sharīʿah* internal control checklist. This checklist may be used when *Sharīʿah* auditors perform *Sharīʿah* audits of IFIs in order to enhance the governance, accountability and transparency of the operation of IFIs.

Bibliography

AAOIFI (2008). *Accounting, Auditing & Governance Standards for Islamic Financial Institutions*. Bahrain: AAOIFI.

Adawiah, E. R. (2007). *Sharīʿah Framework for Sharīʿah Compliance Review, Audit & Governance*, Paper presented in Workshop on *Sharīʿah* Review, Audit and Governance for Islamic Financial Institutions on 30–1 January 2007, Kuala Lumpur.

Arens, A. Elder, R. J. and Beasley, M. S. (2008). *Auditing and Assurance Services*. London: Pearson Prentice Hall.

Chorafas, D. N. (2002). *Modelling the Survival of Financial and Industrial Enterprises: Advantages, Challenges and Problems with the Internal Rating Based (IRB) Method*. London: Palgrave Macmillan.

Grais, W. and Pellegrini M. (2006). *Corporate Governance and Sharīʿah Compliance in Institutions Offering Islamic Financial Services*, World Bank Policy Research Working Paper, 4054.

Guidelines on the Governance of Sharīʿah Committee for the Islamic Financial Institutions. BNM, Kuala Lumpur. Available at: www.bnm.gov.my/guidelines/01_banking/04_prudential_stds/23_gps.pdf, last accessed 20 July 2009.

Humphrey, C., Moizer, P. and Turley, S. (1992). *The Audit Expectations Gap in the United*

Kingdom, Report prepared for the Auditing Research Foundation of the Research Board of the Institute of Chartered Accountants in England and Wales, London, ICAEW.

KPMG (1999). *The KPMG Review Internal Control: A Practical Guide*. Service Point (UK) Ltd.

Mansor, A. M. (2007). *Finding the Right Sharīʿah Auditor*, Paper presented at Seminar on Syariah Audit, Kuala Lumpur.

Rahim, A. (2008). *Sharīʿah Audit for Islamic Financial Services: The Needs and Challenges*, Paper presented at ISRA Islamic Finance Seminar, Mandarin Hotel, Kuala Lumpur.

Shahul, H. and Mulyany, R. (2007). *Sharīʿah Audit for Islamic Financial Institutions (IFIs): Perceptions of Accounting Academicians, Audit Practitioners and sharīʿah Scholars*, Paper presented at the IIUM Accounting Conference, Gombak.

Sikka, P. *et al.* (1998). 'The impossibility of eliminating the expectation gap: Some theory and evidence', *Critical Perspectives on Accounting* 9(3): 299–330.

Sultan, S. A. M. (2007). *Adoption and Acceptance of AAOIFI Standards*, Paper Presented at Workshop on *Sharīʿah* Review, Audit and Governance for Islamic Financial Institutions on 30–1 January 2007, Kuala Lumpur.

Sultan, S. A. M. (2007). *Audit for Sharīʿah Compliance: Developing the Audit Program and a Proposed Methodology*, Paper presented on Workshop on *Sharīʿah* Review, Audit and Governance for Islamic Financial Institutions on 30–1 January 2007, Kuala Lumpur.

10

SHARĪ͑AH REPORT: A POTENTIAL TOOL FOR *SHARĪ͑AH* NON-COMPLIANT RISK MANAGEMENT

Abdou Karim Diaw and Irawan Febianto

10.1 Introduction

It is agreed that *Sharī͑ah*-compliance is the main justification of the existence of Islamic banking and finance. To fulfil this very important requirement, the Islamic Financial Institutions (IFIs) have made various arrangements consisting of the appointment of *Sharī͑ah* scholars with the specific task of supervising their operations. At the national level, some countries have taken the initiative of setting up a national body to cater for the *Sharī͑ah* supervision and the approval of the financial instruments used by the IFIs. That is the case in Malaysia (*Sharī͑ah* Advisory Council) and Sudan (Higher *Sharī͑ah* Supervisory Board). Globally, there are also international organisations such as the Accounting and Auditing Organization for Islamic Financial Institutions (AAOIFI) and the Islamic Financial Services Board (IFSB), which set standards for the governance of IFIs. Since *Sharī͑ah*-compliance is a unique feature of IFI, the conventional risk management techniques may not be adequate to mitigate *Sharī͑ah*-related risk. IFSB specifically treats this risk and provides guidelines for its mitigation (IFSB, 2005). The questions that can therefore arise are:

(i) What are the means at the disposal of the IFIs' stakeholders to measure the *Sharī͑ah*-compliance of these institutions?
(ii) Are these means appropriate to inform adequately the users of IFIs?
(iii) Are these means adequate instruments to mitigate *Sharī͑ah* non-compliance risk?

In the practice of Islamic banking today, the most formal way to inform the users of *Sharī͑ah*-compliance is through *Sharī͑ah* reports, which are a component of the annual report. Therefore, the issues that we try to specifically address in this paper are:

(i) to show the adequacy of the *Sharī͑ah* report as a risk management instrument;
(ii) to know whether the current forms of the *Sharī͑ah* report of Islamic banks are of a nature that provides the users with sufficient information on related *Sharī͑ah* activities.

We do not aim at discussing the reports issued by Sharī͑ah advisers of the banks for internal use, nor will we address the reports of national bodies. The scope will be limited to those reports published in the annual reports and usually produced by what is generally known as the Sharī͑ah Supervisory Board (SSB). Since the report is supposed to be based on the activities carried out by this body, it is imperative to know the rationale, responsibilities and authority of the SSB.

10.2 Literature Review

Islam, as a comprehensive way of life, has provided Muslims with guidance in all matters. In business, the Sharī͑ah has set rules and principles by which the Muslim businessperson must abide. Thus, Islam prohibits ribā (Qur'ān, 2: 275–6), gambling (Qur'ān, 5: 90) and gharar (manipulated uncertainty), but also there are hadiths where the Prophet (pbuh) prohibits gharar. It also prohibits betrayal of all trusts (Qur'ān, 8: 27) and considers it immoral to derive any income by cheating or by fraud (Qur'ān, 4: 29). In addition, the Qur'ān requires the honest fulfilment of all contracts (Qur'ān, 5: 1), and promotes transparency, by recommending putting in writing the contracts meant to take place in a future period (Qur'ān, 2: 282).

To meet these requirements, modern Islamic banks have come up with arrangements whereby specialised bodies monitor all Sharī͑ah matters. One of these bodies is the Sharī͑ah Supervisory Bord (SSB). Almost all Islamic banks have an SSB (Abdel Karim, 1990) with, sometimes, different names depending on the country or the Islamic bank (Hameed, 2007). Thus, the rationale of SSB is quite obvious, since Sharī͑ah-compliance is crucial for IFIs.

The tasks of the SSB are as follows (al Baraka, 2008):

(i) As an expert source on Islamic principles (including fatawā), the board, through a representative, usually the general secretary of the board, supervises the Sharī͑ah-compliance of all the transactions in the bank;

(ii) To devote time and effort to devising more Sharī͑ah-compliant transactional procedures, templates and banking products that enable the bank to adapt to market trends while maintaining a high competitive edge in deposit procedures, investments, and banking services. At the same time, the board gives its opinion on proposed new templates and banking transactions;

(iii) Analysing unprecedented situations that are not covered by fatwā, in the bank's transactional procedures or those reported by different departments, branches and even by customers. This is to ensure Sharī͑ah-compliance before the bank develops any new products or implements any new procedure;

(iv) Analysing contracts and agreements concerning the bank's transactions, as submitted by the chairman of the board of directors or any department/branch within the bank or requested by the board itself so that Sharī͑ah-compliance can be evaluated and maintained.

  (v) Ensuring *Sharīʿah*-compliance in the implementation of all banking trans-
      actions and correcting any breaches;
 (vi) Analysing administrative decisions, issues and matters that require the
      board's approval;
(vii) Supervising *Sharīʿah* training programmes for the bank's staff;
(viii) Preparing an annual report on the bank's balance sheet with respect to its
      Sharīʿah-compliance.

The AAOIFI provided a good definition of the SSB, which we shall consider in
this study (GS IFI, cited in Shahul and Mulyany, 2007):

> A sharīʿah supervisory board is an independent body of specialized jurists
> in *fiqh almua'malat* (Islamic commercial jurisprudence). However, the *sharīʿah*
> supervisory board may include a member other than those specialized in
> *fiqh almua'malat*, but who should be an expert in the field of Islamic financial
> institutions and with knowledge of *fiqh almua'malat*. The sharīʿah supervi-
> sory board is entrusted with the duty of directing, reviewing and supervis-
> ing the activities of the Islamic financial institution in order to ensure that
> they are in compliance with Islamic Sharīʿah Rules and Principles. The
> *fatwas*, and rulings of the sharīʿah supervisory board shall be binding on the
> Islamic financial institution.

In this definition, the responsibilities of SSB are outlined in a general manner,
consisting of 'directing, reviewing and supervising the activities of the Islamic
financial institution'. Chronologically, we can deduce from this statement that
there are two main phases in the activities of SSB: an *ex-ante* audit referred to by
the word 'directing' and an *ex-post* audit that consists of the 'reviewing'.

    Abdallah (1994), who refers very much to the Sudanese experience – one of
the countries following AAOIFI standards – spelled out some elements of the *ex-
ante* audit and advisory role of SSB, which, he says, should include:

  (i) To draft and approve, in collaboration with other concerned departments
     and officials, model contracts and agreements to govern and regulate all
     the bank's activities and dealings.
 (ii) To update and improve the developed models to conform to *Sharīʿah*
     principles, rules and spirit.
(iii) To study and decide on, from a *Sharīʿah* point of view, issues and problems
     submitted by the boards of directors or the general manager.
(iv) To provide advice and instructions to the management of the bank.

On the other hand, for the AAOIFI, the *Sharīʿah* review – *ex-post* audit – is an
examination of the extent of an IFI's compliance, in all its activities, with the
principles of the *Sharīʿah*. This examination includes contracts, agreements, policies, products, transactions, memoranda, articles of association, financial statements, reports (especially internal audit and central bank inspection), circulars,
and so forth (Abdallah, 1994).

The AAOIFI also includes in the responsibilities of the SSB elements such as the calculation of *zakāh*, the identification and disposal of non *Sharīᶜah*-compliant earnings and advising on the distribution of income or expenses among shareholders and investment account holders (see the AAOIFI's example of *Sharīᶜah* report, as cited by Hameed, 2007).

Meanwhile, Bank Negara Malaysia (BNM) issued guidelines on the governance of the *Sharīᶜah* Committee through the Garis Panduan *Sharīᶜah* 1 (GPS-1). The BNM/GPS-1 took effect on 1 April 2005 and requires all IFIs regulated and supervised by BNM to comply with all the points outlined in the guideline. Apart from the GPS-1, Bank Negara Malaysia has also issued another Standard known as GP8-i. Unlike the GPS-1, which focuses more on the issue of governance, the GP8-i is more focused on providing the basis for presentation disclosure of reports and financial statements of Islamic banks in carrying out its banking and finance activities (BNM, 2004).

It is worth noting that the BNM Guidelines, GPS-1, like the AAOIFI, emphasises on the *ex-ante* and advisory role of SC (which is the equivalent of SSB). However, this advisory role is not limited to the board of directors or the management but it could also concern the *Sharīᶜah* Advisory Council of Bank Negara Malaysia (BNM). On the other hand, GPS-1 does not seem to include the *ex-post* audit in the duties of SC, as can be seen in the enumeration of the main responsibilities of SC, which consist of (BNM, GPS-1):

(i) advising the board of directors on *Sharīᶜah* matters in its business operation

(ii) endorsing *Sharīᶜah* compliance manuals that specify the manner in which a submission or request for advice is to be made to the SC, the conduct of SC meetings and the manner of compliance with any *Sharīᶜah* decision

(iii) endorsing and validating relevant documentations to ensure that the products of the IFI comply with *Sharīᶜah* principles in all aspects

(iv) assisting with related parties such as the IFIs' legal counsel, auditors or consultants on *Sharīᶜah* matters for advice upon request

(v) advising on matters that have not been endorsed or resolved to the *Sharīᶜah* Advisory Council of BNM

(vi) providingwritten *Sharīᶜah* opinions in the case where the IFI makes reference to SAC for advice or requests advice and on applications for product approval to the BNM

(vii) assisting the *Sharīᶜah* Advisory Council on reference for advice, such as explaining the *Sharīᶜah* issues involved, and assisting for recommendations for a decision.

In the AAOIFI framework, the SSB enjoys a high level of authority. Its members are appointed by the shareholders and their *fatwās* are binding on the IFI, as is stated in the definition. Similarly, GPS-1 mentioned that the 'IFI is required to adopt and take the necessary measures for the implementation of *Sharīᶜah* Committee's advice'. However, in the Malaysian framework the board of directors appoints the members of SC. Therefore, the SC seems to have less authority than the SSB.

10.3 Research Method

The present study by nature is a textual and descriptive analysis, which aimed at critically analysing how the *Sharīʿah* report is practised in four leading countries in the area of Islamic finance; these are Malaysia, Pakistan, Bahrain and Kuwait. The sources of information include the AAOIFI standards, Bank Negara Malaysia standards, banks' annual reports and legal standards. Content analysis is the key tool, which we intend to use to extract necessary information materials. We will analyse the *Sharīʿah* report of Islamic banks (for the years 2008 and 2009) on the basis of a sample of ten reports in comparison with the standard reports issued by AAOIFI. From these banks, any necessary information for the study will be extracted using exploratory methods, and then will be critically analysed and interpreted using explanatory methods.

10.4 Discussion and Findings

10.4.1. SSB and Sharīʿah *Non-compliance Risk*

As stated earlier, *Sharīʿah*-compliance is a primary concern of Islamic banks. SSB is established to make sure that IFIs comply with *Sharīʿah* principles in their different activities. The IFSB (2005) defines *sharīʿah* non-compliance risk as: 'the risk that arises from Institutions Offering Islamic Financial Services' (IIFS) failure to comply with the *Sharīʿah* rules and principles determined by the *Sharīʿah* Board of the IIFS or the relevant body in the jurisdiction in which the IIFS operate'.

The failure to adhere to *Sharīʿah* rules and principles can be deliberate or unintended. For instance, for the sake of maximising profit, the management could recognise income from unlawful means or distribute profit and loss in a way that is detrimental to investment account holders. On the other hand, the employees of IFIs may fail to properly execute a contract by pure ignorance. Hence, the responsibility of the internal *Sharīʿah* advisors or SSB is crucial to manage such failure. However, the management of this risk requires a particular competence as well as authority and independence. To determine the areas where failure is likely to happen, *Sharīʿah* supervisors need to be experts in *fiqh muamalat* and to at least have working knowledge in banking, finance and audit techniques.

(i)   The IFSB (2005) provides useful guidelines on the events when maximum vigilance is needed as far as *Sharīʿah*-compliance is concerned;
(ii) When accepting deposits and investment funds (liability side);
(iii) When providing finance and carrying out investment services for their customers (asset side).

Another important area mentioned by IFSB is the contract documentation, where due care should be given to the elements pertaining to 'formation, termination and elements possibly affecting contract performance such as fraud, misrepresentation, duress or any other rights and obligations'.

Once the issue of competence of the *Sharī*ah* Supervisors settled, we are faced with another critical issue regarding their authority and independence. *Sharī*ah* Supervisors should have the right to access all sources of information that they deem relevant without restriction. Further, they should be free to express objectively their opinion without any kind of pressure. We are of the view that the appointment of the SSB by the shareholders is of a nature to strengthen this independence.

Abdel Karim (1990) emphasised the importance of independence of the SSB for credibility of IFIs' financial statements. He argued that the *Sharī*ah* report could enhance market discipline in the sense that if the SSB reports any misrepresentation in the Islamic bank's financial statements that are due to a violation of Islamic principles, the consumers of these statements are likely to react in a manner that could be detrimental to the bank's management. In addition to independence, Grais and Pellegrini (2006) discussed the issue of disclosure and maintained that the public disclosure of all information relating to *Sharī*ah* advisories, besides empowering the stakeholders, would provide a forum for educating the public, thus paving the way for a larger role for market discipline in regard to *Sharī*ah*-compliance, and at the same time decreasing the cost that external agents may face in assessing the quality of internal *Sharī*ah* supervision.

Thus, the *Sharī*ah* report, if properly done, could play an important role in mitigating *Sharī*ah* non-compliance risk by making the management and other employees more cautious when dealing with *Sharī*ah*-related matters. Therefore, the question that we try to answer in the following section is whether the current form of *Sharī*ah* report of Islamic banks is sufficient to mitigate *Sharī*ah* non-compliance risk. Thus, Figure 10.1 depicts a Model of Sharī*ah Governance of Islamic banks proposed by this study.

10.4.2. Sharī*ah *Reports: An Analysis*

As we have shown in the previous section and in Figure 10.1, the unique feature of Islamic banks necessitates the inclusion of bodies entrusted with *Sharī*ah* supervision. A logical consequence of this is the need to produce a report that shows how *Sharī*ah*-compliant the various operations of the bank were. Abdel Karim (1990: 36) holds that the *Sharī*ah* report can be justified on the grounds that it:

> [a]ssures readers that the financial statements of the bank were in accordance with Islamic Sharia. It also states whether SSB auditors had access to all the documents and records that they deemed necessary in carrying out their duties. Such a report is meant to give credibility to the information in the financial statements from a religious perspective.

Such assurance is of a nature to enhance and strengthen the stakeholders' confidence in the operations of the Islamic banks. It should be noticed that in this context the stakeholders are quite large and they comprise all those with a vested

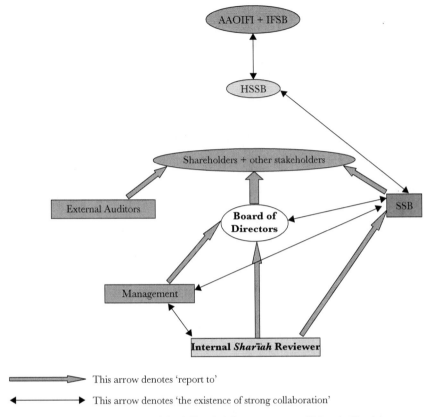

Figure 10.1 A Model of *Sharīʿah* Governance of Islamic Banks

interest in the well-being of Islamic banks such as employees, customers, suppliers, supervisors and the Muslim *ummah* as a whole (IFSB, 2006, Corporate Governance Standards: 27).

Few standards and guidelines have been produced locally (for example, in Malaysia) and globally (for example, by the AAOIFI and IFSB) in relation to *Sharīʿah* reports of Islamic banks. However, the guidelines given by the AAOIFI in this respect are much more detailed, even though we consider it still deficient in some of its aspects. Nevertheless, we shall take it as a benchmark in the process of evaluating the sample of *Sharīʿah* reports in this study, and shall, whenever necessary, voice our opinion with regard to some issues.

The sample is constituted of ten *Sharīʿah* reports of different banks from various countries: six banks from Malaysia (Bank Islam Malaysia Berhad, Bank Muamalat Malaysia Berhad, CIMB Islamic bank Berhad, RHB Islamic bank Berhad, Kuwait Finance House- Malaysia and Al-Rajhi Banking & Investment Corporation-Malaysia), two banks from Bahrain (Albaraka Banking group,

Bahrain Islamic bank), one bank from Pakistan (Meezan Bank Limited) and one bank from Kuwait (Kuwait Finance House). The reports were produced from 2008 to 2009, in the annual reports of the above banks.

In its standard on the *Sharī^cah* Supervisory Board, the AAOIFI outlines the basic elements that must be contained in the *Sharī^cah* report:

a) title
b) addressee
c) opening or introductory paragraph
d) scope paragraph describing the nature of the work performed
e) opinion paragraph containing an expression of opinion on the compliance of the Islamic financial institution with Islamic *Sharī^cah* rules and principles
f) date of report
g) signature of the members of the *Sharī^cah* Supervisory Board.

The table opposite shows us how compliant the sample reports are with AAOIFI's guidelines.

In the example report provided by AAOIFI, there are four items that should be considered in the opinion section:

(i) the contracts, transactions and dealings entered into by the Islamic Financial Institution
(ii) the allocation of profit and charging of losses relating to investment accounts
(iii) the earnings that have been realised from sources or by means prohibited by Islamic *Sharī^cah* rules and principles
(iv) the calculation of *zakāh*.

Apparently, only the Al Baraka Banking Group has attempted to follow the AAOIFI guidelines, with a level of conformity that reaches 100 per cent. The analysis of the different reports shows that Meezan Bank's *Sharī^cah* Advisory report is by far the most comprehensive and the most complete of all (see in the Appendix Meezan Bank).

Meanwhile, there are four Islamic banks that tend to be very brief with a common general statement such as: 'We M.X, . . ., do hereby confirm on behalf of the Committee, that in our opinion, the operations of the Bank for the year ended . . . have been conducted in conformity with *Sharī^cah* Principles.'

It is clear that this kind of report is not of a nature to help the stakeholders of Islamic banks appreciate how *Sharī^cah*-compliant are the operations that are conducted. Despite the confidence that the stakeholders of Islamic Financial Institutions may have about the independence, competence and honesty of *Sharī^cah* Supervisors, much more details are needed to make them stronger in their confidence. Even the Prophet Ibrahim (*pbuh*) asked *Allah* to show him how to resuscitate, although he was a true believer. The story is told in a formidable manner in the *Qur'ān* (2: 260):

Table 10.1 Comparison between the Sample of *Shariʿah* Reports with the AAOIFI Example Report

Elements of AAOIFI Example report / Bank	Title	Addressee	Introductory Paragraph	Scope Paragraph	Opinion a	b	c	d	Date	Signature of All the Members	Level of Conformity
Bank Islam (Malaysia-2009)	✓	✓	✓	✓	✓	✓	✓	✓	✓	✓	90.9 %
Bank Muamalat (Malaysia-2008)	✓	✗	✗	✗	✓	✗	✓	✓	✓	✗	27.3 %
CIMB Islamic bank (Malaysia-2009)	✓	✗	✓	✓	✗	✗	✗	✗	✓	✗	45.5 %
RHB Islamic bank (Malaysia-2008)	✓	✗	✓	✓	✓	×	✗	✗	✓	✗	72.7 %
Kuwait Finance House (Malaysia-2009)	✓	✗	✓	✓	✓	✓	✓	✓	✓	✓	90.9 %
Al-Rajhi (Malaysia-2008)	✓	✗	✗	✗	✗	✗	✗	✗	✓	✗	27.3 %
Meezan Bank Limited (Pakistan-2009)	✓	✗	✓	✓	✓	✓	✓	✓	✓	✓	90.9 %
Al Baraka Banking group (Bahrain-2009)	✓	✓	✓	✓	✓	✓	✓	✓	✓	✓	100 %
Bahrain Islamic Bank (Bahrain-2008)	✓	✓	✓	✓	✓	✓	✓	✓	✗	✓	90.9 %
Kuwait Finance House Group (Kuwait-2009)	✓	✗	✗	✗	✗	✗	✗	✗	✗	✗	18.2 %

✓ denotes that the element is present in the report; × stands for that the element is not present in the report.

And (remember) when Ibrahim said, 'My Lord! Show me how You give life
to the dead.' He (Allah) said: 'Do you not believe?' He (Ibrahim) said: 'Yes
(I believe), but to be stronger in Faith.'

Our analysis has also revealed a sort of passive attitude of some *Sharīᶜah*
Supervisors as reflected in the following statement: 'This opinion is rendered
based on what has been presented to us by the Bank and the Group and its
sharīᶜah Advisor.' (See in the Appendix Kuwait Finance House Report-Malaysia.)
It is evident that the management would never present to the *Sharīᶜah* auditors
elements that could be to its detriment!

> In addition to the risk of material misstatements, the auditor is also respon-
> sible to ensure that he has a reasonable chance of detecting material fraud
> in the financial statements by infusing a dose of healthy professional scepti-
> cism in the conduct of his audit and when there are any suspicions, he
> should follow up until he has investigated the matter to his satisfaction.
>
> (Hameed, 2007: 505)

If this stance is required from the conventional auditor, much more rigour is
expected from the *Sharīᶜah* auditor due to the fact that *Sharīᶜah*-compliance is the
raison d'être of Islamic banks.

This problem can be explained by another related issue. In the case of the
Kuwait Finance House, the SC (for the Malaysian subsidiary) and the *Fatwā*
and *Sharīᶜah* Supervisory Board (for the Group in Kuwait) are constituted of
the same scholars. The language could be a serious barrier if we know that
English is used in Malaysia whereas the *Sharīᶜah* scholars are generally trained
in Arabic.

With respect to AAOIFI's Standard on SSB report (GSIFI No. 1), some comments are necessary, despite the fact that it can be seen as a praiseworthy effort.
Hameed (2007) made pertinent observations on the form as well as the substance
of the proposed report. He raised some confusing elements in the example report
with respect to the arrangement and the content of some paragraphs and the
nature of the work performed. The standard emphasises four important matters: contracts and related documentations in compliance with Islamic *Sharīᶜah*
rules and principles; the allocation of profit and losses related to investment
accounts; the disposal of prohibited earnings; and the calculation of *zakāh*. Given
this scope, the omission of the financial statements is strange, if one takes into
consideration the fact that 'financial statements' is part of the *Sharīᶜah* review
scope as stated in AAOIFI's standards (Hameed, 2007: 552).

Moreover, we can remark that even AAOIFI, in its example report, tends to
imitate too closely the typical report of the external auditors, in particular in the
paragraph on scope, where it is stated that:

> The Example Islamic Financial Institution's management is responsible for
> ensuring that the financial institution conducts its business in accordance
> with Islamic Shari'a Rules and Principles. It is our responsibility to form an

independent opinion, based on our review of the operations of the Example Islamic Financial Institution, and to report to you . . .

(GSIFI No. 1 cited in Shahul and Mulyany, 2007)

This statement seems to narrow down the responsibilities of SSB as defined in another statement in GSIFI No. 1, where it is affirmed that:

> The Shari'a supervisory board is entrusted with the duty of directing, reviewing and supervising the activities of the Islamic financial institution in order to ensure that they are in compliance with Islamic Shari'a Rules and Principles. The fatwas, and rulings of the Shari'a supervisory board shall be binding on the Islamic financial institution.

(GSIFI No. 1 cited in Shahul and Mulyany, 2007)

Hameed (2007) spells out clearly the differences in the responsibilities between the SSB and the auditor on the grounds that the former is concerned with the activities and operations of the Islamic Financial Institutions as a whole; hence its report should have quite a wide scope, whereas the latter is mainly concerned with the IFIs' financial statements. In our view this difference in responsibilities should be reflected in the wording and contents of the SSB's report. In this regard, Meezan Bank *Sharīᶜah* Advisor's report (see Appendix 10.1) is very much progressive in the sense that it informs, in detail, about all the major events that took place in the bank and in which the SSB/*Sharīᶜah* Advisor was involved. These range from products launched to training provided, treatment of prohibited earnings, review of the balance sheet, and so forth; such forms of *Sharīᶜah* reports should be emulated in the industry as it fairly represents the duties carried out by *Sharīᶜah* Supervisors, and enables the users of Islamic financial services to assess the level of conformity of IFI operations to *Sharīᶜah* rules and principles.

Before ending this section, we deem it worthwhile to propose a model of a *Sharīᶜah* report that takes into consideration the positive aspects of the existing models (GSIFI No.1 / AAOIFI, and Meezan Bank Limited *Sharīᶜah* Advisor report) and the observations available to us in the literature (Hameed, 2007). We have attempted to reflect in the proposed report the role of SSB, in particular the *ex-ante Sharīᶜah* audit and the *ex-post Sharīᶜah* audit. This distinction has a clear implication in the structure of the report.

10.5 Conclusion

In this paper we have argued that the SSB, due to its responsibilities in the governance structure of IFIs, has the main role in the management of *Sharīᶜah* non-compliance risk. We have raised the issues of competence, authority and independence of *Sharīᶜah* Supervisors which are crucial for a proper discharge of their duty. A tool at the disposal of SSB that can help in managing *Sharīᶜah* non-compliance risk is the *Sharīᶜah* report. Our view is that a good *Sharīᶜah*

In the name of *Allah*, The Beneficent, The Merciful

***Sharī°ah* Supervisory Board Report**

To the Shareholders of X Islamic Financial Institution

Assalam Alaikum Wa Rahmat Allah Wa Barakatuh

In compliance with the letter of appointment, we are required to submit the following report.

Ex-ante Sharī°ah Audit:

In order to discharge our duties which consist of directing, supervising and reviewing the activities of X Islamic Financial Institution to ensure *Sharī°ah*-compliance in all its activities:

We have held n_1 meetings to discuss issues relating to the operations of X Islamic Financial Institution. In this respect, n_2 *fatwās* have been issued as required by the various questions that we were faced with. (All *fatwās* have been attached to this report.) **Enumeration of the major events of the ended period and what was the role of SSB in these.**

Ex-post Sharī°ah Audit:

To verify that the X Islamic Financial Institution's operations are conducted in conformity with the Islamic *Sharī°ah* rules and principles, as stipulated in our guidelines and *fatwās*:

We thoroughly studied all the reports submitted to us by the Internal *Sharī°ah* Reviewer(s).

We examined, on a test basis of each type of transaction, the relevant documentation and procedures adopted by the X Islamic Financial Institution an opinion as to whether the X Islamic Financial Institution has complied with *Sharī°ah* Rules and Principles and also with the specific *fatwaā*, rulings and guidelines issued by us.

It is the responsibility of X Islamic Financial Institution's management and employees to ensure the application of *Sharī°ah* principles and guidelines issued by the SSB and to ensure *Sharī°ah*-compliance in all activities of the institution.

Based on the review and tests that we have conducted:

In our opinion:

a) The contracts, transactions and dealings entered into by the X Islamic Financial Institution during the year ended . . . that we have reviewed are in compliance with the Islamic *Sharī°ah* rules and principles.
(If any, indicate the nature of violation.)

b) The allocation of profit and charging of losses relating to investment accounts conform to the basis that had been approved by us in accordance with Islamic *Sharī°ah* rules and principles.
If any, indicate the nature of violation.)
(Where appropriate, the opinion paragraph shall also include the following matters:)

c) All earnings that have been realised from sources or by means prohibited by Islamic *Sharī°ah* rules and principles have been disposed of to charitable causes.
(The source, amount and way of disposal, should be disclosed.)

d) The calculation of *zakāh* is in compliance with Islamic *Sharī°ah* rules and principles.

We beg *Allah* the Almighty to grant us all the success and straight-forwardness.
Wassalam Alaikum Wa Rahmat *Allah* Wa Barakatuh
(Names and signature of the members of the *Sharī°ah* supervisory board)
Place and date.

report could enhance market discipline and make the IFIs' managements handle *Sharīʿah*-related matters with more care and rigour. Our study of *Sharīʿah* reports of some Islamic banks from four leading countries in the area of Islamic finance has revealed the lack of harmonisation of *Sharīʿah* reports in the industry. The mainstream Malaysian *Sharīʿah* reports are very brief and are not of a nature to adequately inform the stakeholders of the Islamic banks on the extent of *Sharīʿah* compliance of the operations. The AAOIFI's model, although it does provide some detailed and useful information, is still deficient and needs to be improved in terms of coherence and consistency with respect to the responsibilities and duties of the SSB. The Meezan Bank *Sharīʿah* Advisory report is, in our opinion, a good model. In our analysis, we have raised some issues relating to the supervision of Middle Eastern Islamic banks in Malaysia that need to be properly addressed. We have also proposed a model of *Sharīʿah* report that we consider more consistent with the responsibilities of SSB, and could constitute a good instrument to mitigate *Sharīʿah* non-compliance risk.

We think that the lack of harmony regarding the responsibilities and authority of the SSB at the global level is a main issue that should be tackled as soon as possible. The phenomenon becomes more complicated with the advent of IFSB as standard setter for *Sharīʿah* governance, besides the AAOIFI. Which standard should the IFIs follow? It would be preferable that these two organisations meet to harmonise and outline the scope of interest for each of them, in order to avoid more confusion.

Bibliography

AAOIFI (1999). *Governance Standard for Islamic Financial Institutions No. 2 –Shari'a Review.*

AAOIFI (1999). *Governance Standard for Islamic Financial Institutions No. 3 –Internal Shari'a Review.*

AAOIFI (2004). *Governance Standard for Islamic Financial Institutions No. 1 – Shari'a Supervisory Board: Appointment, Composition and Report.*

Abdallah, Ahmed Ali. (1994). *The Role of Shariah Supervisory Board in Setting Accounting Policies in Islamic Banks: Selected Reading.* London: Institute of Islamic banking and Insurance.

Abdel Karim, R. A. (1990). 'The independence of religious and external auditors: The case of Islamic banks', *Accounting, Auditing & Accountability Journal* 3(3): 34–44.

Ahmad, S. F. (2001). 'The ethical responsibility in business: Islamic principles and implications', in Khaliq Ahmad and AbulHasan M. Sadeq (eds), *Ethics in Business and Management: Islamic and Mainstream Approaches.* London: Asean Academic Press, pp. 189–206.

Bank Negara Malaysia (BNM) (2004). *Guidelines, on the Governance of Sharīʿah Committee for the Islamic Financial Institutions.* BNM, Kuala Lumpur.

Besar, Mohd Hairul Azrin Haji *et al.* (2008). *The Practice of Sharīʿah Review as Undertaken by Islamic Banking Sector in Malaysia,* Proceedings of the Eighth International Business Research Conference, Dubai, UAE, 27–28 March 2008.

Chapra, M. and Ahmed, H. (2002). *Corporate Governance in Islamic Financial Institutions,* Occasional Paper No. 6, Islamic Research and Training Institute, Islamic Development Bank, Jeddah.

Grais, W. and Pellegrini, M. (2006). *Corporate Governance and Sharī*c*ah Compliance in Institutions Offering Islamic Financial Services*, World Bank Policy Research Working Paper 4054, November 2006..

Hameed, S. (2007). *Accounting and Auditing for Islamic Financial Institutions*. Bahrain: AAOIFI.

IFSB (2005). *Guiding Principles of Risk Management*. Kuala Lumpur, Malaysia. Available at: www.albaraka.com.ua, last accessed 16 March 2008.

IFSB (2006). *Guiding Principles on Corporate Governance for Institutions Offering Only Islamic Financial Services (Excluding Islamic Insurance (Takaful) Institutions and Islamic Mutual Funds)*. Kuala Lumpur: IFSB.

Shahul H. and Mulyany R. (2007), *Sharī*c*ah Audit for Islamic Financial Institutions (IFIs): Perceptions of Accounting Academicians, Audit Practitioners and Sharī*c*ah Scholars*. Paper presented at the IIUM Accounting Conference, Gombak.

Appendix

AL RAJHI BANKING & INVESTMENT CORPORATION (MALAYSIA) BHD

(Incorporated in Malaysia)

Company No. 719057-X

REPORT OF SHARIAH COMMITTEE

بِسْــــمِ اللهِ الرَّحْمٰنِ الرَّحِيـــــمِ

In the name of Allah, the most Beneficent, the most Merciful

Praised be to Allah, the Lord of the Worlds and peace and blessings be upon our Prophet Muhammad, and on his family and companions

السلام عليكم ورحمة الله وبركاته

We the undersigned, Dr Salleh Abdullah S. Al Lheidan and Burhanuddin Lukman, in our capacity as members of the Shariah Committee of Al Rajhi Banking & Investment Corporation (Malaysia) Bhd, do hereby confirm on behalf of the members of the Shariah Committee that the operations of the Bank for the financial year ended 31 December 2008 have, in general, been conducted in compliance with Shariah. However, it has become clear to the Shariah Committee the presence of irregularities which must be rectified. The Shariah Committee has communicated to the Bank of the said irregularities and the Bank is in the midst of rectifying these irregularities.

On behalf of the Shariah Committee,

DR SALLEH ABDULLAH S. AL LHEIDAN   **BURHANUDDIN LUKMAN**

Chairman   Deputy Chairman

Sharia Supervisory Board's Report

To the shareholders of

Bahrain Islamic Bank B.S.C.

In The Name of Allah, most Gracious, most Merciful
Peace and Blessings Be Upon His Messenger

Assalam Alaykum Wa Rahmatu Allah Wa Barakatoh

Pursuant to the powers entrusted to the Sharia'a Supervisory Board to supervise the Bank's activities and investments, we hereby submit the following report.

The Sharia'a Supervisory Board monitored the operations, transactions and contracts related to the Bank throughout the year ended 31 December 2008 to express opinion on the Bank's adherence to the provisions and principles of Islamic Sharia'a in its activities by following the guidelines and decisions issued by the Sharia'a Supervisory Board. The Sharia'a Supervisory Board believes that ensuring the conformity of its activities and investments with the provisions of Islamic Sharia'a is the sole responsibility of the Bank's Management while the Sharia'a Supervisory Board is only responsible for expressing an independent opinion and preparing a report thereabout.

The Sharia'a Supervisory Board's monitoring function included the checking of documents and procedures to scrutinize each operation carried out by the Bank, whether directly or through the Sharia'a Internal Audit department. We planned with the Sharia'a Internal Audit department to carry out monitoring functions by obtaining all the information and clarifications that were deemed necessary to confirm that the Bank did not violate the principles and provisions of Islamic Sharia'a. The Sharia'a Internal Audit department audited the Bank's transactions and submitted a report to the Sharia'a Supervisory Board. The report confirmed the Bank's commitment and conformity to the Sharia'a Supervisory Board's opinions.

The Sharia'a Supervisory Board obtained data and clarifications it deemed necessary to confirm that the Bank did not violate the principles and provisions of Islamic Sharia'a. It held several meetings throughout the year ended 31 December 2008 and replied to inquiries, in addition to approving a number of new products presented by the Management. The Sharia'a Supervisory Board discussed with the Bank's officials all transactions and applications carried out by the Management throughout the year and reviewed the Bank's conformity with the provisions and principles of Islamic Sharia'a as well as the resolutions and guidelines of the Sharia'a Supervisory Board.

The Sharia'a Supervisory Board believes that:

1. Contracts, operations and transactions conducted by the Bank throughout the year ended 31 December 2008 were made in accordance with the standard contracts pre-approved by the Sharia'a Supervisory Board.

2. The distribution of profit on investment accounts was in line with the basis and principles approved by the Sharia'a Supervisory Board.

3. No gains resulted from any sources or means prohibited by the provisions and principles of Islamic Sharia'a.

4. Zakah was calculated according to the provisions and principles of Islamic Sharia'a. The Bank distributed Zakah on the statutory reserve, general reserve and retained earnings. The shareholders should pay their portion of Zakah on their shares as stated in the financial report.

5. The Bank was committed to the Sharia'a standards issued by the Accounting & Auditing Organisation for Islamic Financial Institutions (AAOIFI).

We pray that Allah may grant all of us further success and prosperity.

1. Dr. Shaikh A. Latif Mahmood Al Mahmood
   Chairman

2. Shaikh Mohammed Jaffar Al Juffairi
   Vice Chairman

3. Shaikh Adnan Abdullah Al Qattan
   Member

4. Shaikh Nedham M. Saleh Yacoubi
   Member

5. Shaikh Dr. Essam Khalaf Al Onazi
   Member

Bahrain Islamic Bank   Annual Report 2008

Report of Al-Fatwa and Shareea'ah Supervisory Board

By following up the performance of Kuwait Finance House during the year ended 31 December 2009, we certify confidently that all activities were practiced in compliance with Islamic Shareea ah and no violations have occurred, to the best of our knowledge.

Chairman
Sheikh Ahmad Bazie Al-Yaseen

Shareea'ah Board Member
Sheikh Dr.
Khaled Mathkour Al-Mathkour

Shareea'ah Board Member
Sheikh Dr.
Ajeel Jasem Al-Nashmi

Shareea'ah Board Member
Sheikh Dr.
Anwar Shuaib Abdulsalam

Shareea'ah Board Member
Sheikh Dr.
Mohammad Abdul Razak Al-Tabtabae

Shareea'ah Board Member
Sheikh Dr.
Mubarak Jaza Al-Harbi

KUWAIT FINANCE HOUSE (MALAYSIA) BERHAD
(672174-T)
(Incorporated in Malaysia)

REPORT OF SHARIAH COMMITTEE

In the name of Allah, the most Beneficent, the most Merciful.

Praise to Allah, the Lord of the Worlds and peace and blessings be upon our Prophet Muhammad, and on his scion and companions.

Assalamualaikum Warahmatullahi Wabarakatuh.

In compliance with the Guidelines on the Shariah Committee of Kuwait Finance House (Malaysia) Berhad we are required to submit the following report:

We have reviewed the principles and the contracts relating to the transactions and applications undertaken by the Bank and the Group during the financial year ended 31 December 2009. We have also conducted our review to form an opinion as to whether the Bank and the Group has complied with Shariah rules and principles and also with the specific fatwa, rulings, guidelines issued by us.

The Management is responsible for ensuring that the Bank and the Group conduct its business in accordance with Shariah rules and principles. It is our responsibility to form our independent opinion, based on our review of the operations of the Bank and the Group, and to report to you.

We conducted our review which included examining, on a test basis, each type of transaction, the relevant documents and procedures adopted by the Bank and the Group.

We planned and performed our review so as to obtain all the information and explanations which we consider necessary in order to provide us with sufficient evidence to give reasonable assurance that the Bank and the Group have not violated the Shariah rules and principles.

In our opinion:

(a) the contracts, transactions and dealings entered into by the Bank and the Group during the year ended 31 December 2009 have been reviewed by us and are in compliance with Shariah rules and principles;

(b) the allocation of profits and losses relating to investment accounts conform to the basis that had been approved by us in accordance with Shariah rules and principles.

(c) all earnings that have been realised from sources or by means prohibited by Shariah rules and principles, have been disposed to charitable causes; and

(d) the calculation of zakat is in compliance with Shariah rules and principles.

This opinion is rendered based on what has been presented to us by the Bank and the Group and its Shariah Advisor.

We pray to Allah the Almighty to grant us success and the path of straight-forwardness.

Wassalamualaikum Wa Rahmatullahi Wabarakatuh.

Sheikh Prof. Dr. Mohammed Abdul Razzaq Al-Tabtabae (Chairman)
Sheikh Dr. Anwar Shuaib Abdulsalam Al-Abdulsalam (Member)
Sheikh Adnan Ali Ibrahim Al-Mulla (Member)

Kuala Lumpur, Malaysia
8 March 2010

CIMB Islamic Bank Berhad
(671380-H)

Report of the Shariah Committee

The Shariah Committee of CIMB Islamic Bank Berhad (the Bank) was established under the provision of Section 3(5)(b) of the Islamic Banking Act 1983 to advise the Bank and the Group on the operations of their Islamic banking and finance business in order to ensure that they do not involve any element which is not approved by the Shariah.

In advising the Bank and the Group, the Shariah Committee also adopts the views of Shariah advisory councils of Bank Negara Malaysia and Securities Committees from time to time.

The duties and responsibilities of Shariah Committee are to advise the Directors on the operations of the Islamic banking and finance business of the Bank and the Group in order to ensure that they do not involve any element which is not approved by Shariah.

The roles of the Shariah Committee in monitoring the Islamic banking and finance activities of the Bank and the Group are as follows:

a. Review the products and services to ensure conformity with the Shariah principles.
b. Deliberate on Shariah issues pertaining to the day-to-day operations of the Bank and the Group and provide advice accordingly.
c. Form opinions on the Shariah compliance of the Islamic banking and finance operations of the Bank and the Group.

The roles of Shariah Committee with respect to zakat are as follows:

a. Review computation of zakat and approve the amount to be paid according to Shariah.
b. Advise on the payment of zakat to the appropriate authority.

We, Professor Dr Mohammad Hashim Kamali and Associate Professor Dr. Shafaai bin Musa, being two of the members of the Shariah Committee of CIMB Islamic Bank Berhad, do hereby confirm on behalf of the Shariah Committee, that in our opinion, the operations of the Islamic banking and finance business of the Bank and the Group for the financial year ended 31 December 2008 have been conducted in conformity with the Shariah principles.

On behalf of the Shariah Committee.

Professor Dr Mohammad Hashim Kamali   **Associate Professor Dr Shafaai Musa**

Kuala Lumpur
24 March 2009

Report of the Shariah Committee

We, the Shariah Committee of Bank Muamalat Malaysia Berhad, do hereby confirm that in our opinion, the operations of the Bank, to the best of its effort for the year ended 31 December 2008 and to the best of our knowledge, have been conducted in conformity with the Shariah principles.

Signed on behalf of the Shariah Committee,

Azizi Che Seman   **Associate Professor Dr. Mohamad Sabri Haron**

Kuala Lumpur, Malaysia
30 March 2009

report of the RHB Group Shariah Committee

In the name of Allah, The Most Gracious, The Most Merciful

We, Professor Dr. Haji Abdul Samat Musa, Professor Dr. Joni Tamkin Borhan and Dr. Abdulazeem Abozaid, being three of members of Group Shariah Committee of RHB Islamic Bank Berhad, do hereby confirm on behalf of the members of the Committee, that we have reviewed the principles and the contracts relating to the transactions and applications introduced by the Bank during the year ended 31 December 2008.

We have also conducted our review to form an opinion as to whether the Bank has complied with Shariah rules and the principles and also with the specific rulings and guidelines issued by us.

The Bank's management is responsible for ensuring that the financial institution conducts its business in accordance with Islamic Shariah rules and principles. It is our responsibility to form an independent opinion, based on our review of the operations of the Bank, and to report to you.

We have performed our review so as to obtain all the information and explanations, which we considered necessary in order to provide us with sufficient evidence to give reasonable assurance that the Bank has complied with Islamic Shariah rules and principles.

In our opinion:

a)   main sources of income of the Bank during the year ended 31 December 2008 that we have reviewed are in compliance with the Shariah (Islamic Law) rules and principles;

b)   all investments that have been disclosed to us by the Bank conform to the basis that had been approved by us in accordance with Shariah rules and principles;

c)   the contracts and legal documents of the products used by the Bank that we reviewed are in compliance with the Shariah rules and principles;

d)   the products proposals including concept used by the Bank which have been reviewed and advised by us are in compliance with the Shariah rules and principles; and

e)   The Bank is not required to pay Zakat. This should be paid by shareholders on their shareholding.

We beg Allah the Almighty to grant us success and lead us on the right path.

Wassalamu Alaikum Wa Rahmatullahi Wa Barakatuh

PROF. DR. HAJI ABDUL SAMAT MUSA
Chairman of the Committee

PROF. DR. JONI TAMKIN BORHAN
Member of the Committee

DR. ABDULAZEEM ABOZAID
Member of the Committee

Kuala Lumpur
11 March 2009

Unified Shari'a Supervisory Board Report

For the year ended 31 December 2009

In the name of Allah, The Beneficient, The Merciful, Ever Merciful

Praise be to Allah and peace be upon our Prophet Mohamed, His Apostles and Companions

To: Al Baraka Banking Group Shareholders
May peace and God's Mercy and Blessings Be upon You

In accordance with Article (58) of the Articles of Association of Al Baraka Banking Group, we are required to submit the following report:

We have reviewed the principles applied by the Group and reviewed the 2009 Shari'a reports issued by the Group Units' Shari'a Supervisory Boards. We have also reviewed their financial statements when needed. In addition, we examined the Group's financial position as of 31 December 2009 and Statement of Income and their notes. We have queried from some of the Technical's on the points that need explanation and statement. We have also reviewed the process of calculating Zakah in accordance with the Sharia Standard number (35) and Accounting Standard number (9) issued by the Accounting and Audit of the Islamic financial Institutions.

The Group and Units' management are responsible for the execution and implementation of the Unified Shari'a Supervisory Board resolutions and to bring to the attention of the Unified Shari'a Supervisory Board any transactions or issues that require Shari'a approval. The Unified Shari'a Supervisory Board is responsible for supervising the implementation of the resolution from a Shari'a point of view and issue opinion based on the Group and Units' Shari'a reports and financial statements.

The Unit's Shari'a Supervisory Boards, as is clear from their report, have supervised the Units' business activities including examining on test basis documentations and procedures applied by the Group and its Units.

The Units' Shari'a Supervisory Boards, as is clear from their reports, planned and performed reviews so as to obtain all the information and explanations they considered necessary in order to provide them with sufficient evidence to provide reasonable assurance that the Group and its Units have not violated Shari'a Rules and Principles.

In our opinion:

1. The Contracts, transactions and dealings entered into by the Group and its Units during the year ended 31 December 2009 are made in compliance with Shari'a Rules and Principles.

2. The allocation of profit and charging of losses relating to investment accounts conform to the basis that have been approved by the Units' Shari'a Supervisory Boards in accordance with Shari'a Rules and Principles.

3. All earnings realized from sources or by means prohibited by Islamic Shari'a Rules and Principles have been committed by the Management to dispose it off to Charitable Causes.

4. The attached Zakah calculation was prepared in accordance with the provisions and principles of Islamic Sharia according to the Net Invested Fund Method in accordance to Shari'a Standard number (35) and Accounting Standard number (9) issued by the Accounting and Audit of the Islamic financial Institutions and on the basis set out in the resolution of the International Islamic Fiqh Academy that if a company calculate Zakah, the shareholders is committed to pay his Zakah according to that calculation, whatever his intention was. Since the Group and the Units are not empowered to pay Zakah, shareholders should pay their share of Zakah. The Zakah per share is 2.50 US cents. In case of unavailability of liquidity, it is allowed to postponed the Zakah and become a debt until the liquidity become available.

Praise be to God

Issued on 30 Safar 1431 H, corresponding to 14 February 2010 AD.

Executive Committee of the Unified Shari'a Supervisory Board

Dr. Abdul Sattar Abu Ghudah
President Shari'a Supervisory Board

Sh. Abdulla Al Mannea
Shari'a Supervisory Board's Member

Dr. Abdulaziz Al Fowzan
Shari'a Supervisory Board's Member

Dr. Abdullatif Al Mahmood
President Shari'a Supervisory Board

Dr. Ahmed Mohiyeldin Ahmed
Shari'a Supervisory Board's Member

Shariah Advisor's Report

الحمد لله رب العا لمين، والصلاة والسلام على خاتم الأنبياء والمرسلين، محمد المصطفى الأمين، وعلى آله وأصحابه أجمعين، وبعد:

By the Grace of Allah, the year under review was the eighth year of Islamic commercial banking for Meezan Bank Limited. During this year, the bank developed and executed a variety of new as well as established Islamic banking products and transactions after due approval from the Shariah Supervisory Board and/or Shariah Advisor. During the year, the Shariah Supervisory Board (SSB) of Meezan Bank Limited held 2 meetings to review various products, concepts, transactions, processes and their Shariah-compliance, referred to them by the Shariah Advisor.

As part of the Shariah Compliance framework a full-fledged Product Development & Shariah Compliance (PDSC) department is working under my supervision for centralization of Product development activities, new product research, Islamic banking training and Shariah Audit & Compliance functions.

Following were the major developments that took place during the year:

1. **Research & New Product Development:** During the year, the bank has launched a Hajj & Umrah product namely Meezan Labbaik, a product designed for customers to facilitate their holy journey. Several customized Shariah-compliant solutions were provided to new sectors of the industry based on Islamic modes of financing including Tijarah & Istisna. Solution for Islamic Inter-bank financing was successfully developed based on Musharakah & Wakalah with the consensus of other major Islamic banks in Pakistan. An innovative structure was developed for financing transaction with Food Department, Government of Punjab, for the procurement of wheat. Based on the guidelines provided by the Chairman of SSB of the bank, legal documentation of all financing products was further refined as part of the continuous improvement process.

   Furthermore, active research is being done in many areas of business including development of Islamic alternative for the Continuous Funding System (CFS) transactions, Islamic Microfinancing & Agriculture financing, Islamic Benchmark as an alternative to KIBOR, Islamic long-term finance facility (ILTFF) for exporters and new deposit product options for small savers etc.

2. **Investment Banking:** During the year Meezan Bank structured & participated in various Shariah-compliant structured finance transactions such as Liberty Power Sukuk, PIA Sukuk and Amreli Steel Sukuk.

3. **Training & Development:** Several specialized in-house functional-level Islamic banking training sessions were held across all four regions during the year. The number of internal training sessions was increased with 72 Islamic Banking Training Sessions held during the year 2009 (60 sessions during 2008) in which 2234 employees participated across Pakistan. These sessions range from basic level orientation and Islamic Banking Certification to specialized sessions for middle and senior-level management. Furthermore, online self-training modules were developed by the product development & research team of the Bank to provide continuous training to all MBL staff through Intranet. Due to continuous increase in number of branches and employees, the focus on training and development needs to be further enhanced in the coming years. The bank also conducted 24 Islamic banking awareness seminars for corporate customers as well as the general public.

4. **Shariah Advisory:** The PDSC department of the bank is also involved in providing Islamic Financial Advisory Services to different financial institutions interested in offering Islamic banking products & services both in Pakistan and abroad with the objective of promoting Islamic financial products by sharing Meezan Bank's experience, research & success stories. During the year, the bank advised Al-Meezan Investment Management (AMIM), National Fullerton Asset Management Company (NAFA) and KASB Funds, Pak Oman Asset Management Limited for the launch & management of various types of Shariah-compliant Mutual Funds. Being the Shariah Advisor of AMIM, MBL also provided Shariah Advisory Services for matters related to re-composition of KMI - 30 Index (Karachi Stock Exchange Meezan Islamic Index) which is Pakistan's first ever Shariah-compliant Islamic Index. During the year, the Bank entered into 'Shariah Technical Services and Support' agreements with Meezan Cash Fund, Meezan Asset allocation Fund & Meezan Sovereign Fund.

   Islamic Financial Advisory function of the bank also provided advisory for launch of Islamic consumer finance to United Sales (Pvt) Ltd (USL), a subsidiary of Dawlance group under the umbrella of *Diyanat financing*. The Bank also provided product-review advisory to Islamic Relief, UK for their Islamic microfinance program in Pakistan

Review of Assets
The Bank primarily used Murabaha, Ijarah, Diminishing Musharakah, Istisna, Tijarah and Salam for its financing activities during the year.

Murabaha transactions (including Islamic Export Refinance Scheme) constitute around 47% of the total financing portfolio as compared to 45% last year, while the share of Diminishing Musharakah & Istisna increased from 14.5% & 4% to 23% & 8% respectively. However, Ijarah transactions' share moved downward from 23% to 17%. These ratios suggest that the percentage of Murabaha in the overall financing figure has remained at the same level, however the Istisna-based financing has gained popularity. The Bank's total financing portfolio reached Rs. 46.716 billion as on December 31, 2009. All these transactions were executed using Shariah-compliant financing agreements.

It is a matter of great concern that due to excess liquidity, the bank has executed local currency Commodity Murabaha transactions amounting to Rs. 34.499 billion as compared to last two years' figures of Rs. 18.108 billion and Rs. 8.850 billion respectively, while the remaining excess liquidity was used in inter-bank Musharakah. In the absence of short-term placement avenues this mode was inevitably used. However, the Bank, in consultation with other players in the market, should try to explore other opportunities for short-term liquidity management.

Review of Liabilities
On the liability side, the Bank offered different Shariah-compliant deposit products based on the mode of Mudarabah. The total deposits of the Bank reached Rs. 100.333 billion as at December 31, 2009. During the year, the Bank accepted deposits on the modes of Musharakah for short-term liquidity management from inter-bank market and corporate clients.

Throughout the year, the process of the allocation of assets & funds to various deposit pools, announcement of overall profit sharing ratios for Mudarabah based deposits, monthly allocation of the weightages and distribution of income to deposit accounts were monitored and reviewed in accordance with Shariah rules & principles.

Shariah Audit & Compliance Reviews
To ensure that all the products and services being offered by the bank strictly adhere to conjunctions of Shariah, the PDSC department actively monitored various operational activities of the Bank throughout the year. During the year, credit approvals, restructuring of financing facilities, customer-specific transaction process flows, text of Letters of Guarantee (LGs) and security documents were reviewed to ensure Shariah-compliance while offering financing products to the customers.

During 2009, over 400 customer-specific transactional process flows (of Murabaha, Diminishing Musharakah, Istisna, Tijarah & Ijarah) were revised / developed for SME customers and more than 380 Credit approvals and Restructuring of facilities were reviewed. For Corporate customers, over 400 customer-specific transactional process flows (of Murabaha, Diminishing Musharakah, Istisna, Tijarah & Ijarah) were revised / developed, 100 security documents, 120 credit approvals and restructuring of more than 10 clients were reviewed

Summary of Direct Payment in Murabaha Financing for Meezan Bank

MURABAHA FINANCING - DIRECT PAYMENT	2008	2009	Growth
Overall Portfolio	38%	67%	76%
Customer Wise Breakup			
Corporate	28%	60%	114%
SME/Commercial	70%	85%	21%
Region Wise Breakup			
NORTH	56%	88%	57%
SOUTH	46%	81%	76%
CENTRAL	30%	54%	80%

As per the directive of SSB to increase direct payments in Murabaha, it is a matter of appreciation that Bank has increased the overall percentage of direct payments. In the year 2009, a significant growth of 76% was registered in terms of direct payment for Murabaha financing as the overall percentage of direct payment was increased to 67% in the year 2009 against 38% in the year 2008.

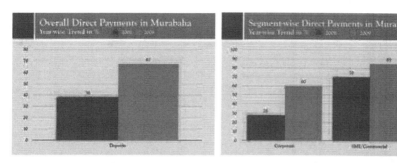

In customer wise break-up of direct payments, a persistent upward trend was witnessed. In SME/Commercial segment the percentage of direct payment increased from around 70% in the year 2008 to 85% in the year 2009. For Corporate customers, a great deal of improvement was observed as the percentage of direct payment jumped from 28% in the year 2008 to around 60% in the year 2009.

Moreover, in Istisna and Tijarah transactions, physical inspection is done in 100% of the cases to take the possession of the goods purchased.

In addition to the above compliance measures, this year Shariah audit & compliance review of 130 branches was conducted in order to get the first hand knowledge of the activities being carried out at these branches. These audited branches had approximately 74% share of total branch financing and approx. 75% share of total deposits of the bank.

During the year, Shariah Audit was conducted in all major branches, to ensure and evaluate the overall Shariah compliance of the bank's operation and their alignment with the guidelines given by Shariah Advisor and the SSB. In the audit process, following areas have been checked:

- Agreements for Murabaha, Ijarah, Diminishing Musharakah, Istisna, Tijarah and Bai Salam
- Declarations, description of Assets, relevant purchase invoices, sequence and order of the documents and time difference between purchases and declaration in Murabaha.
- Murabaha Monitoring Sheets & Delayed Declaration Reports
- Purchase deeds, treatment of ownership related cost & recovery of rentals in Ijarah transactions.
- Ownership ratio in Diminishing Musharakah for Housing and issuance of timely unit sale receipts.
- Investment made in stock with reference to the stock screening criteria.
- Import Finance transactions and related documentation.
- Extensive reviews of client payment, purchase cycle and periodic assessment of client's processes.
- Other related documents and procedures followed by different functional areas.
- Profit-sharing ratio, profit weightages, pool working, asset & deposit allocation for deposit products.

Based on the Shariah review, the Shariah Advisor has directed the Bank's management to provide for income amounting to Rs. 6.666 million earned on certain financing transactions where non-compliance was observed. Moreover, an amount of Rs 1.141 million was provided for charity to eliminate the non-compliant portion and purify the dividend income earned from the investment made in the Shariah-compliant stocks by the bank.

During the period, the Bank returned an amount of Rs. 7.635 million received as dividend income from M/s Faysal Management Services (FMS) as it was identified that the amount received as dividend income from the company was earned out of bank placement at a conventional bank thus rendering this whole amount as non-shariah compliant. Further the management has been advised to direct FMS to ensure that all investments are made in a Shariah-compliant manner.

Murabaha Monitoring System (MMS)

A system for continuous monitoring of Murabaha transactions is in place whereby the branches extending Murabaha financing are required to submit a fortnightly reporting sheet, after thorough review by the branch/departmental management, to the PDSC department for review and continuous monitoring of Murabaha transactions to avoid any mistakes and errors.

Charity

During the year, an amount of Rs. 51.170 million was transferred to the Charity account and an amount of Rs. 14.605 million was disbursed after the approval of the Shariah Advisor. Details of charity are available in note # 18.41. Moreover, as per the directive of SSB a charitable foundation by the name of Ihsan Trust has been established to ensure effective utilization and disbursement of charity funds.

Recommendations

Based on the review of various transactions, it is recommended that:

- For the placement of excess liquidity, the Bank shall explore new avenues of investment instead of only relying on the Commodity Murabaha transactions. Furthermore, the Bank should explore doing Commodity Murabaha transactions through the Commodity Exchange.
- In view of the growing branch network and induction of new employees, the Bank should continue its focus on employees training related to Islamic banking products and services offered by the Bank with specific focus on front-line staff.
- The Corporate, Commercial & SME department and all Regions of the bank shall organize special training workshops for the executives of their financing clients and continue the practice of conducting customer awareness seminars.
- The Bank should try to initiate execution of Musharakah transactions using the approved models of Running Musharakah facility and transaction-based Musharakah with its customers.
- In the area of retail banking, new deposit schemes that could give higher returns and added benefits to lower income segments and senior citizens shall be introduced.
- Efforts should be made to implement Islamic Microfinancing schemes in Pakistan.
- It is recommended that for residential area branches, separate Women-banking counters should be established to facilitate female customers and arrangements should be made to ensure minimal interaction of female staff with male customers at the branches.
- To strengthen the Shariah-compliance framework in the bank, the scope of external audit shall also include the review of bank's activities in light of the guidelines given by the Shariah Supervisory Board, Shariah Advisor, PDSC and SBP guidelines for Shariah compliance issued from time to time.

Conclusion

As per the charter of the Bank, it is mandatory on all of the management & employees to ensure application of Shariah principles and guidelines issued by the Shariah Supervisory Board and Shariah Advisor and to ensure Shariah-compliance in all activities of the bank. The prime responsibility for ensuring Shariah-compliance of the Bank's operations thus lies with the management.

Based on the extensive reviews of sample cases for each class of transaction, related documentation, processes, the profit distribution mechanism for the depositors and management's representation made in this regard, in our opinion, the affairs, activities and transactions, performed by the bank during the year comply with the rules & principles of Islamic Shariah in light of the guidelines and directives given by the Shariah Supervisory Board, Shariah Advisor of Meezan Bank and SBP guidelines related to Shariah-compliance. The non-compliant income identified during the review is being transferred to the charity account.

May Allah bless us with the best Tawfeeq to accomplish His cherished tasks, make us successful in this world and in the Hereafter, and forgive our mistakes.

Wassalam Alaikum Wa Rahmat Allah Wa Barakatuh.

Dr. Muhammad Imran Usmani
Member Shariah Supervisory Board & Shariah Advisor

Dated: Safar 09, 1431 H / January 25, 2010 AD

REPORT OF THE SHARIAH SUPERVISORY COUNCIL

الحمد لله رب العالمين, والعاقبة للمتقين, ولا عدوان إلا على الظالمين, والصّلاة والسلام على سيدنا محمد سيد المرسلين وإمام المتقين, وعلى آله الطيبين الأطهار وأصحابه الهادين الأبرار, ومن تبعهم بإحسان إلى يوم الدين.

السلام عليكم ورحمة الله وبركاته *and Salam Sejahtera*

To the shareholders, depositors and customers of Bank Islam Malaysia Berhad;

In carrying out the roles and responsibilities of the Bank's Shariah Supervisory Council as prescribed in the Guidelines on the Governance of Shariah Committee for Islamic Financial Institutions issued by Bank Negara Malaysia, we hereby submit the following report for the financial year ended 30 June 2009:

1. The Council held nine (9) meetings to review various products, transactions and processes in line with the Shariah requirements and we had also approved the following products:

   i. Current Account based on *Wakalah* Contract.

   ii. Issuance of Murabahah Medium Term Notes.

   iii. An-Najah NID-i Structured Investment Product based on *Mudharabah Muqayyadah* contract.

   iv. Islamic Convertible Redeemable Non-Cumulative Preference Shares (CRNCPS).

   v. Shariah Advisor for Islamic Syndicated Structure Facility based on *Istisna'* contract convertible to *Ijarah Muntahiah Bit-Tamleek*.

   vi. Legal Documentations for Product based on Commodities Transaction from other Institutions.

   vii. Legal Documentations for Islamic Profit Rate Swap (*Musawamah*) and Cross Currency Profit Rate Swap (*Murabahah*) products.

   viii. Structured Product and Legal Documents for Islamic New Frontier Index.

   ix. Legal Documentation for Equity Option Product.

   x. Legal Documentations for Standard Interbank Commodity *Murabahah* Association of Islamic Banking Institutions Malaysia.

Report of the Shariah Supervisory Council (continued)

xi.   Transaction Legal Documentations *Bai' Murabahah Medium Term Notes Issuance Programme*.

xii. Transaction Documents for the Syndicated Business Financing-i Facility.

xiii. Legal Documentations for Personal Financing-i *Tawarruq*.

xiv. Legal Documentations for Business Financing-i *Tawarruq*.

xv.   Legal Documentations for BBA and *Istisna'* House Financing.

xvi. Legal Documentations of *Ijarah Muntahiah Bit-Tamleek* Facility.

xvii. Multiple *Aqad* of Negotiable Islamic Debt Certificate (NIDC).

xviii. Replacement of Novation Agreement.

xix. Variations in Islamic Negotiable Instruments (INI) and Islamic Negotiable Instruments of Deposit (INID).

xx.   Variations in Al-Awfar Savings Account-i and Investment Account-i (previously known as Savings Multiplier) product features.

2.   In addition, the Council in the said meetings also reviewed, adopted and approved several initiatives of the Bank in strengthening the Shariah governance of the Bank which include the following:

i.   *Wakalah* Contract Guideline (Version 1.0).

ii.   *Tawarruq* (Financing) Concept Guideline (Version 1.0).

iii. *Wadi'ah* Contract Guidelines (Version 3.0).

iv.   Revised Terms of Reference for Shariah Supervisory Council.

v.   Terms of Reference for Zakat Committee.

vi.   Business Zakat Payment Guideline (Version 1.0).

vii. Dress Code Guidelines.

viii. Shariah Compliance Training Programme.

3.   The Bank during the financial year has tracked non-*halal* income arising from various sources amounting to RM8,448.62 to be disposed off to charity.

4.   The Bank carried out Shariah compliance review performed by Internal Audit Division and Shariah Department throughout the organisation and the report was deliberated in the Council meeting. The Council hereby confirms that necessary efforts have been taken to rectify the Shariah breaches, and the Bank has also implemented several mechanism(s) to prevent similar Shariah breaches from recurring.

5.   The Bank had approved a structured training programme and the Shariah requirements are briefed to the newcomers during induction programme by Shariah officer.

6.   The Council reviewed the financial statements of the Bank and confirmed that the financial statements and calculation of *Zakat* is in compliance with the Shariah requirements.

It is the responsibility of the Bank's management to ensure that it conducts its business in accordance with Shariah rules and principles as determined by the Shariah regulatory councils and it is our responsibility to form an independent opinion based on our review on the operations of the Bank and to report to you. In performing this, we had obtained all the information and explanations which we considered necessary in order to provide us with sufficient evidences to give reasonable assurance that the Bank has complied with Shariah requirements.

On that note, we, Dr. Ahmad Shahbari @ Sobri Salamon and Mohd Bakir Haji Mansor, being two of the members of the Shariah Supervisory Council of Bank Islam Malaysia Berhad, do hereby confirm on behalf of the Council that in our level best, the operations of the Bank for the financial year ended 30 June 2009 have been conducted in conformity with Shariah requirements. Allah Knows Best.

On behalf of the Council:

....
Dr. Ahmad Shahbari @ Sobri Salamon

....
Mohd. Bakir Haji Mansor

Kuala Lumpur,

Date: 9 September 2009

11

A SURVEY ON *SHARĪʿAH* GOVERNANCE PRACTICES IN ISLAMIC FINANCIAL INSTITUTIONS IN MALAYSIA, GCC COUNTRIES AND THE UK

Zulkifli Hasan

11.1 Introduction

Sharīʿah governance as defined by the IFSB Guiding Principles on *Sharīʿah* Governance System (IFSB-10) is 'a set of institutional and organizational arrangements through which IFIs ensure that there is effective independent oversight of *Shari'ah* compliance over the issuance of relevant *Shari'ah* pronouncements, dissemination of information and an internal *Shari'ah* compliance review' (IFSB, 2009: 2). As an additional layer of governance within the internal structure of corporate governance in IFIs, *Sharīʿah* governance is very important as a mechanism to address a specific type of risk exclusive to IFIs known as *Sharīʿah* non-compliance risk.[1] The significance of *Sharīʿah* non-compliance risk to the Islamic finance industry can be illustrated in the case of falling *sukuk* issuance due to a statement made by the chairman of the AAOIFI *Sharīʿah* Board, the OIC Fiqh Academy declaration on impermissibility of *tawarruq*,[2] the Malaysian High Court judgment on the issue of BBA,[3] and the dispute in the case of the Investment Dar Company KSCC v Blom Development Bank.[4] All of these major cases indicate the very significance of the *Sharīʿah* governance system as a risk management tool to mitigate the *Sharīʿah* non-compliance risk.

Basically, there are several studies that have been conducted on *Sharīʿah* governance in IFIs across jurisdictions. A survey conducted by Grais and Pellegrini (2006) presented *Sharīʿah* board practices in thirteen IFIs, while Maali, Casson and Napier (2006) researched twenty-nine IFIs, and Aboumouamer (1996) studied forty-one IFIs. Another piece of research carried out by the International Institute of Islamic Thought in 1996 and a survey by Hasan in the same year also presented some aspects of *Sharīʿah* board practices (Bakar, 2002). In spite of all of these surveys, it is nevertheless found that the majority of the authors adhered to secondary data and did not address some pertinent and contemporary issues. In fact, the strong growth and rapid development of *Sharīʿah* governance practices all over the world makes the data and the findings in those surveys less relevant and almost insignificant. The recent IFSB survey on the *Sharīʿah* board of IFIs across jurisdictions (IFSB, 2008) presented the findings of *Sharīʿah* governance practices in sixty-nine IFIs from eleven countries, namely Bahrain, Bangladesh, Brunei, Indonesia, Iran, Jordan, Malaysia, Pakistan, Qatar, Sudan and United Arab Emirates. The IFSB Survey, however, mainly demonstrated the perception and behavioural response of IFIs from a macro-perspective.

Due to the lack of literature, fresh data, empirical evidence and a micro-perspective analysis on *Sharī'ah* governance in IFIs, the author undertakes to carry out a comprehensive survey on *Sharī'ah* governance practices that is designed on the international corporate governance and international *Sharī'ah* governance benchmarks. The survey takes into account the main basic elements of sound *Sharī'ah* governance, namely independence, competency, consistency and transparency. Since the nature of this study is explorative in character, the study chooses Malaysia, the GCC countries[5] and the United Kingdom as the case countries in order to provide a comparative overview of the extent of *Sharī'ah* governance practices in three different jurisdictions with distinctive legal environments and *Sharī'ah* governance approaches.

11.2 Methodology

Since the availability of secondary data on *Sharī'ah* governance practices is very limited, a detailed survey questionnaire is generated for sourcing primary data from IFIs excluding Islamic insurance institutions. The survey was distributed to eighty IFIs in Malaysia (twenty), the GCC countries (Bahrain (twelve); UAE (thirteen); Qatar (ten); Kuwait (ten); and Saudi Arabia (nine) and the United Kingdom (six). This survey is divided into eight sections that consist of a general approach to *Sharī'ah* governance, regulatory frameworks and internal policies on *Sharī'ah* governance, roles of the *Sharī'ah* board, and attributes of the *Sharī'ah* board in term of competency, independence, transparency and confidentiality, operational procedures and the *Sharī'ah* board's assessment. These sections are illustrated in Table 11.1; they represent the main elements of a sound and proper *Sharī'ah* governance system as laid down by the AAOIFI Governance standards and the IFSB guiding principles on a *Sharī'ah* governance system.

In designing the questionnaires, the study relied on the OECD Principles of Corporate Governance, the Guidance by the Basel Committee on Banking Supervision on Enhancing Corporate Governance for Banking Organizations, the AAOIFI Governance Standards (for Islamic Financial Institutions) and the IFSB published Standards including the Guidance on Key Elements in the Supervisory Review Process of Institutions offering Islamic Financial Services (excluding Islamic Insurance (*Takāful*) Institutions, the Guiding Principles on Corporate Governance for Institutions Offering Only Islamic Financial Services (Excluding Islamic Insurance (*Takāful*) Institutions and Islamic Mutual Funds and Islamic Mutual Funds) and the Guiding Principles on *Sharī'ah* Governance System.

The response rate of 43.8 per cent out of eighty IFIs is relatively satisfactory and significant. This is affirmed by Sekaran (2003: 237), who considers that a

Table 11.1 Questionnaires on *Sharīʿah* Governance

Questions	Number of Questions
General Approach to *sharīʿah* Governance	**8**
Q1. IFIs that adopt the AAOIFI Governance Standards	
Q2. IFIs that are sensitively aware on the development of *sharīʿah* governance such as the IFSB Guiding Principles on *Sharīʿah* Governance	
Q3. IFIs that have standards or guidelines for *sharīʿah* governance	
Q4. IFIs that develop standard processes for *sharīʿah* compliance, audit, and review of the *sharīʿah* boards' legal rulings	
Q5. IFIs that have professional code of ethics and conduct for members of the *sharīʿah* board	
Q6. IFIs that have an internal *sharīʿah* board	
Q7. IFIs that have institutional arrangement for *sharīʿah* governance	
Q7.1 Internal *Sharīʿah* Board	
Q7.2 *Sharīʿah* Advisory Firm	
Q7.3 Internal *sharīʿah* Board and *sharīʿah* Advisory Firm	
Regulatory and Internal Framework of *sharīʿah* Governance	**4**
Q8. IFIs that have specific rules and policies concerning *sharīʿah* governance	
Q9. IFIs that have written policies or by-laws specifically referring to the conduct of the *sharīʿah* board	
Q10. IFIs that have good understanding on what type of dispute settlement to redress legal matters concerning Islamic finance	
Q10.1 Civil Court	
Q10.2 *Sharīʿah* Court	
Q10.3 Arbitration	
Q11. IFIs that have good understanding on the legal position of the *sharīʿah* board's rulings	
Q11.1 Binding	
Q11.2 Non-Binding	
Roles of the *Sharīʿah* Board	**5**
Q12. IFIs that provide clear authority to their *sharīʿah* board	
Q12.1 Advisory	
Q12.2 Supervisory	
Q13. IFIs whose *sharīʿah* board performs *ex-ante* and *ex-post sharīʿah* governance process	
Q13.1 *Sharīʿah* pronouncements	
Q13.2 *Sharīʿah* review or audit	
Q13.3 Endorsing and validating documentations	
Q13.4 Endorsement of *sharīʿah* compliance	
Q13.5 Overseeing the computation and payment of *zakāh*	
Q13.6 Examining any inquiries referred to by the IFIs	
Q13.7 Developing *sharīʿah* approved instruments	
Q13.8 Acting as a *sharīʿah* highest authority	

Table 11.1 (continued)

Questions	Number of Questions
Roles of the *Sharīᶜah* Board	
Q13.9 Approving model agreements of Islamic modes of financing	
Q13.10 Achieving harmonization on rulings of the *sharīᶜah* boards	
Q14. IFIs whose *sharīᶜah* board performs the *sharīᶜah* audit function	
Q15. IFIs that delegate *sharīᶜah* review functions to the internal *sharīᶜah* compliance unit to assist the *sharīᶜah* board	
Attributes of *sharīᶜah* Board (Competence)	**8**
Q16. IFIs that have policies on fit and proper criteria for the members of *sharīᶜah* board	
Q17 Fit and Proper Criteria	
Q17.1 Academic qualification	
Q17.2 Experience and exposure	
Q17.3 Track Record	
Q18. IFIs that put condition of academic qualification	
Q18.1 Specialised in *muᶜāmalāt*	
Q18.2 Specialised in Islamic Jurisprudence	
Q18.3 Knowledge of Arabic and English	
Q18.4 Knowledge of banking	
Q19. IFIs that put requirement of exposure and experience	
Q19.1 Understanding of *sharīᶜah* rules and principles	
Q19.2 Understanding of general legal and regulatory framework	
Q19.3 Understanding of the impact of the *sharīᶜah* pronouncement	
Q19.4 Skills in the financial services industry	
Q20. IFIs that put requirement of track record	
Q20.1 Good character	
Q20.2 Competence, diligence, capability and soundness of judgment	
Q20.3 Suitability and Exposure to *muᶜāmalāt*	
Q21. IFIs that allows non-*sharīᶜah* background individual as a member of the *sharīᶜah* board	
Q21.1 Well versed in law	
Q21.2 Well versed in economy	
Q21.3 Well versed in finance	
Q21.4 Basic *sharīᶜah*	
Q21.5 Strategic objective	
Q22. IFIs that organize adequate training for *sharīᶜah* board	
Q23. IFIs that have proper assessment of the *sharīᶜah* board	
Attributes of *sharīᶜah* Board (Independence)	**5**
Q24. IFIs that appoint the *sharīᶜah* board through	
Q24.1 Shareholders	
Q24.2 Board of Directors (BOD)	
Q24.3 Management	
Q24.4 Government	
Q24.5 Nomination Committee	

Table 11.1 (continued)

Questions	Number of Questions
Attributes of *sharīʿah* Board (Independence)	
Q25. IFIs that appoint *sharīʿah* board based on contractual basis	
Q25.1 One year	
Q25.2 Two years	
Q25.3 Three years	
Q25.4 Five years	
Q25.5 Permanent	
Q26 IFIs that think the appropriate body for the *sharīʿah* board to be accountable to	
Q26.1 Shareholders	
Q26.2 Board of Directors (BOD)	
Q26.3 Management	
Q26.4 Government	
Q26.5 National *sharīʿah* board	
Q27. *sharīʿah* board remuneration is determined by	
Q27.1 Shareholders	
Q27.2 BOD	
Q27.3 Management	
Q28. IFIs that have mechanism in place to mitigate conflict of interest in relation to *sharīʿah* scholars sitting in various boards	
Q28.1 Restriction on multiple appointment	
Q28.2 Disclosure on *sharīʿah* board's information	
Q28.3 Declaration in writing	
Q28.4 Integrity	
Q29. IFIs that provide full mandate and authority of the *sharīʿah* board	
Q29.1 Article of Association	
Q29.2 Memorandum of Association	
Q29.3 Letter of Appointment	
Attributes of *sharīʿah* Board (Transparency and Confidentiality)	**4**
Q30. IFIs that have a written policy in respect to the preparation and dissemination of *sharīʿah* information	
Q31. IFIs that grant full authority to *sharīʿah* board to have access to all documents, information and records	
Q32. IFIs that publish the *sharīʿah* pronouncements and ensure them available to the public	
Q33. IFIs that ensure their *sharīʿah* board is fully aware of the issue of confidentiality and sensitive information obtained in the course of performing their duties	
Operational Procedures	**10**
Q34. IFIs that have standard operative procedure for *sharīʿah* board	
Q35. IFIs that hold *sharīʿah* board meeting	

Table 11.1 (continued)

Questions	Number of Questions
Operational Procedures	
Q35.1 Weekly	
Q35.2 Monthly	
Q35.3 Quarterly	
Q35.4 Twice a month	
Q35.5 Ad hoc	
Q35.5 Every two months	
Q35.6 Semi-Annually	
Q36. Quorum for the *sharīᶜah* board meeting	
Q36.1 Three	
Q36.2 Seven	
Q36.3 Six	
Q36.4 Two	
Q37. Basis of the decision of *sharīᶜah* board meeting	
Q37.1 Simple Majority	
Q37.2 Two-third majority	
Q37.3 Consensus	
Q38. IFIs that do not grant voting rights to non-*sharīᶜah* background members of the *sharīᶜah* board	
Q39. IFIs that ensure agenda prepared and distributed in advance of *sharīᶜah* Board meetings	
Q39.1 A week in advance	
Q39.2 Two weeks in advance	
Q39.3 A month in advance	
Q39.4 Ten days in advance	
Q39.5 3 days in advance	
Q40. IFIs that have specific arrangement to coordinate the *sharīᶜah* governance process	
Q40.1 Internal *Sharīᶜah* officer	
Q40.2 Company Secretary	
Q40.3 Head of Product Development	
Q40.4 Head of the Legal Department	
Q40.5 Islamic capital market department	
Q40.6 Outsource Company	
Q41. Attendees in the *sharīᶜah* board meeting	
Q41.1 Representative from the Internal *sharīᶜah*-Compliance Unit	
Q41.2 Representative from Risk Management Department	
Q41.3 Representative from Legal Department	
Q41.4 Representative from Product Development Department	
Q41.5 Representative from external legal firm	
Q41.6 Representative from IFIs in the case of national *sharīᶜah* board	
Q41.7 Senior Management	
Q41.8 Executive Director	

Table 11.1 (continued)

Questions	Number of Questions
Operational Procedures	
Q41.9 Managing Director	
Q41.10 Board Risk Committee	
Q41.11 Chief Internal Auditor	
Q41.12 Company Secretary	
Q41.11 CEO	
Q42. IFIs that require their *sharīʿah* board to review the previous rulings	
Q43. IFIs that put mandatory requirement for *sharīʿah* report	
Q44. IFIs that detail out the contents of the *sharīʿah* report to include	
Q44.1 Information on duties and services	
Q44.2 *Sharīʿah* pronouncements	
Q44.3 *Sharīʿah* board activities	
Q44.3 Declaration of *sharīʿah*-compliance	
P45. IFIs that set up independent organizational arrangement for the internal *sharīʿah* audit	
Q45.1 Independent Division/department	
Q45.2 Part of the Internal Audit Department	
Q45.3 Outsource company	
Q45.4 *Sharīʿah* division	
Q45.5 *Sharīʿah* compliance unit	
Assessment of the *Sharīʿah* Board[a]	5
Q46. IFIs whose *sharīʿah* board demonstrates effective organizational accountability	
Q47. IFIs whose *sharīʿah* board communicates effectively with other organs of governance, including the BOD, management and auditors	
Q48. IFIs whose *sharīʿah* board properly identifies and evaluate the organization's exposure to *sharīʿah* non-compliance risk and reputational risk, and effectively communicate that risk information to appropriate bodies in the organisation	
Q49. IFIs whose *sharīʿah* board promotes Islamic ethics and values within the organization	
Q50. IFIs whose *sharīʿah* board promotes continuous improvement of an organization's Shari'ah control processes	
Total Questions	**50**

[a] Q46–Q50 uses Likert scale analysis of 'Strongly Disagree', 'Disagree', 'Neutral', 'Agree' and 'Strongly Agree' to measure the performance level of the *sharīʿah* board.

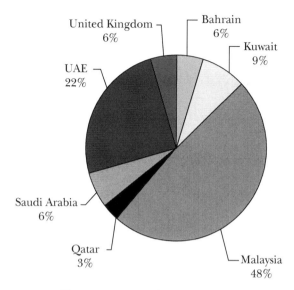

Figure 11.1 The Response Rate

response rate of 30 per cent is acceptable. The survey was launched on 1 April 2009 and ended on 1 June 2009 and the timeline for the survey was extended to 30 December 2009 due to the small response rate. In view of the difficulties in getting response from the industry players and practitioners due to some inherent factors, the feedback of thirty-five IFIs from Malaysia, GCC Countries and the United Kingdom is considered significant and acceptable for this study.[6] Figure 11.1 illustrates the percentage of the response rate according to the case countries.

11.3 Findings

11.3.1 Sharīʿah Board Members

The survey affirms that most of the *Sharīʿah* boards in IFIs meet the minimum requirements of the AAOIFI Governance Standards and the IFSB-10 in that a majority of them consist of three board members (40 per cent). A total of 22.8 per cent of the *Sharīʿah* boards comprise of four members; 17.1 per cent, five members; 5.8 per cent, of six and ten members respectively; and only 2.9 per cent of IFIs engaged only one and two *Sharīʿah* scholars. In Malaysia, the *Sharīʿah* board of the BNM and the *Sharīʿah* Committee (SC) consists of ten members while the trend at the individual IFI level shows that three members are the most preferable practice. A significant number of *Sharīʿah* board members of the BNM and the SAC indicate their functional roles and position as the highest *Sharīʿah* authority. On the other hand, in GCC Countries the practice shows that there are significant variations on the number of *Sharīʿah* board members in IFIs: the majority of them prefer five and three board members. This is similar to the practice of IFIs in the UK, where it is found that *Sharīʿah* boards consist of four and three members respectively.

With regard to female *Sharīʿah* board members, only six out of thirty-five IFIs (17.1 per cent) have female board members; all of them are from Malaysia. This indicates that the board's room in GCC Countries and in the United Kingdom is still male territory. The study presumes that the issue of shortage of *Sharīʿah* scholars specialised and experienced in Islamic finance and *muʿāmalāt* may be overcome by liberalising the practice of accepting female *Sharīʿah* scholars as *Sharīʿah* board members as in the case of Malaysia.[7]

11.3.2 Sharīʿah *Governance Approach*

This section attempts to examine the different approaches of IFIs to *Sharīʿah* governance. The study identifies seven questions in order to explore the state of *Sharīʿah* governance practices in the case countries. Figure 11.2 illustrates the overall findings of IFIs' approach to *Sharīʿah* governance.

As a general observation, Malaysia presents a slightly better general framework of *Sharīʿah* governance by scoring higher on every question compared to the GCC Countries and the United Kingdom. An interesting observation is that, although there is less interference from regulatory authorities compared to Malaysia, IFIs in GCC Countries and in the United Kingdom pro-actively developed their own *Sharīʿah* governance framework. In fact, the majority of IFIs in the GCC Countries have developed their own *Sharīʿah* guidelines and standard processes regarding *Sharīʿah*-compliance. Although some GCC Countries clearly state in their regulations the adoption of the AAOIFI Governance Standards, it is found that only 22.8 per cent had indicated its implementation. In spite of the absence of any provision on the AAOIFI Governance Standards, 22.8 per cent of IFIs in Malaysia on the other hand had indicated the adoption of the standards based on voluntary practices.

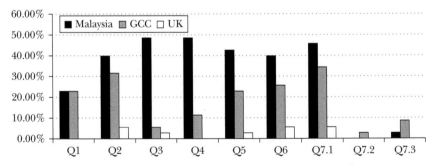

Figure 11.2 Comparative Overview of *Sharīʿah* Governance Approach

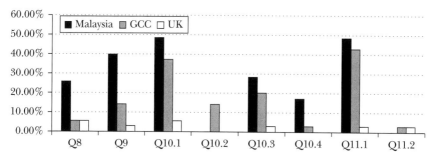

Figure 11.3 Comparative Overview of Regulatory Frameworks and
Internal Policies

11.3.3 Sharī͑ah *Governance and Regulation*

The study classifies Malaysia as the proponent of a 'Regulation-based Approach',
Saudi as a taking a 'Passive Approach', Qatar, UAE, Kuwait and Bahrain as
having a 'Minimalist Approach' and the UK as showing a 'Reactive Approach'
(Hasan, 2010: 82–4). This section tries to explore the general understanding and
perception of IFIs concerning the regulatory and internal framework of *Sharī͑ah*
governance as illustrated in Figure 11.3.

According to the study, 25.7 per cent of IFIs in Malaysia indicated that there
was a comprehensive set of rules and regulation concerning *Sharī͑ah* governance, while only 5.7 per cent of IFIs in the GCC Countries and in the United
Kingdom indicated the same. With reference to internal policies or bylaws, 40
per cent of IFIs in Malaysia claimed that they had written policies specifically
referring to the conduct of the *Sharī͑ah* board. On the other hand, only 14.2
per cent of IFIs and 2.8 per cent of IFIs in the United Kingdom indicated that
they have specific bylaws concerning this issue. The overall IFIs in all jurisdictions rightly viewed that Islamic finance cases were put under the auspices of
civil courts,[8] and most of them agreed that there were other alternative legal
avenues available such as arbitration. With respect to alternative dispute resolution, 51.4 per cent of IFIs posit that there were alternative legal avenues for
Islamic finance disputes in the form of arbitration and 20 per cent in the form
of *Sharī͑ah* authority. A total of 17.1per cent of IFIs in Malaysia and 2.8 per cent
of IFIs in the GCC Countries indicated that, despite arbitration as possible
legal avenues to redress disputes on Islamic finance, the *Sharī͑ah* authority at
the national level also offers alternative dispute settlements. In the aspect of
legal position of *Sharī͑ah* rulings, all IFIs in Malaysia (48.5 per cent) and 42.8
per cent of IFIs in the GCC Countries affirmed that they are bound by the
Sharī͑ah board's pronouncements. Only a small percentage (2.8 per cent) of
IFIs in the United Kingdom and the GCC Countries respectively indicated
otherwise.

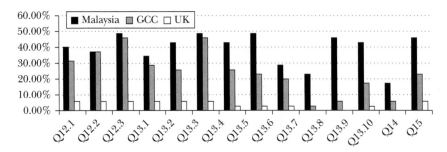

Figure 11.4 Comparative Overview of Roles of the *Sharīᶜah* Board

11.3.4 Role of Sharīᶜah *Board*

The ideal roles of the *Sharīᶜah* board involve *ex-ante* and *ex-post* aspects of *Sharīᶜah* governance and these include *Sharīᶜah* pronouncements (*fatwā*), supervision (*raqabah*) and reviews (*mutabaah*). The survey attempts to clarify the actual functions of the *Sharīᶜah* board in various IFIs in the case countries. Figure 11.4 illustrates the overall finding and comparative overview on roles of the *Sharīᶜah* board.

Some interesting observations arise from the survey on the roles of the *Sharīᶜah* board. Most of the IFIs in Malaysia (40 per cent), the GCC Countries (31.4 per cent) and in the United Kingdom (5.7per cent) pointed out that the *Sharīᶜah* board had only advisory authority while in 2.8per cent of the IFIs in the GCC Countries it had an executive power. This position denotes that the *Sharīᶜah* board is an independent body within the IFIs' governance structure, which has advisory and supervisory authorities. The executive power is still in the hands of the board of directors. The overall findings show that the majority of IFIs' *Sharīᶜah* boards undertook the *ex-ante* task of *Sharīᶜah* governance process. On the other hand, only 11.4 per cent of IFIs in Malaysia, 17.1 per cent of IFIs in the GCC Countries and 5.7per cent in the United Kingdom carried out the *ex-post* task of *Sharīᶜah* governance process, namely, a *Sharīᶜah* review. This position demonstrates a weak *Sharīᶜah* governance practice on the aspect of the *Sharīᶜah* review process, particularly in Malaysia. This weak position nevertheless is compensated for by another approach where 45.7 per cent of IFIs in Malaysia and 5.7 per cent of IFIs in the United Kingdom have delegated the *Sharīᶜah* board's audit functions to their internal *Sharīᶜah*-compliance unit. Unlike Malaysia and the United Kingdom, only 22.8 per cent of IFIs' *Sharīᶜah* boards in the GCC indicated that the functions had been delegated to an internal *Sharīᶜah*-compliance unit.

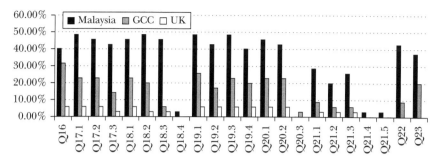

Figure 11.5 Comparative Overview of Mechanism of Competency

11.3.5 Attributes of Sharī‘ah Board Members

11.3.5.1 Appointment Criteria for Sharī‘ah Board Membership

IFIs in various jurisdictions adopt different processes as well as fit and proper criteria for their *Sharī‘ah* boards. This section specifically demonstrates the appointment criteria of the *Sharī‘ah* board as a mechanism to ensure competency practised by IFIs in the case countries. Figure 11.5 illustrates a comparative overview of the mechanism of competency of the *Sharī‘ah* board in all the three jurisdictions.

Most of the IFIs in Malaysia had a comprehensive mechanism to check the *Sharī‘ah* board's competency, with an average of 40 per cent of IFIs having fit and proper criteria as well as criteria of academic qualification, experience and exposure, and track record. IFIs in the GCC Countries (31.4 per cent) and in the United Kingdom (5.7 per cent) demonstrated a similar situation, except for the non-*Sharī‘ah* background of individual members of a *Sharī‘ah* board. Only IFIs in Malaysia (such as the BNM and SC) had appointed non-*Sharī‘ah* scholars as a member of a *Sharī‘ah* board. Interestingly, the BNM has also added extra criteria of strategic objectives to its *Sharī‘ah* board members. In this regard, the BNM has appointed different personnel from various institutions such as court and religious council.[9] As a general observation, this implies that IFIs preferred to have only *Sharī‘ah* scholars and not other individuals who are not specialised in *mu‘āmalāt* or *usul fiqh* as members of a *Sharī‘ah* board for *Sharī‘ah* deliberation.

In terms of the *Sharī‘ah* board's training to strengthen their understanding regarding the internal control process and knowledge of technical aspects of banking and finance, most of the IFIs in Malaysia (42.8 per cent) indicated that they had allocated funds and necessary training for their *Sharī‘ah* board members. A small number of IFIs in the GCC Countries (8.5 per cent) and none in the United Kingdom have initiated the same strategy. The study presumes that the good practice of initiating training for members of the *Sharī‘ah* board by IFIs in Malaysia is influenced by the guidelines on *Sharī‘ah* governance or the BNM/GPS1. A total of 37.1 per cent of IFIs in Malaysia, 20 per cent of IFIs in the GCC

Countries and none in the United Kingdom had conducted an assessment of the *Sharīʿah* board's performance and evaluated their contribution to *Sharīʿah*-compliance aspects. These significant findings demonstrate that the majority of IFIs did not evaluate the *Sharīʿah* board. This position presents a weak governance practice, as the assessment and evaluation of the service of each individual *Sharīʿah* board is crucial for maintaining a standard of competency and avoiding any potential of conflict of interest.

11.3.5.2 Independence

There are various ways of ensuring the professional independence of the *Sharīʿah* board. The survey identifies four important elements of independence, namely method of appointment, remuneration, *Sharīʿah* board mandate and means of mitigating potential conflict of interest. Figure 11.6 presents the market practice as to how IFIs manage the issue of the *Sharīʿah* board's independence.

Figure 11.6 demonstrates a comparative overview of the mechanism of independence practised by the IFIs in the case countries. The overall findings present significant differences concerning the mechanism of independence in Malaysia, the GCC Countries and in the United Kingdom. Most of the IFIs (42.8 per cent) in Malaysia indicated that the appointment was made by the board of directors; only in 5.7 per cent of IFIs in Malaysia was the appointment made by shareholders; in 2.8 per cent of IFIs by the management; and in 8.5 per cent by government. On the other hand, most of the IFIs in the GCC Countries indicated that the appointment was made by shareholders; in 31.4 per cent of IFIs in the GCC Countries appointment was made by the board of directors; and in 2.8 per cent of IFIs by the management and government respectively.[10] In the United Kingdom, the appointment is made by the board of directors (5.7 per cent). While most of the IFIs in the GCC Countries (31.4 per cent) indicated that the appropriate body for the *Sharīʿah* board to be accountable to was shareholders, the practice showed that 28.5 per cent of IFIs' *Sharīʿah* boards were appointed by the board of directors; 17.1per cent of IFIs indicated that their remuneration was also determined by the BOD. This position shows inconsistency between the 'ideal' and 'actual' *Sharīʿah* governance practice, particularly when it comes to the mechanism of independence. Although the practice in Malaysia seems to raise

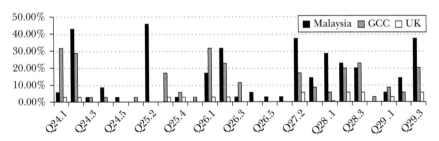

Figure 11.6 Comparative Overview of Mechanism of Independence

an issue of a potential conflict of interest, such conflict is mitigated by requiring all the appointments as well as dismissals to be made subject to the approval from the BNM.

In terms of other mechanisms in place to mitigate a potential conflict of interest, 28.5 per cent of IFIs in Malaysia indicated restrictions on multiple appointments, 22.8 per cent of IFIs in Malaysia indicated restrictions on disclosure of *Sharīᶜah* board's information, and 20per cent indicated restrictions on declarations in writing. This position demonstrates that *Sharīᶜah* governance practice in Malaysia has initiated various means of mitigating a potential conflict of interest of the *Sharīᶜah* board. Interestingly, the enforcement of the restrictions on multiple appointments has significantly produced more *Sharīᶜah* scholars, where more than 180 have been registered as qualified *Sharīᶜah* advisors with the BNM (Ismail, 2009). In the case of the GCC Countries, 5.7 per cent of IFIs indicated that they had a policy of restriction on multiple appointments,[11] 20 per cent of IFIs on disclosure of *Sharīᶜah* board's information, and 22.8 per cent of IFIs on declarations in writing. IFIs in the United Kingdom indicated that they only had a policy on the disclosure of the *Sharīᶜah* board's information and written declarations (5.7 per cent respectively).

With regards to the issue of mandate and authority, most of the IFIs in Malaysia (37.1 per cent) and 20 per cent of the IFIs in the GCC Countries indicated that the power and authority of the *Sharīᶜah* board were mentioned in the letter of appointment. A total of 5.7 per cent of IFIs in Malaysia indicated that the authority was confirmed by an article of association and 14.2 per cent of IFIs by a memorandum of association, while less than 9 per cent of the IFIs in the GCC Countries used both article and memorandum of association. IFIs in the United Kingdom indicated that mandate and authority were clearly stipulated in the article of association (2.8 per cent) and the letter of appointment (5.7 per cent). On the whole, the overall findings imply that some IFIs did not grant a full mandate or fail to provide clear mandate and authority to the *Sharīᶜah* board.

11.3.5.3 Transparency and Confidentiality

The existing literature evidences that *Sharīᶜah* governance practices in IFIs are not very transparent. The survey attempts to explore the mechanism used by IFIs to ensure transparency and to observe confidentiality on the part of their *Sharīᶜah* board members. The survey identifies one question on the aspect of confidentially and three questions on transparency, that is, a written policy on preparation and dissemination of *Sharīᶜah* information, right to access all documents and necessary information and publication of *Sharīᶜah* rulings. Figure 11.7 demonstrates the *Sharīᶜah* governance practices of the case countries concerning the mechanism of transparency and confidentiality.

Figure 11.7 illustrates the *Sharīᶜah* governance practices regarding transparency and confidentiality. These two elements are very important for a good and sound *Sharīᶜah* governance system. The survey demonstrates that 34.2 per cent of IFIs in Malaysia and only 17.1 per cent of IFIs in the GCC Countries indicated that they

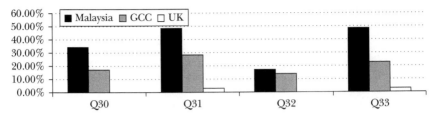

Figure 11.7 Comparative Overview of Mechanism of Transparency and Confidentiality

had a written policy in respect to the preparation and dissemination of *Sharī'ah* information. All of the IFIs in Malaysia indicated that they granted full authority to the *Sharī'ah* board to have access to all documents and information, while this was the case in only 28.5 per cent in the GCC Countries and 2.8 per cent in the United Kingdom. A small number of IFIs in Malaysia (7.16 per cent) and in the GCC Countries (14.2 per cent) and none in the United Kingdom indicated that they had published *Sharī'ah* rulings and made them known to the public.

In terms of confidentiality, all of the IFIs in Malaysia, 22.8 per cent in the GCC Countries, and 2.8 per cent in the United Kingdom indicated that their *Sharī'ah* boards were fully aware of sensitive information obtained in the course of performing their duties. The survey shows that IFIs in the United Kingdom are less concerned about the issues of transparency and confidentiality with respect to *Sharī'ah* governance. Presumably, IFIs in the United Kingdom are bound to comply with the existing corporate laws and related regulation concerning transparency and confidentiality without feeling the need for a separate internal policy on *Sharī'ah* governance. The overall findings tend to suggest that *Sharī'ah* governance practice concerning transparency and disclosure is still low and needs a reform in order to maintain IFIs' credibility and accountability.

11.3.6 Operational Procedures

Different IFIs adopt various processes and procedures on the aspect of *Sharī'ah*-compliance process. The survey attempts to discover the state of operational procedures in the context of *Sharī'ah* governance practices, particularly concerning standard operational procedures, *Sharī'ah* board meeting, quorum, basis of decision, voting rights, preparation and dissemination of documents to the *Sharī'ah* board, the *Sharī'ah* report and its content and the institutional arrangement for a *Sharī'ah* review. Figures 11.8, 11.9 and 11.10 illustrate the different practices of IFIs pertaining to operational procedures on the *Sharī'ah*-compliance process.

Significant variations were found across the case countries concerning the operational aspect of *Sharī'ah* governance practices. Most of the IFIs in Malaysia (34.2 per cent) indicated that they had standard operational procedures for the *Sharī'ah* governance process, while 5.7 per cent of IFIs in the United Kingdom

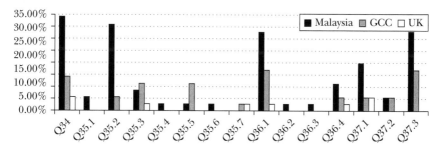

Figure 11.8 Comparative Overview of Operational Procedures (Q34–37)

and 14.2 per cent of IFIs in the GCC Countries indicated the same. IFIs in the GCC Countries indicated a slightly lower standard of practice in terms of providing clear operative procedures of *Sharīᶜah* governance process. In terms of *Sharīᶜah* board meetings, overall the IFIs in the case countries had conducted more than four meetings annually, where 35.2per cent of IFIs in Malaysia and 5.7 per cent of IFIs in the GCC Countries indicated that they had conducted monthly meetings, while 8.5 per cent of IFIs in Malaysia, 11.4 per cent in the GCC Countries, and 2.8 per cent in the United Kingdom held quarterly meetings.[12] A small percentage (2.8per cent) of IFIs in the GCC and in the United Kingdom respectively indicated that they conducted fewer than four meetings annually.

As regards to the quorum for *Sharīᶜah* board meetings, 17.1 per cent of IFIs in the GCC Countries and 28.5 per cent of IFIs in Malaysia indicated that three *Sharīᶜah* board members are required to reach the quorum. Only a minority of IFIs indicated the quorum to be seven and six. With respect to the decision-making process, most of the IFIs in Malaysia (20 per cent), 5.7 per cent of IFIs in the GCC Countries, and 2.8 per cent in the United Kingdom indicated that decisions made at the *Sharīᶜah* board meeting were based on simple majority, while 28.5 per cent of IFIs in Malaysia and 17.1 per cent of IFIs in the GCC Countries indicated that they reached decisions by consensus. This practice demonstrates that the majority of IFIs preferred the decision to be made by consensus rather than by simple or two-third majority.

Figure 11.9 presents a continuation of the survey result pertaining to operational procedures with respect to voting rights, agenda, coordinator and attendees of *Sharīᶜah* board meetings. Most IFIs did not prefer to grant voting rights to non-*Sharīᶜah* experts; however, 17.1 per cent of IFIs in Malaysia and 2.8per cent of IFIs in GCC Countries indicated that they may have voting rights, while the majority of IFIs preferred to give such rights solely to *Sharīᶜah* scholars.

Most of the IFIs in Malaysia (42.8 per cent), 8.5 per cent in the GCC Countries and 2.8 per cent in the United Kingdom indicated that the agenda and documents for a *Sharīᶜah* board meeting were prepared and distributed a week in advance. Interestingly, 5.7 per cent of IFIs in the GCC Countries indicated that they submitted the agenda and document to the *Sharīᶜah* board a month in

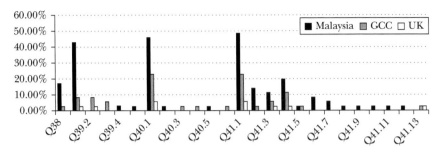

Figure 11.9 Comparative Overview of Operational Procedures (Q38–41)

advance. As regards *Sharīʿah* coordination, most of the IFIs in Malaysia (45.7 per cent),[13] 22.8 per cent of IFIs in the GCC Countries and 5.7 per cent of IFIs in the United Kingdom indicated that their internal *Sharīʿah* officer was responsible for handling the *Sharīʿah* board meeting and *Sharīʿah*-related matters. A minority of IFIs granted this responsibility to a company secretary, the head of product development, the head of the legal department, a representative from the capital market or the outsource company.

With respect to attendees of the *Sharīʿah* board meeting, all of the IFIs in Malaysia, 22.8 per cent of the IFIs in the GCC Countries and 3.7 per cent of the IFIs in the United Kingdom indicated that a representative from the internal *Sharīʿah*-compliance unit was a permanent attendee. Besides that, there were some other parties who were invited to attend the meeting such as a representative from the risk management department (14.2 per cent of IFIs in Malaysia and 2.8 per cent of IFIs in the GCC Countries), from the legal department (11.4 per cent of IFIs in Malaysia and 5.7 per cent in the GCC Countries and 2.8 per cent in the United Kingdom), and from product development (20 per cent of IFIs in Malaysia, 11.4 per cent of IFIs in the GCC Countries and 2.8 per cent in the United Kingdom). The survey finds some interesting observation to the *Sharīʿah* governance practice in Malaysia and in the United Kingdom when some IFIs invited the CEO, the managing director, the executive director, the board risk committee and the chief internal auditor to attend the *Sharīʿah* board meeting.

Almost all of the IFIs in Malaysia (45.7 per cent), 22.8 per cent of the IFIs in the GCC Countries and 5.7 per cent of the IFIs in the United Kingdom indicated that they had conducted a review of *Sharīʿah* rulings. Regarding another aspect of the review, namely the *Sharīʿah*-compliance review, 34.2 per cent of the IFIs in Malaysia and 40 per cent of the IFIs in the GCC Countries indicated that they had established an independent division for this purpose. A small number of IFIs in the case countries indicated that the *Sharīʿah*-compliance review was conducted by the existing internal audit department; some of them had even appointed a *Sharīʿah* advisory firm to perform the task.

Despite the regulatory requirement to submit *Sharīʿah* reports in Malaysia,

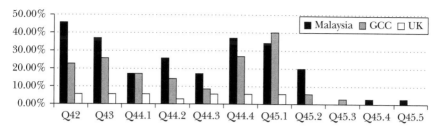

Figure 11.10 Comparative Overview of Operational Procedures (Q42–Q45)

only 37.1 per cent of IFIs indicated that the *Sharīᶜah* board was required to submit a *Sharīᶜah* report. Even in the absence of such a regulatory requirement, as in the case of Malaysia, 25.7 per cent of the IFIs in the GCC Countries, and 2.8 per cent of the IFIs in the United Kingdom indicated that the *Sharīᶜah* report was part of their internal requirement. In terms of the content of the *Sharīᶜah* report, 17.1 per cent of the IFIs in Malaysia indicated that the *Sharīᶜah* report contained information on the duties and services of the *Sharīᶜah* board, 25.7 per cent indicated that it contained information on *Sharīᶜah* pronouncements, 17.1per cent indicated that it contained information on *Sharīᶜah* board activities and 37.1per cent indicated that it contained information on the declaration of *Sharīᶜah*-compliance. Similar situations existed in the GCC and in the United Kingdom where the majority of IFIs indicated that the content of the *Sharīᶜah* report was just a declaration of *Sharīᶜah*-compliance.

11.3.7 Assessments of Sharīᶜah Board

There have been numerous criticisms and negative allegations on the roles and functions of *Sharīᶜah* board. The problem with all sort of criticisms is that such allegations have not been proven or supported by any empirical evidence or reliable data. The survey identifies five questions specifically to address this important issue. These five questions consist of general assessment of IFIs upon their *Sharīᶜah* board in term of organisational accountability, communication with other organ of governance, ability to identify and evaluate *Sharīᶜah* non-compliance risk, contribution to promote Islamic ethics and values as well as *Sharīᶜah* control process. Figure 11.11 illustrates the IFIs' perception upon the performance of their *Sharīᶜah* board in the case countries.

Figure 11.11 demonstrates the IFIs' perception on the roles and functions that are played by the *Sharīᶜah* board in five aspects, namely, accountability, organisational communication, *Sharīᶜah* non-compliance risk, Islamic ethics and values and the *Sharīᶜah* control process. The overall findings in Malaysia indicated that IFIs were generally satisfied with the performance of the *Sharīᶜah* board where 22.8 per cent of IFIs gave a response of Strongly Agree on Q46, Q47 and Q49, 28.5 per cent of IFIs gave a response of Agree on Q48 and Q50, 2.8 per

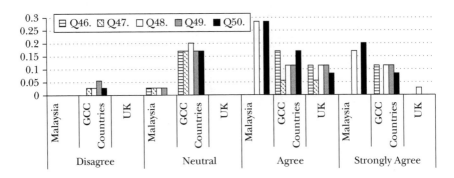

Figure 11.11 Comparative Overview of the Perception of Performance of the *Sharīʿah* Board

cent of IFIs gave a response of Neutral on Q46–50. None of the IFIs in Malaysia indicated a negative perception on assessment of their *Sharīʿah* board. Similarly to IFIs in the United Kingdom, they were positively satisfied with the performance of the *Sharīʿah* board by indicating Agree and Strongly Agree on Q46–Q50.

Unlike Malaysia and the United Kingdom, some interesting observations are found in terms of the perception of the IFIs in the GCC Countries. While the majority of IFIs gave a response of Strongly Agree on Q46 (11.4 per cent) and Q48–50 (11.4 per cent), a small percentage of IFIs indicated that they were dissatisfied with the performance of the *Sharīʿah* board where 2.8 per cent of the IFIs gave a response of Disagree on Q47, Q48 and Q50 and 5.7 per cent of IFIs gave a response of Disagree on Q49. This interesting finding tends to show that some IFIs have identified that the *Sharīʿah* board has neglected some important aspect of *Sharīʿah* governance particularly regarding the effectiveness of organisational communication, identifying *Sharīʿah* non-compliance risk, contributing to Islamic ethics and values as well as the *Sharīʿah* control process. This finding positively affirms that the assessment and evaluation of the performance of the *Sharīʿah* board is of utmost importance to IFIs.

11.4 Conclusion

The survey findings in this study affirm that the IFIs in these three jurisdictions have different and diverse *Sharīʿah* governance systems. They further acknowledge that there are shortcomings and weaknesses to the existing *Sharīʿah* governance framework and practices. Without a proper mechanism and approach to strengthen and improve, the current *Sharīʿah* governance practices may expose IFIs to potential *Sharīʿah* non-compliance risk that would affect the Islamic finance industry significantly. Based on the overall survey findings, the study concludes that the existing *Sharīʿah* governance framework needs major enhancement and improvement, particularly in the aspects of *Sharīʿah* governance approach, regulatory frameworks, internal policies on *Sharīʿah* governance, roles of the *Sharīʿah* board and attributes of the *Sharīʿah* board in terms of competency, independence, transparency, confidentiality, operational procedures and the *Sharīʿah* board's assessment.

As a prerequisite, this paper advocates the regulatory-based approach as the ideal model of *Sharīʿah* governance system. Elements of adequate internal control systems and a functional process design with the necessary checks and balance as well as adequate corporate values, codes of conduct and effective systems used for ensuring compliance and financial and managerial incentives that are consistent with the bank's objectives, performance and ethical values are very important asmatters of consideration in regulating the *Sharīʿah* governance system (Iqbal and Mirakhor, 2007: 285). In addition, elements of a good *Sharīʿah* board such as independence, competence, transparency, disclosure, consistency, well-defined operating procedures, a sound code of ethics and conduct and clear mandate and responsibility are at the heart of strengthening the function of the *Sharīʿah* board.

At the institutional level, within the internal structure of *Sharīʿah* governance in IFIs, the *Sharīʿah* board and *Sharīʿah*-compliance or review unit shall play pro-active roles to take full responsibilities for the aspect of *Sharīʿah* assurance. In this regard, IFIs shall give clear mandate and authority, advisory and supervisory functions that grant them power to undertake *ex-ante* and *ex-post* responsibilities. It is also important to expand the framework of the *Sharīʿah* board's function to not only include technical aspects and legalities of Islamic financial products, but also to promote Islamic values and ethics to Islamic finance practice. With the purpose of ensuring the integrity and competency of the *Sharīʿah* board, a specific code of conduct or ethics for individual *Sharīʿah* scholars shall be regulated that would be able to maintain the credibility and integrity of the profession.

It is strongly believed that the need for the above enhancement of *Sharīʿah* governance practice is crucial, as it would strengthen the performance and credibility of IFIs. In this regard, regulatory authorities shall take the initiative to introduce *Sharīʿah* governance standards or to adopt the existing *Sharīʿah* governance prudential standards for IFIs. It is firmly believed that a sound *Sharīʿah* governance practice would enhance the potential role of Islamic finance in contributing towards corporate reform and mitigating certain types of risk exclusive to IFIs. It is hoped that this exploratory study can further motivate and trigger future research to extend further discourse on the topic of *Sharīʿah* governance in IFIs.

Notes

1. The IFSB-3 defines *sharīʿah* non-compliance risk as 'the risk that arises from IFIs' failure to comply with the *sharīʿah* rules and principles determined by the *sharīʿah* board or the relevant body in the jurisdiction in which the IFIs operate' (IFSB, 2006: 26). In this aspect, Delorenzo (2007: 398–407) illustrates *sharīʿah*-compliance risk by referring to the risk of *fatwā* rejection and differences as a form of operational and regulatory

risk. In addition, Iqbal and Mirakhor (2007: 245) classify *sharīᶜah* risk into two types, namely the risks that are due to non-standard practices of Islamic financial products and the risks that are due to non-compliance with the *sharīᶜah*.

2. The Islamic Fiqh Academy of the OIC issued the final resolution on *Tawarruq* at the nineteenth meeting in Sharjah, United Arab Emirates on 26–30 April 2009, which confirmed its impermissibility.

3. *Arab Malaysian Finance Bhd V Taman Ihsan Jaya Sdn Bhd Ors (Koperasi Seri Kota Bukit Cheraka Bhd, third party) [2008] 5 MLJ 631.*

4. In this case the Investment Dar refused to pay the Expected Profit and to return the Principal Amount of *wakala*-based deposit in the amount of USD10 million. The Investment Dar claims that the *wakala*-based deposit did not comply with the *sharīᶜah* and therefore should be considered void. This case is a timely reminder to IFIs about the essence of *sharīᶜah*-compliance product via mechanism of *sharīᶜah* governance. See *The Investment Dar Company KSCC v Blom Development Bank Sal* (2009) EWHC 3545 (Ch).

5. The value of *sharīᶜah*-compliant assets for Saudi Arabia, the UAE, Qatar, Bahrain and Kuwait alone, worth more than USD262.6 billion, accounted for 41 per cent of the total world *sharīᶜah*-compliant assets (Wilson, 2009). This simply demonstrates the emergence and need of a strong and robust *sharīᶜah* governance framework to address the issues pertaining to *sharīᶜah* matters.

6. This is affirmed by other surveys such as Chapra and Ahmed (2002), where the response rate of the study is only 23.3 per cent (fourteen IFIs out of sixty). A study conducted by Aboumouamer (1996) demonstrates a very minimal percentage of response rate, where only fifteen IFIs in twenty different countries participated in the survey. In addition, only sixty-nine IFIs in eleven countries responded to the IFSB Survey on the *Sharīᶜah* Board of Institutions Offering Islamic Financial Services across Jurisdictions despite getting special assistance from the IFSB full members from fifteen countries (IFSB, 2008).

7. Qudeer Latif, a prominent corporate lawyer in Islamic finance industry, views that the market experiences a shortage of scholars with expert knowledge of finances so that he had to travel to several countries to meet just one Islamic scholar for *sharīᶜah* advisory services (Devi, 2008).

8. In the case of Malaysia, a specific High Court Division known as the *Muʾāmalāt* Bench was established to hear cases pertaining to Islamic finance cases. The implementation of this *Muʾāmalāt* Bench shows a positive result on the increasing numbers of settled cases. From the statistic, it shows that more than 75 per cent of 656 cases had been settled by the court from the year 2003 to 2005 (Hasan, 2007). This position indicates that Malaysia has established a comprehensive Islamic finance framework and this includes how to handle issues related with *Sharīᶜah* governance.

9. The BNM appointed the non-*Sharīᶜah* experts such as a judge and director general of the Department of Islamic Development of Malaysia for purpose of coordination among the various government agencies as well as judicial body (Ismail, 2009).

10. This position affirms the finding by Aboumouamer (1989: 185), where 75 per cent of forty-one *sharīᶜah* board members indicated that their authority was derived from the shareholders.

11. A survey by Unal (2009) affirms the above finding where the top ten listed *sharīᶜah* scholars have monopolised more than 58 per cent of 956 *sharīᶜah* board positions in 271 organizations in twenty-two countries. Some *sharīᶜah* scholars even hold more than seventy *sharīᶜah* board memberships. It is observed that the majority of the *sharīᶜah* board positions were represented by IFIs in the GCC Countries.

12. The survey witnesses a slightly different trend in the GCC Countries with the study

conducted by Aboumouamer (1996: 188), where it revealed that 24.4 per cent of forty-one sharīʿah board members have a weekly meeting, 7.3 per cent have a monthly meeting, 48.8 per cent have a quarterly meeting and 2.4 per cent have semi-annual meetings.

13. In the case of Malaysia, the issue on the remit of various sharīʿah boards at the individual IFIs level as well as the sharīʿah Advisory Council of the BNM and the Securities Commission is resolved by having proper coordination among the sharīʿah officers of these different institutions led by the officers at the Islamic banking and Takaful Department of the BNM (Ismail, 2009).

Bibliography

Abomouamer, F. M. (1989). *An Analysis of the Role and Function of Sharīʿah Control in Islamic Banks*, PhD dissertation, University of Wales.

Bakar, M. D. (2002). 'The *Sharīʿah* supervisory board and issues of *Sharīʿah* rulings and their harmonisation in Islamic banking and finance', in S. Archer and A. A. K. Rifaat (eds), *Islamic Finance Innovation and Growth*. London: Euromoney Books and AAOIFI, pp. 74–89.

Chapra, M. U. and Ahmed, H. (2002). *Corporate Governance in IFIs*. IRTI: Jeddah.

Delorenzo, Y. T. (2007). '*Sharīʿah* compliance risk', *Chicago Journal of International Law 7(2)*: 397–408.

Devi, S. (2008). 'Experts: Scholars and harmony in short supply', *Financial Times*, 17 June. Available at:, www.ft.com/cms/s/0/4b67288c-3c0f-11dd-9cb2-0000779fd2ac,dwp_uuid=282ce812-36c3-11dd-bc1c-0000779fd2ac.html, last accessed 19 December 2008.

Grais, W., and Pellegrini, M. (2006). *Corporate Governance and Stakeholders' Financial Interests in Institutions Offering Islamic Financial Services*, World Bank Policy Research Working Paper No. 4053.

Hasan, Z. (2010). 'Regulatory framework of *Sharīʿah* governance system in Malaysia, GCC countries and the UK', *Kyoto Bulletin of Islamic Area Studies 3(2)*: 82–115.

Hasan, Z. (2007). *Impact of Globalisation to Islamic Financial Institutions in Malaysia: Sharīʿah and Legal Framework*. Sharīʿah Law Report, 2.

IFSB (2006). *Guiding Principles on Corporate Governance for Institutions Offering Only Islamic Financial Services (Excluding Islamic Insurance (Takāful) Institutions and Islamic Mutual Funds.* Kuala Lumpur: IFSB.

IFSB (2008). *Survey on Sharīʿah Boards of Institutions Offering Islamic Financial Services Across Jurisdictions.* Kuala Lumpur: IFSB.

IFSB (2009). *Guiding Principles on Sharīʿah Governance System in Institutions Offering Islamic Financial Services.* Kuala Lumpur: IFSB.

Iqbal, Z, and Mirakhor, A. (2007). *An Introduction to Islamic Finance: Theory and Practice*, Singapore: John Wiley and Sons (Asia).

Ismail, N. (2009). *Manager, Islamic Banking and Takaful Department, the Central Bank of Malaysia.* Interview, 24 June.

Maali, B., Casson, P., and Napier, C. (2006). 'Social reporting by Islamic banks', *ABACUS* 42(2): 266–89.

Sekaran, U. (2003). *Research Methods for Business: A Skill Building Approach.* Hobohen, NJ: John Wiley and Sons Inc.

Unal, M. (2009). *Sharīʿah Scholars in GCC – A Network Analytic Perspective – Updated*, Germany: Funds@Work. Available at: www.funds-at-work.com/fileadmin/downloads/Sharia-Network_by_Funds_at_Work_AG.pdf.pdf, last accessed 18 January 2010.

Wilson, R. (2009). *The Development of Islamic Finance in the GCC.* Kuwait: The Centre for the Study of Global Governance, LSE, London.

12

TOWARDS GENUINE *SHARĪʿAH* PRODUCTS WITH LESSONS OF THE FINANCIAL CRISIS

Abdulazeem Abozaid

12.1 Introduction

According to financial analyses, the current financial crisis has basically been caused by excessive dealing in interest and by trade of debt securities.

In fact, these two practices are unanimously prohibited in Islam and are related to *ribā*, one of the gravest sins a Muslim may ever commit. However, some Islamic banks have developed and marketed as *Sharīʿah*-compliant some products that are to observers and financial experts similar in substance and economic implications to the conventional interest-bearing loans. Developers and proponents claim the legitimacy of these products on the basis of locating some juristic statements that indicate their acceptability. However, the opponents of these products argue that, since its very establishment, *fiqh* literature has not been free from irregular opinions; it has also been, on the other hand, plagued with extreme and twisted interpretations by researchers in an attempt to seek legal grounds for their arguments. Sadly enough, the contemporary juristic debates and arguments over these issues have not yielded any substantial results nor solved the problem. This is evidenced by the ongoing persistence of Islamic banks in offering the same controversial products despite the many juristic criticisms raised as well as by overruling the resolutions of the largest representative of contemporary *Sharīʿah* scholars, namely the International Fiqh Academy.

Therefore it is perceived indispensable nowadays to depart from the classical juristic approach and to adopt a new approach to tackling the so-called controversial Islamic banking products. The suggested approach for judging the Islamic banking products depends on examining their implications and investigating any possible essential similarities with the prohibited conventional banking products. This step is necessitated in fact by the perceived fatal implications of Islamic banking and finance having an evidenced convergence with conventional banking.

These implications on the emerging industry of Islamic banking include the following:

(i) vulnerability of Islamic banking to the same financial threats inherent in conventional banking;

(ii) having the Islamic financial law being reduced to one establishing itself on mere technicalities rather than reason and justice;

(iii) risking the public image of the Islamic *Sharīʿah* in general and the Islamic financial system in particular;

(iv) losing the public's confidence in Islamic banking.

Undoubtedly, such implications are fatal enough to urge decision makers in Islamic finance to take urgent steps towards re-evaluating the current Islamic products on the basis of the described approach, so as for Islamic banks to remove the bad products from their shelves.

12.2 The Proposed Approach is Rooted in the *Sharīʿah*

The essence of the entire Islamic law is predicated on the philosophy of retention of good and prevention of evil. This is evidenced by the *Qur'ānic* verse (7: 157): '*Allah* makes lawful for believers all that is good and prohibits for them all that is bad and harmful.'

It is from this verse that a major principle of Islamic law has been derived, namely *al-maṣlaḥa vs al-mafsadah* (Ibn al-Subki, 2004; Al-Shatibi, n.d.). The former means good or public benefit, and the later means bad and evil. Besides the above *Qur'ānic* verse, reflection on *Sharīʿah* texts has also led *Sharīʿah* scholars to reach the conclusion that *Sharīʿah* rules admit *maṣlaḥa* and prohibit *mafsada*.

This notion of recognition of good and prohibition of evil has been used by jurists as one of the *Sharīʿah* sources valid for judging new matters on their validity that have no direct textual authority. To explain, if a new matter on which the *Sharīʿah* texts are silent is needed to be looked into in order to determine its *Sharīʿah* value, then it can be judged against its own harms or benefits. Should it be found beneficial to society, it can be positively ruled as lawful. Conversely, if it is found harmful to society or found that it carries more harms than benefits, it then can be ruled as *ḥarām*.[1]

Beside the validity of the principle of *maṣlaḥa* and *mafsada* to function as a *Sharīʿah* source for judging new matters, it can also be used by contemporary scholars as a benchmark against which conflicting juristic opinions with equal *Sharīʿah* authority can be weighed and evaluated. If we want to opt for the strongest or the most appropriate past juristic opinion among the available conflicting ones, we can simply choose the one we may consider more conducive to the realisation of *maṣlaḥa* and the prevention of evil, since *Sharīʿah* rules are naturally characterised by upholding good and avoiding evil (Abdulazeem, 2006: 52–3).

Similarly, the same benchmark can be used to examine the current contemporary conflicting *fatwās* in Islamic banking and finance and the products designed on their bases. Any product that is found to involve evil more than good must be rejected, and the *fatwā* allowing it must be overruled. This is again nothing but an application of the above *Qur'ānic* verse to which all contemporary *Sharīʿah* scholars have no choice but to submit.

However, the issue that may arise here relates to the practicality of this approach since the same banking product may be considered by some as beneficial whereas others may deem it harmful! It is here, in fact, where lessons of experience, like the ones derived from the current financial crisis, manifest themselves as hard practical evidence that leave no room for disagreement or dispute. Once the conventional banking products that led to the crisis are identified, an analysis of the controversial Islamic products can be made. If substantial similarities between the two are located, the same *Sharīʿah* stand on these conventional products must be extended to the controversial Islamic banking products in question.

12.3 Reasons for the Occurrence of the Financial Crisis

According to many analyses and reports on the current financial crisis, it can be concluded that the following are the primary factors behind its occurrence:

(i) interest- based financing with all its forms and structures
(ii) dealing in bonds and the circulation of debt securities.

However, for sake of brevity, our study will mainly discuss issues related to the first factor, that is, interest-based financing, considering that debts represented in bonds and debt securities are sub-products of the interest-based debts.

12.3.1 Locating Similarities of Islamic Banking Products to the Conventional Interest-based Financing

A thorough and fair analysis of the current Islamic banking products will identify some products that are similar at their core and to conventional transactions. *Eina* and *tawarruq* in some Islamic banks, for example, constitute the basis for many of their products, although the essence of these two transactions can hardly distinguish itself from that of conventional loans. These products include personal financing, corporate financing, home financing, credit cards and overdraft facilities. Sale of debt, on the other hand, is practised in some Islamic banks in a variety of products like 'Islamic Private Debt Securities', 'Islamic Factoring' and 'Islamic Accepted Bills'.

Below is a brief description of these sales along with some examples of the products structured on their basis.

12.3.1.1 Eina *Sale (Back-to-back Sales)*

Eina connotes a sale contract whereby a person sells an article on credit and then instantly buys it back at a lesser price for cash. Example: 'A' asks for a loan of $10 from 'B'. 'B', instead of asking for interest on this loan, applies a contrivance. He sells an article to 'A' for $12 on credit and then buys it back from him for $10 cash. So, 'A' departs with $10 in hand but indebted to 'B' for $12.

Such a mechanism suggests that the article itself is not meant for purchase, but rather it is used only as a tool to provide cash with some return. To illustrate, it makes no difference to the one seeking finance to conclude the sale contract on a car, a house or anything else. Furthermore, an *eina* sale is conducted sometimes on assets that one party may not be effectively willing to sell or buy, like the bank's premises or equities in cases when the bank is financier. This confirms the fact that this sale contract is fictitious and not real. Moreover, practically, *eina* transactions rarely involve the actual possession of the item sold or official documentation of the contract.

Proponents of *eina* argue that its permissibility can be attributed to the *Shafi'i* school. However, this is not true as the *Shafi'i* school has only ruled on the validity of the *eina* contract and not its permissibility, and a valid contract is not necessarily permissible.[2]

As for the applications of *eina*, it is the underlying contract in products like cash financing, home financing overdraft facility and credit cards. The following is a description of both *eina*-based home financing and personal financing.

Home Financing

Some Islamic banks offer *eina*-based home financing under the term of BBA, an Arabic term for '*bai' bithaman ajil*', which means 'deferred payment sale'. Technically, BBA refers to a sale contract (practised mainly in Malaysia) whereby a person 'A' who does not have enough cash to pay the full price of his house of choice will pay only about 10per cent of the full price. In return, 'A' gets from the seller of the property a 'Beneficial Ownership', which reflects a commitment on the part of the owner to conclude the sale upon payment of the balance (90 per cent). After paying the 10 per cent and obtaining the beneficial ownership, 'A' sells the house as represented by the beneficial ownership to the Islamic bank for a cash price equivalent to the outstanding amount (90 per cent) of the house price. So, if the total price was $100,000, then the selling price between 'A' and the Islamic bank would be $90,000. Afterwards, the Islamic bank immediately sells the house, which is represented by the beneficial ownership, back to 'A' on a deferred payment basis at a mark-up, say for $120,000 over a period of five years.

The $90,000 paid by the Islamic bank as the purchase price will be extended to the property developer in conclusion of the sale contract with 'A'. 'A', however, remains indebted to the Islamic bank for the $120.000 – the price in the last sale contract.

Resemblance of BBA Home Financing to Conventional Mortgage

This mode of finance, apart from the technicalities followed therein, is hardly differentiated from the conventional mortgage used in home financing. The only difference an observer may locate is the way cash is advanced from the bank to the client. In the conventional mortgage it is through an explicit conventional loan while in BBA it is through the technicalities of *eina*. A further examination of BBA contract particulars and terms of agreement will even enhance convergence of BBA with mortgage.[3]

Had the bank acquired the house first from the property developer or its original owner and genuinely taken the property risk and then sold it to the client, the financing would then be construed as a real trade business and thus it would lawfully entitle the bank for profit. However, the bank in BBA home financing acquires the house from the customer and then immediately sells it back to him or her at a higher price without taking any property risk.

Eina-based Personal Financing

Conventionally, personal financing simply functions on the concept of interest-bearing loans. However, since charging interest on loans is prohibited in Islam, some Islamic banks have resorted to Eina as a presumably lawful alternative. To explain the mechanism, the Islamic bank would sell an asset to the client seeking finance on a credit basis and then it would immediately repurchase the same asset on a cash basis. The amounts of the two prices depend on the required financing and the bank rate of profit for the repayment period. The cash price would be handed to the client who will become indebted to the bank for the credit price.

Similarity of *Eina* to Interest-based Financing

Obviously *eina* is implemented in some Islamic banks for the purpose of providing clients with cash yet in a securely profitable manner to the bank. Therefore, as far as the substance of *eina* is concerned, this transaction is similar to the interest-based loan.

Had *eina* been a real sale contract, it would not be free from risks that are normally associated with sale contracts. Besides, it would then entail a real interest of the client in the commodity of sale. However, in most applications of *eina*, the underlying asset subject to the dual sale is inconsequential and typically not related to the purpose of financing and it may originate from the customer or the bank.

Moreover, the sequence of contracts in *eina* is not accidental but rather it is something predetermined in order to reach the end set in advance, that is, to legalise charging clients upon providing them with cash. Obviously, sale contract is used in *eina* for what it was not originally designed for. The sale contract was originally designed to acquire things for their own use, to trade in order to generate profit and even as a means to obtain cash through the disposal of some properties. However, with *eina* the sale contract is used for a different purpose all together. Since its very initiation it involves a known and deliberate determined loss in the asset acquired. So, the loss is known to materialise at the time that the asset is acquired and not only when the asset is sold, as is the case in selling one's property when cash is needed. In other words, it is not a genuine sale contract but one that is designed to be immediately followed by a subsequent sale contract to reverse and thus cancel the legal consequences of the former sale. Transfer of title from the seller to the buyer and price from the buyer to the seller is the major legal consequence of a sale contract, and it is immediately reversed by the following sale contract in the *eina* transaction. What remains out of the two consecutive sale transactions in *eina* is only the indebtedness of one contractor to the other.

Had this flow of action been lawful, Islam, the practical and rational religion, would have legalised loans with interest in the first place, not bothering individuals with the need to follow certain technicalities to reach the same end result. Obviously, *eina* cannot be construed as the *Sharīʿah* substitute to loan with interest because *eina* places no input or value whatsoever in economy and has one single implication similar to that of a conventional loan, which is the creation of debt liability against the extension of cash.

12.3.1.2 Tawarruq-*based Financing*

The meaning of *tawarruq* is to purchase a commodity from one party on credit and then sell it immediately to another for cash. Thus, *tawarruq* shares the same objective of *eina* as both are meant for extending cash money. However, *tawarruq* remains technically distinguished from *eina* as in the latter the commodity is resold to its original seller while in *tawarruq* it is sold to a third party. Its proponents basically claim its permissibility on the grounds that it comprises two independent and non-related sale contracts and the sale contract is unanimously permissible.[4]

Tawarruq in Islamic Banks

The mechanism of *tawarruq* that is practised in some Islamic financial institutions[5] is a slightly modified version of the original form of the *tawarruq* described above. In this institutional *tawarruq*, the bank purchases some commodity from the market, typically a metal from the London Metal Exchange (LME), and then sells it to the customer on a *murābaḥah* basis (at cost plus a mark-up) for deferred payment. Subsequently, the bank, as the customer's agent, sells the metal on LME for immediate cash. In result, the bank gains *murābaḥah* profit and agency fees, the customer obtains immediate cash and remains committed to repaying the outstanding debt that he or she has incurred when acquiring the commodity from the bank on a *murābaḥah* basis.[6]

Similarity of *tawarruq* to Interest-based Financing

As with *eina*, the bank in *tawarruq* acts as a financier who makes a secured profit from the clients he or she finances and not as a real trader who takes market risks, although taking market risk is, as commonly known, the dividing line between sale and *ribā*, profit and interest. Moreover, in both transactions, *tawarruq* and *eina*, the bank knows that the client has no interest in the commodity but to resell it immediately, either to the bank as in *eina* or to a third party but through the bank's mediation, as in *tawarruq*. These facts about *tawarruq* and eina eliminate real differences between the two; and more generally, they eliminate differences between both of them on one side and the interest-bearing loan on the other, reducing differences to only technicalities followed in the execution of the two. It is envisaged that of *eina* or *tawarruq* is not considered as ḥarām, it would then be easily and comfortably resorted in order to circumvent the prohibition of *ribā*. Anyone wishing to legitimately provide interest-loaded loans would simply execute *eina* or *tawarruq* with people seeking finance, so *ribā* would be 'lawfully' practised! Therefore, claiming the permissibility of such transactions contradicts the *Sharī'ah* objective meant from the prohibition of *ribā*.

Furthermore, the absence of substantial differences between eina/tawarruq-based financing in Islamic banks on the one hand and conventional loans on the other, annuls the justification for burdening clients seeking finance from Islamic banks with extra costs due to extra procedures. Clients of Islamic banks willingly accept bearing extra cost in return for obtaining *Sharī'ah*-compliant products but with a product like *eina* or *tawarruq* they ultimately end up paying the cost of the useless technicalities followed by some Islamic banks to unjustifiably claim legitimacy of these products!

Logically, it makes no sense for the *Sharī'ah* to prohibit *ribā* and then accept from its followers to circumvent such prohibition by some technique like *eina* or *tawarruq*. Definitely *Sharī'ah* would then have contradicted itself and acted against its very principles and objectives, besides acting against logic and sound reason. Thus, *Sharī'ah* would then fail to convince its followers, before outsiders, of its rationality and validity, which have always been some of its cornerstones in proving and defending its authenticity.

12.3.1.3 Economic Analysis of Eina and Tawarruq

Both *eina* and *tawarruq* create in favour of the Islamic bank a debt liability out of a transaction in which the bank advances to the client an amount less than the amount the client has to repay in the future. This is exactly the economic purport of conventional loans as therein the client repays to the conventional bank an amount larger than the advanced lent money. In fact, it is wrong to consider *eina* and *tawarruq* as similar to the acceptable debt-creating commodity-financing instruments like the *Sharī'ah*-compliant *murābahah*. In other words, the debt that *eina* or *tawarruq* creates is not similar to the debt a genuine, commodity-based financing creates. This is because the latter is a result of a real economic activity in which the bank sells to customers their desired commodities in a manner hat involves risk and provides no guarantee of return. In other words, the bank in a *Sharī'ah*-compliant *murābahah* functions as a real trader mediating between the commodity suppliers and their consumers, which is not the case with either *eina* or *tawarruq* as their clients are not real consumers.

Anas Zarka, a prominent Islamic economist, points out the similarity in the economic results and implications between *eina* and *tawarruq* on the one hand and the practices of *ribā* on the other by saying:

> [T]awarruq leads to the same end results of the usurious practices of *ribā* before Islam, which involved increasing debts in return of their postponement, so debts were given the power to increase and multiply by themselves without them being associated with genuine sale of commodities or services. This, in turn, creates a gap between the real economic sector and the financial sector, which is one of the characteristics of the *ribā*-based economics. (Zarka, n.d.: 3)

Commenting on the technicalities-driven nature of *eina* and *tawarruq* sales, Zarka says:

> *Eina* involves a temporary engagement with a commodity which is imme-
> diately resold to its original owner, rendering the outcome a mere con-
> ventional financing. *Tawarruq* also involves the same thing, except that the
> commodity is resold to a third party. Obviously, in both *eina* and *tawarruq*
> the commodity in exchange is not meant for itself; rather, any commodity
> that can be easily resold with minimum loss will do. (Zarka, n.d.: 2)

Another bitter fact about *eina* and *tawarruq* is that the Islamic banks practising
them and their likes have not been helpless to design some instruments through
which they could restructure debts with increase or roll them over, although the
Sharīʿah does not allow creditors to increase the debt on debtors. As a matter
of fact, *eina* and *tawarruq* have mainly been the tools adopted to reschedule
non-performing debts, which may themselves have resulted from former *eina*
or *tawarruq*! However, interestingly enough, increasing debts via rolling them
over or rescheduling have been some of the practices of conventional banks that
contributed to the occurrence of the credit crisis of 2007–10 that originated in the
United States. In result, such application of *eina* and *tawarruq* further reflects their
convergence with conventional loans.

In relation to this point, Zarka stresses that the most important *Sharīʿah* reason
behind prohibiting conventional borrowing, or *ribā*, is to block the means to the
practice of rolling over or rescheduling of debts with increment:

> Linking permissible indebtedness to genuine sales mainly helps block the
> means to the creation of new debts in repayment of old debts. However,
> *eina* and *tawarruq* are potential means to create larger debts for the mere
> purpose of settling old smaller debts and thus, they are similar to *ribā*-based
> borrowing. (Zarka, n.d.: 3)

Al-Jarhi, another prominent Islamic economist, points out that

> [*T*]*awarruq*, like *eina*, opens the doors for the debts resulting from Islamic
> financing to acquire the same characteristics of conventional debts. This is
> because debts resulting from Islamic financing are not tradable by nature
> and cannot increase in case of temporary insolvency. They can only be
> rescheduled without any extra charge. However, by virtue of *tawarruq*,
> banks will be able to increase debts on defaulters via initiating *tawarruq*
> transactions with them, and this process may be repeated over and over,
> so one *tawarruq* may give birth to subsequent *tawarruq*(s). *This will potentially
> expose Islamic financial industry to the same credit crises of the conventional financial
> industry'*. (Al-Jarhi, 2010: 24)

(emphasis added)

Considering the economic implications of a product like *eina* or *tawarruq*, Al-Jarhi
states:

If *tawarruq* spreads, economy will have an act of money market, where
spot money commands higher value over deferred money, the difference
in value being in fact nothing but interest, though it is not given the same
name. As a result, people, motivated by the price of money, will economize
on the use of money, and they will substitute the real productive resources
for money, though the latter is inherently non-productive. This in turn will
reduce the economic efficiency and will let the society forgo production
through the real productive resources'. (Al-Jarhi, 2010: 24)

In the final analysis, if excessive conventional lending is deemed, among other
things, potentially responsible for economic downturns as evidenced by the recent
financial crisis, then *eina* and *tawarruq*, and any similar Islamic banking products
that are economically no different from conventional loans in essence and practices, are potential factors for the creation of a financial crisis. Undoubtedly,
the market implications would have been the same if the conventional banks
in America had used *eina* or *tawarruq* for financing their customers instead of
the standardised conventional loans and then traded the debts resulting from
eina and *tawarruq* locally and overseas on the same terms on which the original
debts were traded. For debt trading has also been practised in Islamic finance as
discussed below.

13.3.2. Debt Trading Practices in Islamic Finance

Debt trading that involves sale of debt at discount or a mark-up is held unanimously[7] unlawful in Islam.[8] However, there are some opinions in the modern
literature of Islamic banking and finance that unjustifiably differentiate, in prohibition, between commercial debts, that is, debts resulting from sale or any other
commutative contract, and non-commercial debts, that is, debts resulting from
loan contracts. So, according to this opinion, which is rooted in the Malaysian
model of Islamic banking and finance, the debts resulting from *eina* and *tawarruq*
are tradable. Consequently, debt creation and then its trading can be given a
Sharīʿah clearance and be labelled as *Sharīʿah* compliant!

In an attempt to justify such arbitrary differentiation between these two categories of debt, it has been argued that when the holder of commercial debt
securities sells them at discount, he is effectively relinquishing part of the profit
he previously made in the commercial transaction that created the debt, so the
buyer of the commercial debt securities is in reality getting a profit and not an
interest![9]

To refute this argument it can be simply said that in the whole *fiqh* literature
there exists no single opinion that supports such division of debts. On the contrary, jurists assert that the debt to which *ribā* injunctions are applicable is any
financial liability that has been created as a result of loan, commutative contract
or damage done to others' properties (Ibn Abideen, 1987: 4/160; Al-Dasuqi,
n.d.: 3/61).

Besides, to exclude commercial loans from prohibition is against the very *Sharīʿah* objectives of subjecting sale of debt to *ribā* rules. This is because *Sharīʿah* rejects the very principle of exchanging a sum of money for more or less money in consideration of time, and this irregular opinion breaks this rule.[10]

Furthermore, if the seller of the commercial debt is allowed to relinquish part of his profit, then why is it not that the seller of the non-commercial debt be also allowed to relinquish part of his principle?! And what if the seller of the commercial debt had made no profit to relinquish in the underlying transaction, would not he be allowed then to sell his commercial debt?!

Effectively, both the seller of a non-commercial debt and the seller of a commercial debt are doing the same thing, that is, leaving to the buyer part of their debts in return for cash payment of debt. The buyer of either debt, in his turn, holds the debt security until maturity in order to claim its nominal value or to sell it at a later time with a profit margin.

To summarise, both debts are the same, and the *Sharīʿah* has subjected the sale of debt, in general, to certain rules that would nullify the common market practices of debt securities trading. Excluding commercial debts from prohibition renders selling debt arising from sale-based financing legitimate. This means that debts arising from the controversial Islamic financing products like *eina* and *tawarruq*, which are, as proven above, no different from conventional lending, would be lawfully tradable. Consequently, both identified crisis-causing elements, that is, *ribā*-bearing lending and debt trading would be somehow labelled *Sharīʿah*-compliant.

12.4 Conclusion: the Criterion of the Non-*Sharīʿah*-compliant Transaction

The preceeding discussion leads to the conclusion that Islamic banking and finance has harboured some products that failed to show real differences from conventional financing, with differences being reduced to only the terminology used and the technicalities followed in their execution. In other words, they share the same essence and economic implications. However, it is the essence of conventional financing, not its terminology nor its technicalities, which have caused the financial crisis.

Therefore, in order for an Islamic financial product to be rightly and logically labelled as *Sharīʿah*-compliant, it must be genuinely distinguishable from the prohibited conventional financing products. However, conventional financing is mainly characterised by the absence of risk taking and with principal as well as profit being guaranteed, which is the meaning of *ribā*. Consequently, a genuine *Sharīʿah*-compliant product must admit risk and never provide the financier with any capital or profit protection. In other words, any financing mode is unlawful if it is structured in such a way that it secures a guaranteed return to the financier without taking any risks, or when the financier acts in reality as a creditor who merely provides money without being involved in the investment process, that is, when the economic substance is interest-bearing debt. This will render the product non-*Sharīᶜah*-compliant regardless of any Islamic name it may be given, and regardless of its legal form and any sound technicalities followed in its execution.

In fact, the current financial crisis has proven beyond doubt that conventional products are not free of defect. Hence, Islamic banks must be extremely cautious when borrowing or mimicking conventional concepts and products, and they have to realise that some conventional products are not possibly able to be Islamised; any attempt to Islamise the un-Islamisable will yield a conventional product but under an Islamic cover.

The current financial crisis has indeed presented Islamic banking with a priceless lesson, a lesson that helps it to identify its non-genuine *Sharīᶜah* products. For the relative success Islamic banks have achieved should not close their eyes to the fact that among their products exist ones that are hardly distinguishable from the conventional products that took the blame for the occurrence of the crisis. If the good performance of Islamic banks and other circumstantial conditions have temporarily veiled these threatening products, this does not mean they do not exist.

Indeed, Islamic banks do not need a financial crisis of their own in order to reform their products, and the time has really come for Islamic banks to take a lesson from the current financial crisis, not on the level of filtering their clients, but rather on the level of filtering their products in light of their essence as explained above.

Finally, the recent crisis should also make Muslims more appreciative of the teachings of their religion and more observant about their right applications, as this crisis has manifested itself as practical evidence that what Islam has prohibited is nothing but evil.

Notes

1. Among the major schools of Islamic jurisprudence, Imam Malik is known to be the leading proponent of upholding *maṣlaḥah* as one of the sources of *sharīᶜah*. He uses the term 'al-masalih al-Mursala' to connote interests that have not been covered by other sources of *sharīᶜah*. On the other hand, the majority of other jurists reject it as a source of *sharīᶜah*; they practised it without theoretically admitting its authority as an independent source of the *sharīᶜah*. However, Al-Ghazali (who is from the *Shafiᶜi* school), uses the term *Istislah* (seeking the better rule for public interest) but never claims it as the fifth source of *sharīᶜah*. He also restricts its application to situations that are deemed necessary to serve the interest of the public.
2. For details on this matter see Abdulazeem (2004).
3. See for mortgage mechanism: Abdulazeem (2004: 576).
4. For *Fiqh* discussion on the permissibility of *Tawarruq* see Abdulazeem (2008a).
5. This transaction is mostly practised in some Islamic banks of Arab Gulf countries.
6. See, for example, the mechanism of *Tawarruq* in Abu Dhabi Islamic Bank.
7. Some juristic stands on the matter, like that of the *Shafiᶜi*' school, have been misinterpreted. For details on this matter see Abdulazeem (2008b).

8. Ibn Abideen, *'Hashiyat Ibn A'bideen'*, 4/160 (Dar Ihiya' al-Turath al-Arabi, Beirut, 1987); Al-Dasuqi, *'Hashiyat al-Dasuqi'*, 3/61 (Dar Ihia'a al-Kutub al-Arabiyyah, Undated); Al-Hattab, *'Mawahib Al-Jalil'*, 4/368 (Dar al-Fikr, Beirut, 1987); Al-Bahuti, *'Kashaf Al-Qina'*, 3/307 (Dar Al-Fikr: Beirut, 1402 AH); Al-Sherbini, *'Mughni Al-Muhtag'*, 2/71 (Dar al-Fikr, Beirut. Undated).

9. See for debt trading justifications *Resolutions of the Securities Commission Syriah Advisory Council*, Malaysia; Sano Moustapha (2001: 50).

10. See for *Fiqh* details on these matters, Abdulazeem (2004: 275).

References

Abdulazeem, Abozaid (2004). *Contemporary 'Eina is it a Sale or Usury*. Dar al-Multaqa: Aleppo.

Abdulazeem, Abozaid (2004). *Fiqh Al-Riba*. Beirut: Al-Risalah.

Abdulazeem, Abozaid (2006). 'The devotional dimension in interest-oriented *Shari'ah* rulings', *Journal of Islam in Asia*, 3(1): 52–3 (article in Arabic).

Abdulazeem, Abozaid (2008). *Contemporary Islamic Financing Modes between Contracts Technicalities and Shari'ah Objectives*. Eighth Harvard University Forum on Islamic Finance, Harvard Law School – Austin Hall, USA, 19–20 April 2008.

Abdulazeem, Abozaid (2008). 'Examining the new applications of sale of debt in the Islamic financial institutions', *Journal of Islam in Asia* 5(2): 1–30 (in Arabic).

Abdulazeem, Abozaid (2010). 'Contemporary Islamic financing modes between contracts technicalities and Shari'ah objectives', *Islamic Economic Studies* 17(2): 55–75.

Al-Bahuti (1402 AH). *Kashaf Al-Qina'*. Beirut: Dar Al-Fikr.

Al-Bugirami (undated). *Hashyat*. Diyar Bakr: Al-Maktabah Al-Islamiyyah.

Al-Dasuqi (undated). *Hashiyah*. Cairo: Dar Ihia'a al-Kutub al-Arabiyyah.

Al-Hattab (1987). *Mawahib Al-Jalil*. Beirut: Dar al-Fikr.

Al-Jarhi, Mabid Ali (2010). *The Organized Tawarruq'*, unpublished Paper in Arabic.

Al-Shatibi (undated). *Al-Muwafaqaat*. Beirut: Dar al-Fikr.

Al-Sherbini (undated). *Mughni Al-Muhtaj*. Beirut: Dar al-Fikr.

Ibn Abdeen (1987). *Hashiyat (Rad al-Mukhtar ala al-Dur al-Mukhtar)*. Beirut: Dar Ihiya' al-Turath al-Arabi.

Ibn al-Subki (2004). *Al-Ibhaj*. Beirut: Dar al-Kutub al-Ilmiyyah.

Mohd Ariffin, Noraini, Archer, Simon and Abdel Karim, Rifaat Ahmed (2009). 'Risks in Islamic Banks: Evidence from empirical research', *Journal of Banking Regulation* 10(2): 153–63.

Resolutions of the Securities Commission, Syriah Advisory Council, Malaysia.

Sano, Koutoub Moustapha (2001). *The Sale of Debt as Implemented by Islamic Financial Institutions in Malaysia'*, Research Center, International Islamic University Malaysia.

Zarka Anas (undated), *Tawarruq Train*, unpublished paper in Arabic.

INDEX

Page numbers in *italics* refer to figures and tables

EU Authorised Representative: Easy Access System Europe Mustamäe tee 5
0, 10621 Tallinn, Estonia gpsr.requests@easproject.com

Printed and bound by CPI Group (UK) Ltd, Croydon, CR0 4YY
16/04/2025
01846987-0001